Finishes

MITCHELL'S BUILDING SERIES

The volumes in this series of standard text books have been completely re-written and re-illustrated by specialist authors to bring them into line with rapid technical developments in building and the consequent revision of syllabuses. All quantities are expressed in SI units and there are tables giving imperial conversions. Also included are the main CI/SfB classifications with cross references to the relevent volumes and chapters in *Mitchell's Building Series*.

The series will be invaluable to students preparing for the examinations of the RIBA, RiCS, IQS and IOB. It provides an ideal text for the Ordinary and Higher National Certificates, and the City and Guilds of London Institute courses in building. It is also a useful reference for practising architects, surveyors and engineers.

The six related volumes are:

ENVIRONMENT AND SERVICES
Peter Burberry Dip Arch MSc ARIBA

MATERIALS
Alan Everett ARIBA

STRUCTURE AND FABRIC Part 1
Jack Stroud Foster FRIBA

STRUCTURE AND FABRIC Part 2
Jack Stroud Foster FRIBA
Raymond Harington Dip Arch ARIBA, ARIAS

COMPONENTS
Harold King ARIBA
revised by Derek Osbourn Dip Arch (Hons) RIBA

FINISHES
Alan Everett ARIBA

See also
INTRODUCTION TO BUILDING
Derek Osbourn Dip Arch (Hons) RIBA

FINISHES

This volume, previously part of *Components and Finishes*, considers the performance requirements for Finishes for buildings and the effectiveness of typical solutions. It includes 62 drawings, 35 tables and a comprehensive index. References to sources of more detailed information are made throughout the following chapters:

1 Floorings
2 Plastering
3 Renderings
4 Wall tiling and mosaics
5 Integral finishes on concrete
6 Thin surface-finishes
7 Roofings

MITCHELL'S BUILDING SERIES

Finishes

Alan Everett *ARIBA*

B T Batsford Limited   London

© Alan Everett 1979
ISBN 0 7134 3335 3
New edition 1979
Reprint 1987

Printed in Great Britain by
Anchor Brendon Ltd Tiptree Essex
for the publishers
B T Batsford Limited
4 Fitzhardinge Street, London W1H 0AH

Contents

Acknowledgment

The author and the publishers acknowledge with thanks the Controller of Her Majesty's Stationery Office for permission to quote from the Building Regulations 1976 and the Directors of the Building Research Establishment, the British Standards Institution, and research and development associations for permission to quote from their publications.

I am particularly grateful to the undernamed experts for correcting and improving my original typescript:

Floorings

A J Beere MICorrT, AIMF of Tretol Protective Coatings Limited (*Resin-based floorings*)
J Bick of the Hardwood Flooring Manufacturers Association
R T Gratwick BEM, AIOB of the Polytechnic of North London (*Maintenance*)
R H Harrison of Stuarts Granolithic Company Limited
V Marriott of Marriott and Price Limited (*Terrazzo floorings*)
J E Moore FRIBA of the Polytechnic of North London (*Sound control*)
J W Murray ARIBA, AIArb of the Mastic Asphalt Council and Employers Federation
S L Scarlett-Smith MA (Cantab) of Armstrong Cork and Company Limited   (*Sheet floorings*)
E J Sigall MInst Marketing of Langley (London) Limited
F Vaughan BSc, FICeram FGS of the British Ceramic Tile Council
W J Warlow of the Building Research Establishment (*Introduction*)
R P Woods BAFor(Cantab), FIWSc of the Timber Research and Development Association

Plastering and Renderings

T F Harvey
T McEwan of British Gypsum Limited
J F Ryder BSc of the BRE

Wall tiling and mosaics

F Vaughan BSC, FICeram FGS of the British Ceramic Tile Council

E J Sigall MInst Marketing of Langley (London) Limited

Integral finishes on concrete

B W Shacklock MSc, FICE, MIStructE, MInstHE of the Cement and Concrete Association

Thin surface-finishes

R S Hullcoop of ICI Limited
J E Todman CGLI, Full Technical Certificate, of the Polytechnic of North London
T Whiteley BSc, ARIC of the BRE

I am grateful for the work of the late Harold King who prepared chapter 18 in the 1971 edition of *Components and Finishes* which is basis of chapter 7 in this book.

My sincere thanks are due to Derek Osbourn Dip Arch (Hons), RIBA for his expert help in updating chapter 7, particularly for revisions to many drawings.

I also thank those listed in the 1971 edition of *Components and Finishes* who assisted Harold King in 1971, and subsequent contributors notably: David Clegg ALA, of the SfB Agency UK Ltd for classifications, D Anderson and Son Ltd, Permanite Ltd for tables 33 and 34; and Universal Asbestos Cement Ltd for drawings. I am extremely grateful to Thelma M Nye for her patience, encouragement and expert editorial advice.

Infinite thanks are again extended to my wife.

I should be grateful to anyone who is kind enough to draw my attention to any errors and to suggest ways in which the book may be improved.

London 1979   A E

British Standards and Codes of Practice are obtainable from
The British Standards Institution
Sales Department
101 Pentonville Road
London N1 9ND

SI units

Quantities in this volume are given in SI units which have been adopted by the construction industry in the United Kingdom. Twenty-five other countries (not including the USA or Canada) have also adopted the SI system although several of them retain the old metric system as an alternative. There are six SI basic units. Other units derived from these basic units are rationally related to them and to each other. The international adoption of the SI will remove the present necessity for conversions between national systems. The introduction of metric units gives an opportunity for the adoption of modular sizes.

Full details of SI Units and conversion factors are contained in the current edition of the *AJ Metric Handbook*.

British Standards, Codes of Practice and other documents are being progressively re-issued in metric units, although at the time of going to press many of those concerned with Building Construction have yet to be metricated. In addition, it should be noted that new Codes of Practice are now contained in British Standards and are no longer issued as separate documents.

Multiples and sub-multiples of SI units likely to be used in the construction industry are as shown in Table 1 below:

Multiplication factor	Prefix		Symbol
1 000 000	10^6	mega	M
1 000	10^3	kilo	k
100	10^2	hecto	h
10	10^1	deca	da
0·1	10^{-1}	deci	d
0·01	10^{-2}	centi	c
0·001	10^{-3}	milli	m
0·000 001	10^{-6}	micro	μ

Further information concerning metrication is contained in BS PD 6031 *A Guide for the use of the Metric System in the Construction Industry,* and BS 5555:1976 *SI units and recommendations for the use of their multiples and of certain other units.*

Quantity	Unit	Symbol	Imperial unit × Conversion factor = SI value		
LENGTH	kilometre	km	1 mile	=	1·609 km
	metre	m	1 yard	=	0·914 m
	millimetre	mm	1 foot	=	0·305 m
			1 inch	=	25·4 mm
AREA	square kilometre	km²	1 mile²	=	2·590 km²
	hectare	ha	1 acre	=	0·405 ha
			1 yard²	=	0·836 m²
	square metre	m²	1 foot²	=	0·093 m²
	square millimetre	mm²	1 inch²	=	645·16 mm²
VOLUME	cubic metre	m³	1 yard³	=	0·765 m³
	cubic millimetre	mm³	1 foot³	=	0·028 m³
			1 inch³	=	1 638·7 mm³
CAPACITY	litre	l	1 UKgallon	=	4·546 litres

Table 2   Imperial/SI conversions

—continued

Quantity	Unit	Symbol	Imperial unit × Conversion factor = SI value		
MASS	kilogramme	kg	1 lb	=	0·454 kg
	gramme	g	1 oz	=	28·350 g
			1 lb/ft (run)	=	1·488 kg/m
			1 lb/ft²	=	4·882 kg/m²
DENSITY	kilogramme per cubic metre	kg/m³	1 lb/ft³	=	16·019 kg/m³
FORCE	newton	N	1 lbf	=	4·448 N
			1 tonf	=	9 964·02 N
				=	9·964 kN
PRESSURE, STRESS	newton per square metre	N/m²	1 lbf/in²	=	6 894·8 N/m²
	meganewton per square metre	MN/m²† or N/mm²	1 tonf/ft²	=	107·3 kN/m²
			1 tonf/in²	=	15·444 MN/m²
			1 lb/ft run	=	14·593 N/m
			1 lbf/ft²	=	47·880 N/m²
			1 ton/ft run	=	32 682 kN/m
	*bar (0·1 MN/m²)	bar			
	*hectobar (10 MN/m²)	hbar			
	*millibar (100 MN/m²)	m bar			
VELOCITY	metre per second	m/s	1 mile/h	=	0·447 m/s
FREQUENCY	cycle per second	Hz	1 cycle/sec	=	1 Hz
ENERGY, HEAT	joule	J	1 Btu	=	1 055·06 J
POWER, HEAT FLOW RATE	watts	W	1 Btu/h	=	0·293 W
	newtons metres per second	Nm/s	1 hp	=	746 W
	joules per second	J/s	1 ft/lbf	=	1·356 J
THERMAL CONDUCTIVITY (k)	watts per metre degree Celsius	W/m deg C	1 Btu in/ft²h deg F	=	0·144 W/m deg C
THERMAL TRANSMITTANCE (U)	watts per square metre degree Celsius	W/m² deg C	1 Btu/ft²h deg F	=	5·678 W/m² deg C
TEMPERATURE	degree Celsius (difference)	deg C	1 deg F		$\frac{5}{9}$ deg C
	degree Celsius (level)	°C	°F	=	$\frac{9}{5}$ °C+32

* Alternative units, allied to the SI, which will be encountered in certain industries

† BSI preferred symbol

Table 2   Imperial/SI conversions

1 Floorings

BS 3589 1963 *Glossary of general building terms* defines flooring as 'the upper layer providing a finished surface to a floor, which latter provides a lower load-bearing surface'. References include:

Floor finishes for houses and other non-industrial buildings, National Building Studies Bulletin 11, HMSO

Guide to the choice of wall and floor surfacing materials. A costs-in-use approach (NBA) Hutchinson Benham

Floors – Construction and Finishes
P.H. Perkins
Cement and Concrete Associations

Architects' and Specifiers' Guide – Floorings
A 4 Publications

Floor finishes, Specification, The Architectural Press Ltd

Flooring, D. Phillips, A Design Centre Publication Macdonald and Co (Publishers) Ltd

Floors, Factory Building Study 3, HMSO

Flooring for industrial buildings, The Engineering Equipment Users' Association, Constable and Co Ltd

Other references, including British Standards and Codes of Practice, are given under the respective headings.

PERFORMANCE CRITERIA

Selection of floorings is facilitated by the *UPEC system* adopted by the Agrément Board which grades *premises,* and gives details of tests for grading the *performance* of various types of floorings under four headings. See table 3. A flooring is considered suitable if its grading under each performance heading is not numerically lower than that of the premises in which it is intended to be used.

Other factors which must be taken into account in selecting floorings include: appearance, comfort criteria, and cost.

We now consider in turn: Wear; Cleaning and surface protection; Comfort criteria; Special requirements; Costs.

Deteriorating Agent	Classification	Gradings of 'Premises' and 'Performance of Floorings'
Walking	U (*usure*)	1 – 5
Indentation and impact wear	P (*poinçonnement*)	1 – 3
Water	E (*eau*)	0 – 3
Chemicals	C (*chemiques*)	0 – 3

Table 3 UPEC classifications

Wear

Good resistance to wear caused by pedestrains and vehicles is almost always a primary requirement – surfaces are often deemed to be worn out when quite superficial deterioration mars their appearance.

Wear is greatest where traffic is concentrated, where it starts, stops, and in particular where it turns, and it is an advantage if floorings can be renewed locally in such areas. It is often economical to eliminate causes of serious deterioration such as badly designed legs to furniture and steel tyred trucks. Gravel and other gritty paving should be separated from entrances to buildings by hard paving. Immediately inside buildings grit and moisture, which are particularly damaging to materials such as magnesium oxychloride, should be removed from footwear by doormats wide enough to ensure that both feet make contact with them.

Cleaning and surface protection

The effective lives of most floorings depend very much on how well they are looked after and in selecting materials it is most important to know how much effort and care will be expended in cleaning and maintenance when the building is in use.

Floor Maintenance: Materials, their cost and usage, J.K.P. Edwards, Butterworths is a good reference. The tables of flooring materials on pages 24—61 recommend treatments for each material. It is important that the correct treatments are applied. For example, polishes and seals which contain solvents damage rubber and mastic asphalt and unsuitable detergents can cause considerable harm to some floorings. Manufacturers' instructions should be carefully followed and tried out on small areas. Instructions should be displayed for the maintenance staff to read.

In deciding upon floorings it should be borne in mind that if too many different treatments are required in one building wrong treatments are more likely to be given to some surfaces.

In design of buildings it is important to realize that it is often difficult to clean and treat floors without scraping and dirtying the lower parts of walls and fixed furniture. These parts should therefore be hard and easily cleaned.

Smoothness, which makes floorings easier to keep clean, is obtained by fine abrasion; pores can then be filled and the final polish given by a polish or seal

Polishes

Wax Polish protects surfaces from abrasion partly by absorbing grit but is too soft for heavy traffic. The finish looks well after buffing. Too many layers of polish darken surfaces and become slippery and require periodic removal and renewal. Solvent wax polishes are not suitable on rubber, mastic asphalt, thermoplastic tiles and similar materials and they may attack the adhesives used for fixing tiles which are themselves resistant to solvents.

Water-wax and/or synthetic resin emulsions can be used on all floorings although water-sensitive materials should be sealed first. They are easy to apply, eg with a mop, and may provide gloss without buffing. Gloss can also be obtained without slipperiness.

Seals

The original seal used on wood flooring was *button polish (shellac)* which is fairly easily scratched and stained. Modern seals give good protection for long

periods before requiring renewal but they do not penetrate surfaces and are too rigid for application on flexible floorings.

Surfaces to be sealed must be dirt, dust and wax-free. Slow curing, up to forty-eight hours, is a disadvantage in buildings such as hospitals. Regular cleaning with soap or detergent and water is usually sufficient to maintain seals in good condition for long periods. Floor seals include:

Oleo-resinous These one-can products, made from a drying oil such as tung oil and a phenolic or other resin, are easily applied, but drying by atmospheric oxidation is rather slow. They are usually yellowish in colour. Being soft they show wear more readily than other seals, but worn patches are easily made good.

Epoxy ester Similar to oleo-resinous seals but they are more glossy and harder wearing.

Resin solutions These consist of resins in volatile solvents. They are quick drying but less hard than other seals.

One-can urea formaldehyde — self cure These seals are more transparent and wear better then the foregoing. However, like those mentioned below, they tend to stick wood blocks and strips together and cause cumulative movement. One way of stopping this is by waxing floors before they are sanded.

Two-can modified urea formaldehyde — organic solvent An acid hardener is mixed in immediately before use of two-can seals. This finish is of excellent appearance and hard wearing, although difficult to repair if allowed to wear through. Penetration is insufficient on terrazzo, quarries and clay tiles.

One-can polyurethane — moisture curing Humid conditions are necessary to form a hard yet flexible coating which is suitable for timber, cork and magnesium oxychloride. It is too difficult to remove from linoleum and penetration is insufficient on terrazzo, quarries and clay tiles.

Two-can polyurethane (also available pigmented) has excellent resistance to wear and staining but is slow hardening. It is unsuitable on terrazzo, quarries and clay tiles.

Two-can epoxy resin This type is rather slow in hardening and is usually yellowish, but has excellent resistance to wear and staining.

Synthetic rubber seals These are suitable for the same uses but are generally cheaper then two-can polyurethanes and give good all round performance.

Water based seals usually consist of acrylic polymer resins. They are recommended for use on thermoplastic and vinyl-asbestos tiles, flexible PVC, rubber, porous linoleum, terrazzo, marble and asphalt.

Sodium silicate and silicofluoride dressings are suitable only on concrete floorings. See page 28

'Comfort' criteria

Although to some extent subjective, comfort assessments are influenced by the temperature, resilience, colour, pattern and texture of the floor, by the temperature and humidity of the atmosphere and by the footwear and activities of the users.

The properties which affect the 'comfort' of floors are:
1 sound control
2 resilience
3 freedom from slipperiness
4 warmth
5 appearance.

Softness, quietness, resilience and warmth tend to go together, for example in cork. At the other extreme, hardness, noisiness and coldness are associated for example in concrete and clay tiles.

1 *Sound control*

Soft floorings which are not masked by furniture can contribute to the absorption of air-borne sound in a room. Thus at the middle frequency of 500 Hz coefficients for carpets on felt vary from 0.25 to 0.50 according to thickness. (For comparision the absorption of *acoustic* ceiling tiles is 0.70 to 0.90 according to type.)

Soft floorings also absorb impact sound and reduce its transmission through floors. *Floating floors* comprising panels of tongued and grooved strip or boards or heavy screeds on resilient underlays, reduce the transmission of impact sound if they are isolated at their edges from surrounding walls and columns. See *MBS: E and S,* chapter 6.

Floor finishes are generally of little value in reducing the transmission of air-borne sound through floors — the extent to which this occurs depending mainly upon the mass of the floor as a whole and that of the surrounding walls.

2 *Resilience*

'Dead' floors are tiring to walk on and resilience is particularly necessary for dancing, gymnastic and similar activities. Thus, wood is more resilient than concrete and wood strips laid on joists or battens are more comfortable than wood blocks laid on concrete. On the other hand, very deep pile carpet is tiring to the feet.

3 *Freedom from slipperiness*

Slipping on floors is a major cause of injuries in buildings, in particular to children, physically handicapped and elderly persons. Accidents are more likely to occur in badly lit conditions, at sharp corners, thresholds and on stairs and ramps, on surfaces made uneven or polished by wear or where the degree of slipperiness suddenly changes. Unexpected conditions are dangerous, eg where polish is transferred on footwear from a polished surface on to materials such as terrazzo and where a floor which is dull in appearance is slippery. Gloss and slipperiness are not related. Moisture dirt and grease reduce friction and are particularly hazardous on rubber, PVC and some clay tiles.

Stair treads of hard stones, terrazzo and timber require non-slip nosings or insets. Resistance to slip is increased by frequent joints, as in mosaic, by embossed surfaces and by the temporary depression of soft materials such as cork. It is important that inherent non-slip properties should not be lost by too liberal application of wax polish, especially on timber and linoleum. Non-slip resin-based floor polishes or seals are preferable.

4 *Warmth*

Effective 'warmth' depends upon the temperature of a surface, its thermal conductivity, thermal capacity, the temperature of the air near the surface, and whether shoes are worn. Dampness reduces the thermal insulation of porous floorings and increases the transfer of heat from shoe to floor. Parts of the body not in contact with floors are cooled by radiation to cold surfaces. Contrariwise hot floors can be uncomfortable and floor warming should not raise the surface temperature above 25°C.

5 *Appearance*

Floor coverings are an important factor in determining the 'scale' of a room and whether it is gay or formal, warm or cold and so on.

Floor finishes are often condemned because they have lost a surface pattern, faded or worn unevenly. Monochromes, especially black and white and glossy surfaces show the slightest mark whereas marbled, jaspé and similar patterns help to camouflage even marks made by black rubber soles.

Patterns and colours should be chosen from large samples. To ensure matching throughout a contract the material should be obtained in one batch and a proportion of additional material should be ordered for future repairs.

Special requirements

Industrial floors

Typical requirements are high resistance to impact, trucking, thermal shock and constant wet conditions.

Underfloor warming

Generally underfloor warming which does not cause discomfort to occupants does not present insuperable problems. Stones, ceramics and concrete which have high thermal capacity are ideal but manufacturers of other floor finishes and of adhesives should be consulted. Some organic materials soften, embrittle or shrink, especially if they are overlaid with carpets of similar insulation.

Resistance to water

Where floor surfaces are likely to be constantly wet the choice of floorings excludes magnesite, linoleum, cork carpet, wood products, most composition blocks, and all adhesives.

Floors in shower baths and other wet floors require tanking, usually with mastic asphalt.

Resistance to freezing

External paving must be frostproof, eg mastic asphalt, tarmacadam, fully vitrified ceramics and good quality stones and concrete.

Freedom from dusting

Dust arising from abrasion must be avoided particularly where precision work is performed. Concrete floorings tend to produce dust. Ceramic tiles do not, but care must be taken in selecting the jointing material.

Resistance to chemicals

No flooring or jointing material can resist all possible combinations of chemical attack, and in buildings such as food processing factories and laboratories spillage should either be avoided or arrangements made for its prompt removal. In such situations paviors and vitrified ceramic tiles with chemical resistant bedding mortars and jointing materials combine high resistance to chemicals with resistance to trucking and thermal shock. Floors should be laid to a fall of 1 in 60, or up to 1 in 40 where dangers of slipping or of trucks rolling do not arise. A chemical resistant membrane, eg of acid resistant mastic asphalt or polythene sheet may be required below the flooring as a second line of defence.

Valuable references are BRE Digest 120 *Corrosion-resistant floors in industrial buildings* and CP 202: 1972 *Tile flooring and slab flooring.*

Fire properties

Floors do not generally present a serious fire hazard, but non-combustible floorings may be required in escape routes.

Resistance to sparking

Sparks can arise from impact by metals on hard surfaces or from friction on electrically non-conductive materials such as PVC and rubber. Where gases with a low flash point occur, as in operating theatres, electrically anti-static materials must be used. Expert advise should be sought for specific cases. *Anti-static precautions: flooring in anaesthetising areas* MOH Hospital Technical Memorandum no. 2, 1965 deals with the subject.

Ordinary grades of ceramic tiles, PVC, rubber, cork and asphalt and some sealing treatments are poor conductors of electricity but conductive grades are available. Terrazzo is often used as an electrically conductive floor. Electrical bonding by copper strips or by a special adhesive or coating on the underside of floorings is required to give uniform conductivity throughout a floor. Floor polishes or seals must not be allowed to reduce anti-static properties.

X-ray resistance

Ordinary floorings do not resist X-rays and a lead or other resistant barrier may be needed.

Costs of floorings

Initial costs of floorings vary as much as 50 to 1 and difference in serviceable lives can be of the same order. Low initial cost is often associated with rapid deterioration, high maintenance costs and high *cost-in-use*. The fact that timber, composition blocks, terrazzo, cork and natural stones being homogeneous throughout their thickness can be resurfaced, substantially reduces their cost-in-use.

THE BASE

Generally, bases must be rigid and stable: few, if any, finishes can withstand constant movement. They must be level (see page 19), and for thin floor coverings which mirror the slightest irregularities, they must be smooth.

Bases for floorings which will transmit or be damaged by moisture must be sufficiently dry. BRE Digest 163 describes a simple apparatus comprising a hygrometer which measures the relative humidity of a small volume or air enclosed so it is in equilibrium with the surface. If the reading taken after at least four hours (preferably 12 hours) is in the range 75 to 80 per cent it is safe to lay all floorings. This section deals with damp-proofing requirements in 'solid' concrete floors and 'suspended' timber floors at ground level where no water pressure exists.

Solid floors at ground level

References are:
CP 102: 1963   *Protection of buildings against water from the ground*
CP 204: 1970   *In-situ floor finishes*
BRE Digest 54   *Damp proofing solid floors.*

Dampness may lead to uncomfortably humid atmospheric conditions, a 'cold floor', surface discolouration, and decay of organic materials in underlays, adhesives and floorings. Rising damp, either as liquid or vapour which penetrates through flooring units or through the joints between them is often only remarked upon when condensation appears on the underside of an impervious mat, or where water which evaporates leaves salts on a surface. Incidentally, perishable materials may remain sound where they are able to 'breathe' but decay rapidly if moisture is trapped by superimposed impervious materials.

Concrete and cement/sand screeds are not vap-our-proof even if a waterproofing admixture is included in their composition. Only mastic asphalt and pitch mastic are completely vapour-proof. Table 5 gives damp-proofing requirements for floorings on solid floors. According to their position damp-proofing membranes are called:
(i)   sub-base membranes
(ii)   sandwich membranes or
(iii) surface membranes.

(i)   *Sub-base membranes*

Damp-proof films with lapped joints can be laid on a sub-grade blinded with fine material before the base concrete is laid. CP 102 states that polyisobutylene film can provide a vapour seal and polythene film at least 0.13 mm thick with lapped joints is of value under thermoplastic and vinylasbestos tiles, although it does not always afford sufficient protection to water-sensitive materials such as magnesuim. oxychloride, PVA emulsion-cement, flexible PVC, cork or timber.

The membrane must be below base concrete which includes heating elements but in other cases because it takes about four weeks for every 25 mm thickness of concrete to dry out, it is usually best to place the membrane above the base concrete.

(ii)   *Sandwich membranes*

These are laid between a concrete base and a screed. Four examples are:

(a)   *Hot bitumen or coal-tar pitch* at least 3mm thick and soft enough to avoid brittleness in cold weather, without being tacky in hot weather. (Softening points should be 50-55°C and 35-45°C respectively.) If the concrete is too damp or dusty, pinholes may develop in the membrane. It should be primed with bitumen solution or emulsion, or with a solution of coal-tar pitch for a hot pitch membrane.

(b)   Three coats of *Bitumen solution, bitumen-rubber emulsion* or *tar-rubber emulsion* at least 0.5 mm thick.

(c)   *Bitumen sheet* damp-proof course to BS743 with sealed joints.

(d)   *Plastics films* as for sub-base membranes.

Floor finishes	Resistance of finish to damp	Minimum damp-resisting requirements[1]
16 mm mastic asphalt 16 mm pitch mastic	No material, dimensional or adhesion failure	No additional protection normally required[2]
Concrete including terrazzo Clay tiles	No material, dimensional or adhesion failure if sulphates are not present	A sandwich membrane is recommended on wet sites[2]
Cement/rubber latex Cement/bitumen Composition blocks laid in cement mortar	No material or dimensional failure Generally no adhesion failure	
Wood blocks dipped and laid in hot soft bitumen or coal-tar pitch covering whole area	Material, dimensional and adhesion failure may occur in wet conditions	
Thermoplastic tiles PVC, vinyl-asbestos tiles	In wet conditions dimensional and adhesion failure may occur. Thermoplastic tiles may be attacked by dissolved salts	
Magnesium oxychloride	Softens and disintegrates in wet conditions	A sandwich membrane is essential
PVA emulsion/cement	Expands when damp	
Rubber and flexible PVC Linoleum and cork carpet Cork tiles	Loses adhesion and expands when damp	
Wood blocks laid in cold adhesive Wood strip and boards Chipboard	Expands and may rot	

[1] Damp-proof membranes must be continuous with damp-proof course in walls
[2] A damp-proof membrane is always required below floor warming

Table 4   Damp-proofing requirements for floorings on solid floors
(Includes information from BRE Digest 54)

(iii)   Surface membranes

Damp-proof underlays or floor finishes of 16 mm mastic asphalt and pitch mastic are water and vapour-proof and eliminate the need to wait for base concrete and screeds to dry. Pitch-epoxy resin coatings are slightly permeable to water vapour and are not able to 'bridge' cracks which may form in the surface to which they are applied.

Suspended timber floors at ground level

A properly constructed floor comprising tongued and grooved timber boards on joists, supported on sleeper walls or piers with damp-proof courses, built off a concrete slab laid on hardcore can provide a dry floor if there is adequate sub-floor ventilation to remove water vapour which rises through the site concrete (see MBS: S and F part 1). However,

16

the thermal insulation provided by the boards must be supplemented by insulating boards or quilt or by reflective foil.

Floor screeds

References are :
BRE Digest 104, *Floor screeds*, HMSO
D of E Advisory Leaflet 5, *Laying floor screeds*, HMSO.

Screeds to receive floorings are laid, usually on a concrete base, for one or more of the following purposes.
1 To provide a degree of level and smoothness to suit a particular flooring, where this is not provided by the structural base with or without a *levelling compound* applied to it.
2 To raise levels.
3 To provide falls. To maintain a minimum stipulated thickness most parts of the screeded area will be wastefully thick and where possible it is better to form falls in the structural base.
4 To accommodate services. Ideally services should be readily accessible and cracking is likely to occur where screeds are reduced in thickness above embedded pipes.
5 To accommodate floor warming installations.
6 To provide thermal insulation.
7 To provide insulation against transmission of impact sound, in the form of *floating screeds.*
8 To provide a nailable base for certain floorings.
9 To form part of the structure of certain precast concrete floor systems.

Generally, if floor finishes are liable to be damaged, by damp, a damp-proof membrane is necessary, see page 15

Screeds on timber bases.

Screeds would not normally be laid on timber bases but if they are the timber must be rigid, dry and adequately ventilated below. The upper surface of timber must be protected by bitumen felt or building paper and wire netting or light expanded metal should be fixed at about 200 mm centres and so that no part of the mesh rises more than 6 mm above the surface of the timber.

Screeds are considered in the following order:
Concrete screeds:
    cement – dense aggregate
    modified cement and sand screeds

    lightweight concrete screeds
Synthetic anhydrite screeds.

Cement: dense aggregate screeds

The thickness of cement – dense aggregate screed must relate to their strength, the degree of bond with the base and where applicable the strength of the base. Screeds which are *monolithic* with sound bases can be very thin. Those which are laid separately must be thicker and *unbonded* screeds, in particular *floating* screeds on compressible layers, must be sufficiently thick to be strong in their own right. They are also more liable to crack and curl upwards at the edges of slabs. Screeds are described under these headings:
1 *Monolithic screeds* (on green concrete)
2 *Bonded screeds* (on hardened concrete)
3 *Unbonded screeds*

1   *Monolithic screeds* By laying screeds on green concrete within three hours of placing, differential shrinkage between the screed and base is minimized and success is guaranteed. However, an early decision to lay monolithically must be made and the screed must be protected during subsequent building operations.

2   *Bonded screeds on hardened concrete* The fact that cement aggregate screeds often fail to bond fully to hardened concrete bases may be acceptable for light duty floors, very thick screeds and where the floor finish is of rigid units such as quarries and in such cases the concrete base need only be brushed with a stiff broom just before it hardens. To obtain maximum bond the aggregate in the base concrete must be exposed without loosening the large particles. This can be done by water spray and brushing the hardened concrete, but after the normal delay before laying the screed the dirty surface is usually very difficult to clean, and mechanical hacking[1] just before laying the screed is preferable.

Whether the surface is prepared to give partial or maximum bond it should be thoroughly cleaned and wetted (preferably overnight), any surplus water removed, and not more than twenty minutes before laying the screed a thin coat of cement grout should be well brushed into the damp surface of the base. Alternatively, a proprietary *bonding agent* can be

[1] It is not practicable to hack precast concrete units and screeds should be considered to be 'partially bonded'.

used, but it remains necessary to remove surface laitance and to wet concrete before it is applied. Agents based on polyvinyl acetate, however, are not suitable in persistently damp conditions.

3 *Unbonded screeds* These screeds must be at least 50 mm thick as shown in table 6. Greater thicknesses are necessary for heated screeds and for those laid on resilient layers. Great care should be taken in the design and laying of screeds which incorporate floor warming installations. For those including electrical cables *The Electric Floor Warming Design Manual*, obtainable from the Electricity Council, 30 Millbank, London, S W 1 should be consulted.

'Floating screeds' for sound insulation must be at least 65 mm thick and 75 mm thick if they are heated. Wire mesh will not prevent curling but it may restrain drying shrinkage. Resilient layers with a nominal thickness of 25 mm should not be reduced to less than 10 mm under the dead load of the floor

and they must be turned upwards at their edges so the screed is isolated from walls and columns. Adjacent edges of quilts should be closely butted and great care must be taken to prevent mortar from seeping into or bridging the installation at any point.

Materials for cement: dense aggregate screeds Portland cement to BS 12 *Portland cement (ordinary and rapid hardening)* is usually satisfactory. Aggregate should comply with BS 882, 1201 *Aggregates from natural sources for concrete (including granolithic)* and BS 1199 *Building sands from natural sources,* zones 1, 2 or 3.

To minimize drying shrinkage, the most common cause of failure, the cement: aggregate ratio should not exceed 1 : 3 and the driest mix which can be thoroughly compacted with the means available should be used. A sample squeezed in the hand should ball together without water being forced out. Low water : cement ratios become practicable by the use of workability aids and mechanical compaction.

Type	Base	Thickness mm	Bay size*
Monolithic	Concrete less than 3 hours old	12 – 25	—
Bonded	Sound, clean concrete more than 3 hours old but not including water repellent admixture	40† min	10 m² max and length not exceeding 1½ × width for screeds to receive thick finishes and heated screeds only – see page 19
Unbonded	Damp-proof membrane or concrete which is weak, contaminated or includes water repellent admixture	50 min *unheated* 65 min *heated*	
	Resilient quilt for *floating floor*	65 min *unheated* 75 min *heated*	

*Joints must also be provided in monolithic and bonded screeds over movement joints in the structure.
†Where bays are very small, eg for terrazzo, minimum thickness can be 25 mm.

Table 5 Thicknesses and bay sizes for dense concrete screeds

Mixes Suitable mix proportions by weight are shown in Table 6 below:

Thickness of screed mm	Cement	Fine Aggregate (dry sand or crushed stone graded 5 mm down)	Coarse aggregate (graded 10 down)
up to 40	1	3* – 4½	–
40 to 75			
over 75	1	1½	3

*The richer 1 : 3 mix is preferred for screeds for thin floorings such as PVC (vinyl)-asbestos and flexible vinyl tiles.

Where weight batching is not practicable, cement should be batched by hole bags, accurate gauge boxes should be used for measuring the aggregate and proportions should be adjusted to compensate for *bulking* (see *MBS: Materials*, page 165).

Mixing Thorough mixing is most important to obtain optimum strength, and a mechanical mixer is advisable.

Laying It used to be thought preferable to lay all screeds in bays to control shrinkage cracking but drying from the upper surface of screeds often caused bays to curl upwards at their edges and it was necessary either to relay or to grind down the raised parts in order to prevent them showing through thin floorings such as vinyl sheet and tiles. It is now recommended by the PSA that *bonded* screeds for thin floorings (other than heated screeds), should be laid in as large areas as possible. Random cracks can then be easily repaired. However, *bonded* and *unbonded* screeds to receive thick floorings, and those including heating, should be laid alternately in bays 'chess board fashion' with close butt vertical joints. Adjacent bays should be laid at intervals of at least twenty-four hours, the edges of the first laid bays being wetted and brushed with cement grout. Shrinkage will accommodate local thermal expansion and expansion joints need only be provided to coincide with those which are in the structure.

Screeds must be thoroughly compacted preferably with a beam vibrator, particular attention being paid to edges of bays and especially to the corners. Where trowelling is required to give a true surface it should be delayed for some hours when it will be accompanied by a ringing sound. Premature or excessive trowelling brings laitance to the surface which will craze and dust. For some finishes a screedboarded or a wood floated surface suffices, but a very smooth trowelled surface is necessary for thin floorings such as linoleum and vinyl sheet.

The *tolerances for level* given for floor finishes in CP 204 would apply to screeds for thin finishes. Acceptable deviations from datum could be ± 15 mm over large open areas and local variations in level ± 3 mm in any 3 m. Differences of level between adjacent bays should not exceed ± 1 mm, and less where thin flexible coverings will be laid.
BS 1134: Part 2: 1972 describes a profilometer which records movements of a wheel over surfaces.

Curing The screed must be kept well above freezing point until it is hard and kept damp for at least seven days until it is strong enough to withstand the stress arising from drying shrinkage.

Drying The slower the rate of drying the lower is the risk of cracking and curling, and the temptation to accelerate drying must be resisted for at least the first four weeks. Water sensitive finishes should not be laid until screeds are sufficiently dry. A rough rule is to allow four weeks for every 25 mm of screed (or concrete) – above the damp-proof membrane in normal weather but the test described in BRE Digest 18 and CP 203 should be used (see page 15). Drying by underfloor warming should not commence for at least four weeks and then only at a reduced temperature. It is important to note that drying will not occur below the elements while the heating is in operation.

Modified cement and sand screeds

Proprietary screeds which include metallic soaps or other water repellents dry slowly but those which contain emulsions of bitumen, polyvinyl acetate, acrylic resins and/or synthetic rubbers are usually thinner than cement/sand screeds and dry more quickly. Screeds of this type may set quickly, adhere well and be laid to a feather edge, resist cracking and some are *self smoothing*.

Lightweight concrete screeds

Screeds of aerated, lightweight aggregate or no-fines concretes [1] are particularly useful in saving weight where thick screeds are required to provide falls or to accommodate services. Broadly, thermal insulation improves, strength reduces and shrinkage increases with decreasing density. No-fines concrete, however, has low shrinkage. Table 7 gives recommended thickness and other information.

Synthetic anhydrite screeds

Screeds of 1 synthetic anhydrite (anhydrous calcium sulphate: 2½ specially graded aggregate (by volume) can be laid to minimum thicknesses of 25 mm for normal use, 30 mm for electric floor warming and 40 mm on compressible layers. Although more costly for equal thickness than cement/sand screeds:
(a)   the base need not be prepared to provide bond
(b)   almost all the water used combines as water of crystallization and moisture-sensitive floorings can sometimes be laid as soon as ten days after the screed is laid
(c)   very low drying shrinkage means that screeds can be laid in large areas without cracking or curling.

[1] Lightweight concretes are discussed in *MBS: Materials* chapter 8

Type	Usual minimum thickness mm	Remarks
Aerated	40 plus 15–20 *monolithic* dense topping on screeds less than 1280 kg/m³ and if heavy wear is likely before floor finish is laid	Mixing and laying should be done by specialist firms
Lightweight aggregate 'weak' eg exfoliated vermiculite, perlite	50 plus 15–20 *monolithic* dense topping*	Mixing and laying should be done in strict accordance with the aggregate manufacturers' instructions eg: *Bonded* screeds are laid on fresh neat cement grout 'Weak' mixes should not be tamped or vibrated
'strong' eg expanded clay, shale or slate, foamed slag, sintered pulverized fuel ash (pfa)	40 including 10 *monolithic* dense topping* if floor finish cannot distribute point loads sufficiently	*Note* Absorbent aggregates are slow in drying but pfa *no-fines* mixes dry more quickly than dense mixes
No-fines eg 1 Portland cement: 10 sintered pfa (*Lytag*) 6 mm single size (by volume)	25 *bonded* or 51 (including reinforcement) *unbonded* plus 10 dense topping* in each case	

* Not richer than 1 cement : 4 sand to minimize risk of shrinkage cracking

Table 7   Lightweight concrete screeds

On the other hand, synthetic anhydrite loses strength in damp conditions and bases must be dry before screeds are laid, If the calcium sulphate dries out before it is thoroughly hydrated dustiness and low strength may result.

Dry underlay systems on concrete bases

A proprietary dry floating floor to receive non-rigid light duty floorings consists of 6 or 8 mm sheets of hardboard with rebated edges which are bonded with PVA adhesive when they are laid mesh side up on 13, 16 or 19 mm heat tempered bitumen insulating fibre building board which is laid loose on the subfloor. 2 mm gaps should be left between adjoining insulating boards, 10 mm gaps around rooms and 3 mm gaps between rooms and at every 10 m in corridors. Joints between hardboards and insulating boards should not coincide. Subfloors should be dry and reasonably smooth, although the insulating board accepts a degree of unevenness.

The boards should be stored flat on the site for a few days to allow them to adjust to the ambient humidity.

Alternatively, chipboards with t and g joints to all edges are laid on foamed polystyrene boards, at least 12 mm thick, separated from the base by polythene foil. Chipboards should not be more than 610 mm wide with end joints staggered. If 12 mm gaps are left adjacent to all walls, columns etc. the system has some value in reducing the transmission of impact sound.

TYPES OF FLOORINGS

The range of floorings includes materials as diverse as wool, cork, plastic, timber, granite and steel with widely differing appearance, performance, and initial and maintenance costs. Common types of materials are either: A *Laid while 'plastic'* or B *'Preformed'*.

A   **Floorings laid while 'plastic'**

    A I   *Without joints*

        1   Mastic asphalt
        2   Pitch mastic
        3   Cement rubber-latex
        4   Cement-bitumen emulsion
        5   Cement resin
        6   Polyurethane resin
        7   Epoxide resin
        8   Polyester resin

See text page 22 and table 9 pages 24-27

    A II   *With joints*

        1   Concrete floorings
           (i)   Plain
           (ii)   Granolithic
           (iii)   Terrazzo
        2   Magnesium oxychloride (magnesite)

See text page 22 and table 11 pages 30-31

B   **Preformed floorings**

    B I   *Sheet supplied rolled*

        Adhesives
        1   Linoleum
        2   Cork carpet
        3   Printed linoleum
        4   Flexible vinyl
        5   Rubber

See text page 32 and table 13 pages 38-41

    B II   *Boards* (other than timber)

        1   Plywood
        2   Chipboard
        3   Hardboard

See text page 32 and table 14 pages 42-43

    B III   *Timber floorings*

        1   Blocks
        2   Blocks, end grain
        3   Boards
        4   Strip
        5   Overlay strip
        6   Parquet
        7   Parquet panels
        8   Mosaic

(Plywood — see B II *Boards*)
See text page 32 and table 15 pages 44-47

    B IV   *Clay and precast concrete floorings*

        1   Bricks
        2   Paviors
        3   Quarries
        4   Vitrified ceramic floor tiles
        5   Fully vitrified ceramic floor tiles
        6   Mosaic
        7   Concrete, precast
        8   Terrazzo, precast

See text page 34 and table 16 pages 50-51

    B V   *Composition blocks*
See table 17 pages 52-53

    B VI   *Stones*

        1   Granites
        2   Sandstones
        3   Limestones
        4   Marbles
           (mosaic see B IV *Clay and precast concrete floorings* table 16)
        5   Slates
        6   Quartzite

See text page 36 and table 18 pages 54-55

    B VII   *Other tile and slab floorings*

        1   Linoleum
        2   Cork
        3   Rubber
        4   Thermoplastic ('asphalt') tiles
        5   Thermoplastic vinylized tiles
        6   Vinyl-asbestos
        7   Flexible vinyls
        8   Asbestos-cement
        9   Mastic asphalt
       10   Cast iron
       11   Steel

See table 19 pages 56-61

    B VIII   *Glass mosaic* See table 16, pages 50-51

    B IX   *Carpets and felts* See text page 36

A Flooring laid while 'plastic'

A I *Without joints* see table 9 page 24

These floorings are able to move sufficiently at ordinary temperatures to accommodate slight structural movements without cracking. The following notes supplement the information given in table 9.

1 *Mastic asphalt* Grades are:
 I *'Special hard'* – for ambient temperatures 25 to 35°C, schools, showrooms, etc.
 II *'Light duty'* – more liable to indentaion.
 III *'Medium industrial'* – not resistant to heavy trucking.
 IV *'Industrial-factory'* – resistant to heavy trucking and thermal shock.

Special grades are: coloured; for use at low and high temperatures eg over floor warming installations; for chemical and mineral oil resistance; non-slip; anti-static and spark-free grades.

An isolating membrane laid loose with lapped joints is essential for mastic asphalt up to 20 mm thick on bases of : timber; concrete or screeds of open texture or containing fine cracks or which have received a surface treatment, eg sodium silicate. A membrane is also required for any thickness of mastic asphalt on timber, roofs and on bases which would cause 'blowing' or which would cause the mastic to cool too rapidly during laying and where a polished surface is required.

Membranes can be black sheathing felt complying with BS 747 *Roofing felts (bitumen and fluxed pitch)*, Type 4A (i) or *glass fibre sheathing* where the base concrete is in direct contact with the ground.

Mastic asphalt should be heated to a temperature between 200 and 220°C preferably in a mechanically agitated mixer, as near the point of laying as possible to minimize cooling before it is laid.

Slight shrinkage occurs during cooling and thermal shock causes cracking, particularly of Grade I material. During laying and for 3 or 4 days the ambient temperatures should be 5 to 10°C.

2 *Pitch mastic* Generally properties and laying are similar to those for asphalt.

3 *Cement rubber-latex*

4 *Cement-bitumen emulsion*

5 *Cement-resin.*

6-8 *Resin-based in-situ floorings* These recently much developed materials, are characterized by toughness, resistance to abrasion and most chemicals, and give dustless and easily cleaned surfaces. Some products are self-levelling to a degree although their high cost precludes their use in sufficient thickness to make levelling screeds unnecessary; Bright colours and coloured flakes suspended in a clear matrix are available.

A II *Floorings laid while plastic, with joints*

Floorings which shrink or are inflexible and which should be laid with joints to accommodate movement include concrete and magnesium oxychloride.

1 *Concrete floorings* Concrete finishes must be of high quality concrete, the principles for obtaining which are stated in *MBS: Materials,* chapter 8. Good appearance, resistance to abrasion and avoidance of cracking, dusting, loss of bond with the base and other defects demand careful specification and supervision and skilled workmanship by specialist layers. In particular, aggregate should be clean and well graded, water: cement ratio should be low, mixing, compaction and curing should be thorough. Resistance to wear depends to a large extent on the skill displayed in trowelling. Over-trowelling brings laitance to the surface leading to *dusting.* Adequate temperature, while maintaining the requisite water content, must be maintained for at least seven days' curing and the flooring must not be brought into use until it is sufficiently strong.

Concrete finishes can be classed as either *integral finishes* on concrete clabs or *applied toppings* laid *monolithically* with, *bonded* to, or *unbonded* to the base. Structural slabs, such as domestic garage floors. at least 100 mm thick, can be finished by a tamping beam, float, trowel or by mechanical surfacers, as soon as the concrete has been thoroughly compacted and is sufficiently stiff to avoid an excess of laitance being bought to the surface.

Toppings may be of *plain, granolithic* or *terrazzo* concrete and will normally be laid on concrete bases. Falls should be formed in the base concrete so the thickness of the finish is uniform. Thicknesses above 40 mm should be laid in two courses, both at least 20 mm thick, the upper course immediately following the first course.

Services should be laid in the base concrete or in ducts, rather than in the concrete topping.

(i) *Plain* concrete toppings with ordinary aggregates provide utilitarian finishes for light and medium duty. They should be laid as recommended for granolithic finishes for best results.

Information concerning granolithic and terrazzo finishes is summarized in table 11, page 30.

(ii) *Granolithic* Useful references are *A specification for granolithic floor topping laid in in-situ concrete* (Cement and Concrete Association) and BRE Digest 47.

Granolithic is a utilitarian finish in which superior resistance to abrasion is a primary requirement and aggregate must be hard and tough. Coarse aggregate should comply with BS 1201: 1971 *Aggregates for granolithic concrete floor finishes* and the fine aggregate should comply with BS 1198-1200: 1955 *Building sands from natural sources.* (Crushed materials may contain dust and it requires more mixing water to give a workable mix) Proportions of topping granolithic should be 1 : 1 : 2 (by weight) subject to small adjustments to compensate for *bulking* of sand and to obtain a satisfactory overall grading from 10 mm down. Mixing should be done by machine.

The methods for laying are similar to those for screeds and thicknesses depend upon similar considerations, although here functional requirements are considerably more exacting.

Monolithic finish As with screeds the best adhesion to the base is obtained by laying granolithic within three hours of the base having been placed or sooner in hot weather. It must be emphasized that the description 'monolithic' cannot apply to finishes laid at a leter stage. Although an early decision to adopt the method, and protection during subsequent building operations are essential it should be used wherever possible particularly where granolithic is laid over heating elements.

For floors in contact with the ground a monolithic finish becomes possible if the damp-proof membrane is laid on blinding below the base concrete. For suspended in-situ floors the finish can be taken to contribute to the structural thickness. Monolithic finishes need be only 10-25 mm thick.

Bonded finish ('separate construction') The rules for obtaining the maximum bond between screeds and concrete bases more than three hours old apply to granolithic finishes and they should be strictly observed. See page 17.

Unbonded finishes Where finishes are laid on concrete bases which are contaminated with oil, or containing a water repellent, or where they are laid

on separating membranes a thickness up to 75 mm is needed, but even with prolonged damp curing the possibility of slabs curling upwards at their edges must be accepted.

Joints Granolithic should be laid in bays of the sizes given in table 8, the lengths of which should not exceed 1½ x widths. Vertical butt joints should occur over construction joints in the base and movement joints must be provided to correspond with any in the base.

Construction	Thickness mm	Maximum bay size m²
Monolithic	10 – 25 max	30 on concrete base 150 mm thick 15 on concrete base 100 mm thick
Bonded *floors* *stairs* treads and risers where forms are used risers where forms are not used	40 min 20 min 15 min	15 and length not exceeding 1½ × width
Unbonded	up to 75	2

Table 8 Thicknesses and bay sizes for granolithic floorings

Finishing surfaces After the topping has been levelled and fully compacted, and is set, it must be trowelled at least three times during the next 6 to 10 hours to produce a hard and dense surface free from laitance, and with as much coarse aggregate just below the surface as possible. Usually about two hours after the first trowelling the surface should be retrowelled to close any pores, laitance which arises being removed and not trowelled back into the surface. The final trowelling, usually being the third and sometimes the fourth, is delayed until considerable pressure is needed to make an impression on the surface.

Granolithic must be protected against drying winds and strong sunlight and as soon as it is

Material, form and references	Base	Properties	Appearance
1 Mastic asphalt Binder – natural and/or derivative bitumen Aggregate – 'natural rock' or crushed limestone, or coarse siliceous grit for acid-resisting grade Mineral fillers and grit Pigments – optional BS 1076 : 1966 Table 2 *Limestone aggregate* BS 1410 : 1966 *Natural rock asphalt aggregate* BS 1451 : 1966 *Coloured (limestone aggregate)* CP 204 : 1970[1] : Section 4	1 Floated and slightly roughened concrete 2 Wood boards No damp-proof membrane required in an unheated floor	Wear varies with aggregate – good to excellent. Non-dusting Hardness – indented by point loads – special grade required in hot positions, eg over underfloor heating Resilience – low but tolerates slight movement if laid on sheathing felt Slippery – if wet or polished Warmth – moderate Quiet – moderate Water and vapour proof Chemical resistance – damaged by oils, greases, acids, sugar solutions – but special grades available. High resistance to alkalis at normal temperatures	Colours – natural black, dark red and brown. Green is costly Textures – matt, polished (Heavily gritted material is less easily polished)
2 Pitch mastic Binder – coal tar-pitch Aggregate – limestone or siliceous grit Chalk – up to 15 per cent Pigments – optional BS 1450 : 1963 *Black pitch mastic flooring* BS 3672 : 1963 *Coloured pitch mastic flooring* CP 204 : 1970[1] : Section 5	Floated and slightly roughened concrete (not timber) No dpm required	Similar to mastic asphalt but superior resistance to mineral oils and inferior resistance to alkalis More brittle at low temperatures and softer at high temperatures – not suitable over floor warming	As mastic asphalt

3 Cement rubber-latex
Binder – rubber latex – natural or synthetic and Portland or high alumina cement
Pigments
Aggregate – cork, rubber, wood and/or stone
Mineral fillers
 	
CP 204 : 1970[1] : Section 6
	1 Floated concrete
	
	2 Timber, if strong, rigid and thoroughly seasoned
	
	3 Other firm strong bases
		Wear – good resistance
		Resilience – more comfortable than concrete
		Non-slip, moderately warm and quiet
		Water resistance – low to medium
		Good resistance to burns
		Resistant to dilute alkalis
		Resistance to oils and greases:
		  natural rubber – low
		  synthetic rubber – good
		Suitable over floor warming
		Good adhesion to base
			Colours – wide range
			
			Texture – smooth
			
			Pattern – with marble aggregate resembles terrazzo if buffed

4 Cement-bitumen emulsion	A dpm is required	Wear – good resistance, non-dusting	Colours – black and dark colours

Table 9   A I Flooring laid while 'plastic' – without joints

TABLE 9

Thickness mm	Laying	Surface treatment		Average Cost factor[2]
		Initial	Maintenance	
15 min – underlays 15 – 20 – Grades I and II 20 – 30 – Grade III 35 – 50 – Grade IV	Materials must not be over-heated Float in one coat for ordinary thicknesses Metal armouring may be incorporated in mastic asphalt Thicknesses up to 19 mm are laid on black sheathing felt or glass fibre sheeting where the base is in direct contact with the ground	Matt finish – trowel with fine sand or stone dust Polished finish – apply special water-wax emulsion (not polishes which contain solvents)	Sweep – avoid oiled sweeping compounds Wash – warm water and neutral detergent, or small quantity of washing soda for very dirty floors. Rinse Non-solvent polish can be applied Strip occasionally	18
May require to be thicker than mastic asphalt for equivalent uses	An isolating membrane is essential on a timber base and on concrete which contains fine cracks, is porous or of open texture Adequate ventilation is necessary to remove toxic fumes from pitch mastic	As mastic asphalt May be buffed to expose aggregate		18
4 – 12 Can be laid to 'feather edge'	Dampen absorptive concrete Prime with latex and cement for heavy duty. On timber base fix galvanized wire netting. Apply finish by trowel as soon as priming coat has set	May be buffed (in two stages) to remove laitance and expose the aggregate Non-oil or solvent emulsion polish only	Sweep frequently, avoid oiled sweeping compounds Wash – warm water and mild soap. Do not over-scrub Non-solvent polish on natural rubber type flooring	25
13	Prime screed Apply finish by trowel	——	Sweep Wash	14

– continued

Material, form and references	Base	Properties	Appearance

Aggregate – sand and crushed granite	See previous page	Resilience – more comfortable than concrete
		High resistance to burns
		Resistance to:
		  solvents – very low
		  acids and oils – low
		  alkalis – high
		Suitable over floor heating	

5 **Cement – resin** Binder – cement and polyester resin Aggregate – sand, crushed stone etc		Wear – good resistance Resilience – very low Fairly good resistance to acids, alkalis and oils Non-slip Suitable over floor heating	Texture – slight
6 **Polyurethane resin** Binder – polyurethane resin Vinyl chips or other fillers One and two-part types	Screed Rigid plywood A dpm is required	Wear – good resistance Non-slip Resilience – good Good resistance to water and oils Moderate resistance to acids and alkalis Low resistance to burns Normally suitable over floor heating	Colours – wide range Texture – 'orange peel' with chips Pattern – plain or chips in transparent binder
7 **Epoxide resin** Binder – epoxide resin Hardener Aggregate Mineral fillers	Screed – must be level (particularly for self-levelling grades), clean and free from laitance Rigid plywood A dpm is required	Wear – high resistance particularly for trowelled type 'Trucking grades' available Non-dusting Adhesion to base – excellent – good for repairs to existing floors Has chemical set and hardens within 48 hours Excellent resistance to water, acids, alkalis, oils and some solvents Can be resilient and non-slip High resistance to burns Can be suitable over floor heating Some anti-static grades available	Depends upon pigments and aggregates used Self-levelling grades tend to be glossy
8 **Polyester resin** Binder – polyester resin Catalyst Aggregates, fillers, glass fibres Pigments	Screed – must be level Rigid plywood A dpm is required	Wear – good resistance Resilience – very low Good resistance to water, acids, oils Moderate resistance to alkalis High resistance to burns Not suitable over floor heating Resin may shrink and hair-crack in curing	Colours – wide range

General considerations in selecting, laying and maintenance are discussed on page 22

Table 9   A I Flooring laid while 'plastic' – without joints

TABLE 9

Thickness mm	Laying	Surface Treatment		Average cost factor[2]
		Initial	Maintenance	
Can be laid to 'feather edge'			Do not use strong detergents for about six months	
3 – 10	Apply by trowel	—	Sweep Wash	18
2 – 3	Various specialized methods	—	Sweep Wash Wax polish is unnecessary and makes it difficult to 'reglaze' worn parts	35–40
2 self-levelling grades 2 sprayed grades 3 – 6 trowelled grades	Prime surface Fill hollows with epoxy resin – sand Spread or trowel Some grades can be sprayed using specialized equipment	Two coats of wax or silicone polish should be applied on self-levelling grades Surfaces of some grades can be ground to resemble terrazzo	Sweep Wash with soap or detergent Polish to maintain good appearance of self-levelling grades	50–70
2 – 6	Trowel	Surface can be ground to resemble terrazzo	Sweep Wash – warm water and soap or detergent Polish – polyacrylate non-slip emulsion	36–46

[1] *General reference:* CP 204 : 1970 *In situ floor finishes*
[2] Approximate cost relationships for typical floorings 'as laid', based on granolithic = 10

sufficiently hard it should be protected continuously for seven days, or longer in cold weather, with

1 canvas, straw mats or 50 mm of sand kept damp

2 impervious sheets securely held in position, lapped 75 mm and overlapping the edges of slabs. This method is necessary for coloured concrete

3 a proprietary curing medium.

Drying should be delayed as long as possible to reduce the likelihood of shrinkage cracking. Artificial heating should not be used for at least six weeks and then temperature should be increased slowly. Steel wheeled trollies should not use floors for at least 28 days.

Non-slip properties can be obtained by trowelling in non-slip granules, or later, surfaces can be mechanically or chemically roughened.

Hard materials such as ferrous aggregate, and surface applications of solution of sodium silicate, magnesium or zinc-fluoride improve resistance to abrasion but oleoresinous seals are more effective. Surface treatments applied in accordance with CP 204 and the manufacturers' instructions can be effective on newly hardened concrete, or on old floors if they are clean and dry.

(iii)   *Terrazzo* (Properties and requirements are summarized in table 11). – In-situ terrazzo floor toppings are described in CP 204 : 1970 *In-situ finishes*. Information on the subject can be obtained from The National Federation of Terrazzo-mosaic Specialists, 111 Wardour Street, London, WC1.

This 'quality' floor (and wall) finish although initially costly provides a hard wearing washable surface in a very wide range of colour combinations. It consists of white or coloured cement with crushed marble aggregate, laid usually on a screed on a concrete base and later ground and polished. It can be slippery when wet or where floor polish is transferred to it from adjacent floorings. For safety the finish should not be smoother than 'fine grit'. Carborundum or bauxite grit can be incorporated in, or trowelled into, mixes. Non-slip inlays are often included in the front edges of stair treads. If polish is ever used, it should be wax-free.

Terrazzo is often used in entrance halls to public buildings, food shops, lavatories and in hospitals. It is especially suitable for anti-static floors, see page 14.

The principles for obtaining sound granolithic finishes apply generally to terrazzo. It can be laid in three ways, ie *monolithically* on a green concrete base or on a screed which may be either *bonded* or *unbonded* to a concrete base. The thickness of screeds must be greater and panel sizes smaller as bond with the base reduces, see table 10.

Construction	Thickness[1] minimum mm	Panel size[2] maximum m[2]
Monolithic	15	dividing strips over all construction joints
Bonded *floors*	15 on 25 mm screed	
stairs treads risers strings	15 10 6	1
walls and skirtings	6 on 12 mm render	
Unbonded	15 on 50 mm screed	

[1] thickness should be greater if maximum aggregate size exceeds 10 mm
[2] length of panel should not exceed twice the width. Re-entrant angles must be avoided.

Table 10   Thicknesses and panel sizes for terrazzo finishes

Monolithic construction – To ensure complete adhesion and to minimize the likelihood of shrinkage cracking, where possible terrazzo should be laid directly on structural concrete bases within three hours of their having been placed, and after they have been brushed with a stiff broom to remove water and laitance. Panels of monolithically laid terrazzo can be larger than with other methods of laying but difficulties may arise in protecting the finish from following trades and the method is not widely used.

Bonded construction Where terrazzo is not laid directly on green concrete it must be laid on a screed preferably within three hours of its having been laid. If the screed is older (it should not be older than 48 hours), a neat cement slurry should be brushed into the surface immediately before laying the terrazzo.

Unbonded construction Where the base is hard, or bond is prevented by contamination or water repellents, the terrazzo topping must be laid as described for bonded construction but on a screed at least 50 mm thick, reinforced with light mesh reinforcement and laid on a bitumen felt, building paper or polythene separating layer lapped 50 mm at the joints.

Toppings The marble aggregate should be clean, angular — not elongated or flaky, and free from dust. Nominal sizes are:

Italian code	Nominal sizes mm
$\frac{1}{5}$	2 – 5
$\frac{1}{6}$	4 – 6
2	5 – 9
3	9 – 19
4	12 – 20
5	22 – 25

These sizes can be used individually or in combinations, eg for a fine mix 1 part 3-5 mm : 1 to 1½ parts 5-6 mm. The larger the size of aggregate the less risk of cracking and particles less than 3 mm should not be used. The cement: aggregate ratio varies with the grading and maximum size of the aggregate, but should not exceed 1 : 2 by volume.

Toppings may either be laid as mixes which include all the aggregate or by the *seminar method* as mixes containing only fine aggregate into the upper surfaces of which the larger particles are beaten and rolled in. Metal, ebonite or plastic strips should be securely anchored in the screed to divide toppings into panels, see table 10, and wherever cracks are likely to form due to structural movements. Expansion and contraction joints in the main structure. must of course, be carried through the flooring and be suitably finished on the surface. After tamping, compaction with a heavy roller, trowelling, and re-

moval of laitance to achieve a dense surface with a regular distribution of aggregate and minimum of cement matrix visible, the flooring must be damp cured. (See *Granolithic floorings*.) Canvas, hessian and sawdust curing media are very liable to stain terrazzo and where white or coloured cement is used plastics sheets are essential.

Finishing surfaces Terrazzo is sometimes sur- fifiently hard for grinding and polishing within four days of laying. It is best done by machine except for small areas, and in the following sequence: Grind with coarse abrasive stone with water; wash the floor; clean out voids and fill them with neat cement paste. Damp cure and keep the floor free from excessive temperature changes for at least three days before polishing with a fine abrasive stone with water.

Where possible artificial heat should not be turned on in the building for 6 to 8 weeks and the temperature should then be increased slowly.

Heavy traffic should not be allowed on the floor for at least two days.

Maintenance and cleaning Before opening to traffic, terrazzo should be scrubbed with an acid and alkali-free soap and allowed to stand overnight. The following day the surface should be scrubbed vigorously with hot water and rinsed. Subsequently surfaces should be kept clean with soft soap and rinsed. Strong detergents should not be used and some disinfectants contain phenols and cresols which stain terrazzo.

A II 2 *Magnesium oxychloride* (magnesite) Properties and requirements are summerized in table 11. This comparatively low-cost finish consisting of calcined magnesite, wood or mineral fillers pigments and sometimes silica, talc or powered asbestos, gauged with a solution of magnesium chloride, can be laid in plain colours and in mottled and terrazzo effects. However, colours are dull and the material has been largely supplanted by preformed floorings. If the surface is protected by oil or wax, resistance to wear is moderate to high and the floor is free from dusting. It is slippery if highly polished but abrasive grit can be incorporated in the finish to give a non-slip surface. Wood-fillers make the floor-ing moderately warm and resilient. Magnesium oxychloride is not seriously affected by alkalis, non-drying oils, fats, grease and organic solvents, but it

Material, form and references	Base	Properties	Appearance
1 Concrete finishes (i) *Self-finish* (ii) *Plain Topping* (iii) *Granolithic* *Cement*: usually Portland cement BS 12: 1971 *Aggregate*: BS 1201:1973 *Aggregates for granolithic concrete floor finishes*; BS 1198–1200:1955 *Building sands from natural sources* CP 204:1970: Section 2 *In-situ floor finishes*	Concrete roughened to receive bonded finishes for which concrete should not contain water proofer (Not timber)	Cold, hard, noisy Subject to 'dusting' Resistant to alkalis, mineral oils and many salts Slippery when wet if abrasive is not incorporated in surface. Rounded aggregate is more slippery than angular aggregate	Grey, utilitarian
(iii) *Terrazzo* *Cement*: usually white or coloured Portland cement *Aggregate*: marble or spar CP 204:1970: Section 3 *In-situ floor finishes*		Cold, hard, noisy Slippery when wet, if machine polished, washed with soap, or if polish is applied Does not 'dust'	Resembles a mosaic of polished marble chippings divided into panels by strips
2 Magnesium oxychloride (Magnesite) Calcined magnesite and magnesium chloride with wood or mineral and asbestos fillers and pigments to comply with: BS 776:1972 *Materials for magnesium oxychloride (magnesite) flooring* and BS 1014:1961 *Pigments for cement, magnesium oxychloride and concrete* CP 204:1970: Section 7 *In-situ floor finishes*	1 Dry and non-porous concrete, tiles, etc 2 Timber flooring with galvanized wire netting fixed to it	Moderately hard, warm and quiet 'Dusts' if not protected Slippery if highly polished but abrasive can be incorporated Deteriorates in damp conditions Tends to 'sweat' Not recommended with underfloor warming	White and plain colours, mottled and terrazzo effects

General considerations in selecting and laying these floorings are discussed on page 22.

Table 11   A II Floorings laid while 'plastic' – with joints

gradually disintergrates if it is continuously exposed to water or to acids and salts.

Magnesium chloride absorbs moisture from the air and 'sweating' may occur in humid atmospheres. It corrodes metal and stains plaster and should be separated from them by at least 25 mm of uncracked, dense concrete or by a bituminous coating, It is difficult to ensure that floor warming systems remain fully coated and CP 204: 1970 *In-situ floor finishes* does not recommend their inclusion in magnesite.

TABLE 11

Thickness mm	Laying	Surface treatment		Approximate cost factors[1]
		Initial	Maintenance	
10 – 25 *monolithic* 40 *bonded* 75 *unbonded*	(i) Base self-finished with trowel float or tamping board (ii) Plain toppings (iii) Granolithic toppings well compacted in bays defined by dividing strips and trowelled when set Damp cured at least seven days	Surface hardener may be applied eg sodium silicate (see page 28) When flooring is dry polyurethane or synthetic rubber seals	Renew hardener or seal when necessary Sweep and wash	5 (19 mm cement: sand) 10 (19 mm granolithic)
12 min terrazzo* laid *monolithically* on structural concrete base 15 min terrazzo* topping laid *monolithically* on 25 mm screed bonded to base or on lightly reinforced 50 mm screed on isolating membrane * Greater thicknesses needed if aggregate is larger than 10 mm	Trowelled and well compacted in bays defined by dividing strips Damp cured Surface ground, filled, cured and reground	See *Terrazzo Tiles* page 300		54 – 60
10 – 65 on concrete 15 – 45 on timber	Isolate from plaster and metals (punch home nails in boards, and fill) Trowelled in one or two coats preferably in bays defined by dividing strips Damp cured	Proprietary dressing	Sweep Damp mop mild alkaline soap may be used occasionally Do not use household cleaning powders or sweeping powders Wax polish or drying oil	15 – 25

[1] Approximate cost relationships for typical floorings 'as laid', based on granolithic = 10

Magnesium oxychloride can also be used as an underlay for thin sheet and tile floorings.

Concrete bases should be finished reasonably free from ridges and hollows but be slightly roughened with a stiff broom. They should be thoroughly dry when the finish is laid. Galvanized wire netting should be laid on timber bases and fixed at about 200 mm centres with galvanized clout nails. Other nails should be left proud of the base at the same centres.

One coat work is generally 10 to 25 mm thick, and thicknesses greater than 40 mm are laid in two coats, each being not more than 20 mm thick. CP 204 recommends that 6 mm plastics or hardwood dividing strips should be incorporated at not more than 7600 mm centres.

Drying must be delayed for at least 24 hours and light traffic should not be permitted for three days, or longer in cold weather. Heavy traffic should not be permitted for some weeks. Maintenance invloves sweeping, damp mopping and treatment with a polish or seal.

B Preformed Floorings

B 1 *Sheet supplied rolled* (See table 13, page 38.) These preformed materials can be laid rapidly with few joints (and these can be welded in (vinyl) PVC sheets). Being thin, a level and very smooth base is needed, although smoothness is less important with materials which have resilient backings. The wear performance of thin materials depends upon flatness of the base, their thickness, the type and intensity of traffic and on maintenance. Edges of sheets must be protected.

All resilient materials are more flexible and easier to handle and bond to the base when they are warm. The base must be clean, dust-free and dry. Sheet floorings require damp-proof membranes in solid ground floors. Some of them will rot in damp conditions and adhesives will fail. Adhesives prevent sheets curling up at the edges, discourage creep and generally improve performance and appearance of thin floorings.

Adhesives must hold various different materials in place while resisting the stresses imposed by traffic and by movements of the flooring and base. It is important to know that no adhesive can act as a damp-proof membrane.

Water-based adhesives, e.g. starch, casein and lignin are lowest in cost but their brittleness limits their use to porous materials such as linoleum, cork and fabric-backed PVC in dry conditions. The gum-spirit adhesives are also fairly low in cost and suitable for porous surfaces but although insoluble in water some products are attacked in damp conditions.

Bitumen emulsions and solvent solutions are suitable for thermoplastic and vinyl-asbestos tiles but not for all types of flexible PVC floorings. Synthetic latex adhesives withstand normal damp and alkaline conditions. Natural and synthetic rubber-resin solutions used for laying rubber floorings must be applied to both the base and flooring and allowed an exact drying time before the surfaces are brought together. Although more costly than the aqueous product they have very high immediate and final bond strengths.

Floorings should not be washed until adhesive is thoroughly hard.

B II *Boards* (See table 14, page 42.)

Suitable boards of appropriate thickness can perform the dual function of supporting traffic and other loads between joist or batten or over other supports and providing a wearing surface of good appearance with few joints.

B III *Timber floorings* (see table 15, page 44.)

General references are:

CP 210 : Part 2 : 1972 *Wood flooring (Board, strip, block and mosaic)*

Timber selection by properties Part 1 : Windows, doors, cladding and flooring PRL. HMSO

Timber floorings, The Timber Research and Development Association (TRADA)

BRE Digest 18, *Design of timber floors to prevent dry rot,* HMSO

MBS : Materials, chapter 2, *Timber.*

Timbers of widely differing properties, appearance and costs can be used in various ways in buildings of almost all types, whether they be residential, educational, industrial or public. Timber is hard wearing (resistance in any one species increases with density), and resilient, more so where fixed on joists or battens rather than a solid base. Resistance to acids and alkalis varies from moderate to high, but polishes and in particular seals, provide protection from them, and also from staining, dirt and water. Timber flooring must be correctly seasoned and also designed to accommodate the moisture movement which is inevitable in service. To prevent fungal attack, timber which is not exclusively heartwood of an inherently durable species must be kept with a sufficiently low moisture content, or be treated with a preservative. Some timbers which are suitable over floor warming are listed in table 12, but they are not recommended where carpets with insulating underfelts are to be used.

Quarter sawn timber has less movement in its width, gives better wear and may have more attractive appearance than plain-sawn timber, However, its high cost is unlikely to be justified except in cases such as softwood gymnasium floors, where freedom from splintering is essential. End grain timber is even more resistant to wear than quarter sawn timber.

A notable advantage of timber flooring is that it can be repeatedly resurfaced, provided any tongues or dowels are well below the surface.

Moisture content of timber BS 1297: 1970 *Grading and sizing of softwood flooring* specifies a maximum moisture content of 22 per cent for air-dried timber and 15 per cent for kiln-dried timber. CP 201 gives 18 per cent. If considerable shrinkage is to be avoided where flooring is installed in modern buildings lower moisture contents requiring kiln seasoning are necessary. Moisture contents likely to occur in service are:

No heating	14 – 18%
Intermittent heating	12 – 15%
Continuous heating	11 – 12%
High degree of central heating	9%
Over underfloor heating	6 – 9%

Selection of timber Table 12 based on FPRL Bulletin no. 40 classifies some timbers for uses as strips, boards or blocks (but not end grain blocks) in respect of wear and other proporties.

Specialist subcontractors should be consulted, as both availability and cost vary considerably.

Timber	HI	LI	HP	NP	LP	RS	G	CA	FH	B	D	SM
African mahogany					LP				FH			
African walnut											D	
Afrormosia				NP				CA	FH			SM
Afzelia				NP				CA	FH			SM
Agba					LP				FH			SM
Brush, box	HI					RS		CA				
Burma teak				NP					FH			
Douglas fir					LP		G					
East African olive											D	
European beech		LI	HP				G					
European birch					LP							
European oak			HP					CA		B	D	
Greenheart	HI											
Guarea				NP			G		FH	B		
Gurjun				NP			G	CA				
Idigbo					LP							SM
Iroko				NP				CA	FH			SM
Japanese maple	HI					RS	G			B		
Keruing				NP			G	CA				
Loliondo		LI	HP				G		FH	B		SM
Missanda		LI	HP						FH			SM
Muhuhu	HI		HP						FH		D	SM
Muninga				NP			G		FH			
Niangon					LP							
Opepe				NP				CA	FH			
Panga panga			HP						FH		D	SM
Parana pine					LP							
Purpleheart			HP								D	
Redwood					LP							
Rhodesian teak	HI		HP					CA	FH	B	D	SM
Rock maple	HI		HP			RS	G			B		
Sapele				NP			G			B	D	
Scots pine					LP							
Utile				NP								
Wallaba	HI											
Western hemlock					LP		G					
Yew											D	

HI	*Heavy duty industrial*	including trucking and other impact loads as in factories, mills, workshops and warehouses.
LI	*Light duty industrial*	including trucking of a light nature, e.g. clothing and food processing establishments.
HP	*Heavy pedestrian*	Intensities of more than 2000 persons per day, usually concentrated in traffic lanes, e.g. in public institutions, barracks and corridors in large schools and colleges.
NP	*Normal pedestrian*	Intensities of less than 2000 persons per day, eg in assembly halls, schools and college classrooms, hospital, shops and offices.
LP	*Light pedestrian*	Residential and domestic buildings, small classrooms and offices.
RS	*Roller skating rinks.*	
G	*Gymnasia*	(softwoods rift sawn only)
CA	*High impermeabilty to chemicals and acid.*	
FH	*Suitable over floor heating.*	
B	*Ballrooms.*	
D	*Decorative*	
SM	*Small movement.*	

Table 12 Timbers for flooring

The base Timber must be protected from moisture by damp-proof membranes in solid ground floors, and by damp-proof courses and ventilation below suspended floors (see *MBS: Structure and fabric part 1*). Timber fillets embedded in concrete are required to be either treated in accordance with BS 3452: 1962 *Copper-chrome water-borne wood preservatives and their application*, or pressure impregnated with copper-chrome-arsenate. Any surfaces which are exposed by cutting must be thoroughly treated with a 10 per cent aqueous solution of the preservative.

The relative humidity of air trapped on the surface of concrete infill between fillets should not exceed 75-80 per cent when wood flooring is laid.

Laying Good quality flooring should not be delivered to a site, or fixed before windows are completely glazed, the heating installation has been tested and the building has been maintained at its normal temperature with correct ventilation for at least a week.

A gap must be left for expansion between timber flooring and walls and columns. This can be concealed by a skirting which should not be fixed to the flooring. Where underfloor heating is installed the flooring should be laid in contact with the concrete filling between fillets to obtain maximum thermal transmittance.

Surface treatment See CP 209: 1963 *Care and maintenance of floor surfaces Part 1 – Wooden flooring.*

Good appearance and cleanliness of floors is obtained by fine sanding and filling the pores of the wood to reduce absorption. *Wax polish* gives good appearance but is soft and requires frequent renewal. *Button polish (shellac)* provides a filler coat before wax polishing but is too easily scratched and stained to serve as a durable finish.

Seals – see page 12 – are preferable for heavy duty, or where liquids are likely to be splashed. They are very tough and normally only require to be kept clean during a long life which can be prolonged by applications of resin-emulsion polish. Ordinary paste wax polish on sealed floors makes them dangerously slippery.

Penetrating or *dust-allaying* oils hold dirt and are only suitable for heavy duty and where appearance is unimportant.

B IV *Clay and precast concrete floorings*

Information concerning these floorings is summarized in table 16, page 48. Both clay and concrete products are hard, noisy and 'cold', have high thermal conductivity and capacity and are suitable over under-floor warming installations. Concrete products are lower in cost but the better clay products have the following advantages:

(i) very high resistance to chemicals, except hydrofluoric acid and strong hot caustic alkaline solutions.

(ii) they are harder and more resistant to abrasion than concrete products and are 'non-dusting'

(iii) colours are permanent and can be very intense and tiles can be glazed.

(iv) there is a much wider range of sizes, shapes, textures and colours.

Thermal movement of clay products is about half, and the modulus of elasticity about 1.5 to 3 times that of other products.

Bedding systems CP 202: 1972 *Tile flooring and slab flooring* describes methods for laying various units on different bases and for stated conditions of use.

(i) *Bedding in cement: sand mortar bonded to the base.* This traditional method is for heavy traffic. Concrete bases should be at least four weeks' old and screeds at least two weeks' old. They should not contain water repellent admixtures. After dipping the more absorptive units in clean water, but not soaking them, they are drained and beds should be 15 mm thick for tiles of 10 mm or less and 15 to 20 mm thick for thicker units.

To improve adhesion a light dusting of dry cement can be trowelled into the upper surface of the bedding or either a slurry of neat concrete or a cement-based adhesive can be applied to the backs of the tiles before they are laid. The backs of concrete tiles are usually painted with neat cement slurry.

Unfortunately, where units are bonded rigidly to bases, loss of bond with 'arching' or 'ridging', particularly of the thinner units, sometimes occurs, for one or more of the following reasons:

1 Shrinkage of the concrete base in drying. (Defects are likely to show in the first twelve months).

2 Shrinkage of the concrete base in cold weather. (Thermal movement of concrete is two to three times that of fired clay.)

3 Rapid local thermal expansion of tiles caused by steam or hot water hosing.

4 Creep deflection of concrete structural floors.

The expansion of ceramics, particularly the less dense materials, with absorption of moisture which occurs most rapidly in the first weeks after they leave the kiln (see *MBS: Materials,* chapter 6) may contribute to compressive stresses in tiling.

The risk of 'arching' and 'ridging' of tiles which are bonded to subfloors can be reduced by providing *movement joints* as described below, and by the following methods of laying, which permit some relative movement between tiles and subfloor.

CLAY AND PRECAST FLOORING

(ii) *Separating layer method* This method is suitable internally, except on stairs, on true and smooth concrete bases. Units can be laid as above but on the bedding mix 15 mm thick and at least as thick as units up to 25 mm thick, separated from from the base by polythene film[1], bitumen felt[2] or building paper[3] with 100 mm lapped joints or by damp-proof membranes. See figure 1.

(iii) *'Thick-bed', semi-dry method* To prevent bond with reasonably level concrete bases damped if necessary to reduce suction, a lean mix, 1 cement: 4 sand containing only sufficient water so it retains its shape when squeezed in the hand is tamped down at least 25 mm thick. For a bedding thicker than 40 mm a 1 cement: 1½ dry. 10 mm 'down' coarse aggregate:3 dry sand mix (by weight) should be used. (If proportions are batched by volume bulking of sand should be allowed for.) A slurry of 1 cement:1 fine sand of creamy consistency is applied about 3 mm thick immediately before the units are well beaten down. The backs of concrete tiles are painted with a 1:1 slurry. Joints should be grouted within four hours of laying.

(iv) *'Thin-bed', cement based adhesive method* On a sufficiently level, and dry base, dry tiles are well tamped on an adhesive which should comply

[1] 500 grade for most conditions
[2] BS 747
[3] BS 1521

with Appendix B of CP 212, Part 1 and be not more than 5 mm thick. The method is not recommended on screeds over underfloor heating. This, and the following proprietary products, should be used in strict accordance with the manufacturer's instructions.

(v) *Bedding in rubber-latex cement mortar* This method is practicable on any base, including metal decking. The mortar, which resembles rubber-latex cement flooring, accepts some movement and is resistant to mildly corrosive conditions.

(vi) *Bedding in bitumen emulsion: sand* The base is primed with the compound (BS 3940 *Adhesives based on bitumen or coal tar*) which is spread to a minimum thickness of about 10 mm.

Joints Joints must be sufficiently wide to accommodate some movement and variations in size of units, about 152 mm square and up to about 15 mm for larger and less accurate units. It is important that joints are completely filled in order to prevent penetration of liquids, to support their top edges and evenly distribute stresses between units. When the bedding has set ordinary joints are grouted with 1 cement: 1 fine dry sand, by volume, and those in mosaic with neat cement.

Movement joints should be taken through the tiles and bedding as indicated in figure 1. They are topped with an elastic but suitably hard sealant

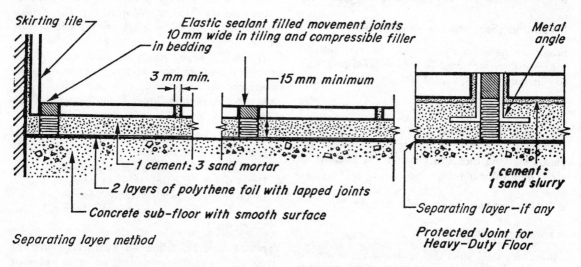

1   *Laying of clay and precast concrete flooring*

(see CP 202 and *MBS: Materials,* chapter 16). Movement joints should be avoided where there is heavy traffic but if they occur they should be protected with metal angles — see figure 1. Compressible back-up materials are used to control the depth of sealant and the way it deforms, and fillers are used to fill the remaining joint. Sometimes one material fulfils both functions. They must be compatible with the sealant. A barrier such as polyethylene film may be needed to prevent elastic sealants sticking to the back-up or filler material. For light duty where a watertight seal is not required, preformed strips such as cork, cork-rubber or rubber-bitumen can be used. They should be keyed into the bedding.

Clay units CP 202 recommended that where units are bedded 'solid', movement joints should be provided to perimeters,[1] over supporting beams and walls, over structural movement joints, and at 4.5 m centres. However, units bedded on a semi-dry mix, at ground level and which will not be subjected to large and rapid changes in temperature or humidity, usually do not require perimeter joints in floors which do not exceed 6 m in one direction. In such floors any intermediate joints can be at 9 m centres.

Concrete units — laid by any method — require perimeter joints[1] where floors exceed 15 mm in any direction and intermediate joints at 15 m centres.

B V *Composition blocks* (See table 17, page 52)

B VI *Stones* (See table 18, page 54)

Stones are hard, 'cold' and noisy but very suitable for underfloor warming. They have good resistance to oils but may be stained if they are not sealed.

B VII *Other tiles and slabs* (See table 19, page 56)

These units include heavy-duty cast iron slabs, semi-rigid materials such as compressed cork and thermoplastic tiles and tiles cut from sheet materials which are also provided in rolls.

B VIII *Glass mosaic* (See table 16, page 50)

B IX *Carpets and felts.*

[1] Where movement joints are required to perimeters they should also be provided around columns, machine bases, steps, etc.

References include:

Product selection for architects: Carpets, RIBA Journal, January 1970

BS 3655: 1963 *Code for informative labelling of carpets, carpeting and rugs* deals with size, construction, fibre content and cleansing.

BS 4223: 1967 specifies *A method for the determination of constructional details of carpets with a yarn pile.*

BS 4334: 1968 *Selected tests for carpets*

BS 5557: 1978 *Textile floor coverings* is a useful reference.

Carpets vary widely in quality, which is generally related to initial cost. Low initial cost is often associated with high *cost-in-use*. It should be noted that durability and deterioration in appearance are not directly related. The materials used for pile, backing and underlay all influence performance. A high pile is not always an advantage in wear but the weight of pile, including that woven into the backing, and the number of tufts per 100 mm^2 are guides to durability.

With correct and regular maintenance the better quality carpets are extremely durable, but all carpets are damaged by grit, by rubber soles and pointed heels to shoes, and by pointed legs to furniture.

Use-category gradings adopted by *The British Carpet Centre* are valuable aids in the selection of carpets.

The BCC system grades Axminster and Wilton woven carpets produced in this country and non-woven carpets manufactured by members of *The Federation of British Carpet Manufactureres* as suitable for:

1 Light domestic, eg bedrooms,
2 Light to medium domestic,
3 General domestic and/or light 'contract' use,
4 Heavy domestic and/or medium 'contract' use.
5 Luxury domestic and/or heavy 'contract' use.
   (Carpets in this category usually have only one stated use.)

Types of carpets Machine made carpets (hand made carpets are not considered here) are either *woven or tufted:*

Woven carpets In Axminster-type carpets the pile is woven with the backing and is always cut, the method permitting a large number of colours to be used. In Wiltons the pile is woven into the backing: the number of colours is restricted. Plain coloured woven carpets are usually Wiltons and their pile is usually denser than Axminsters.

Woven carpets are made in *body widths* of 457 mm to about 1 m and *broadloom widths* up to 4.572 m in thicknesses of 6 to 9 mm.

Tufted carpets Here the looped or cut pile is stitched into a jute backing and secured with latex. Patch repairs are more easily made than with woven carpets. A good quality carpet may have a PVC primary backing and an expanded PVC secondary backing, both of which include glass fibre reinforcement..

Types of pile Cut pile has a matt appearance but tends to *shade* and *track*. *Cording* or *loop pile* does not shade and the irregular appearance of *cut loop* minimizes tread marks and shading.

Types of carpet fibres Fibres which are used alone or in various conbinations include:

Wool fibres are resilient and warm and do not soil easily. They do not ignite easily and are self-extinguishing, but wool is costly and is attacked by moths if it is not specially protected. A *'Woolmark'* is awarded to pure wool carpets of specified quality.

Nylon is strong, tough and very hard wearing, but is less soft and resilient than wool. It soils but is easily cleaned, and it melts at high temperatures.

Polypropylene, although cheap, has comparable durability to nylon and cleans well. It is difficult to dye and tends to flatten quickly.

Acrylic is not as soft as wool but is resilient, wears well and is easily cleaned.

Rayon has low strength and resilience but is cheap and provides bulk in carpets.

Organic fibres can be treated to render them antistatic but:

Stainless steel fibres are included in some carpets to eliminate static electricity which can arise when all animal or synthetic fibres are walked on.

Felts These consist of fibres needled into a jute hessian backing.

Fixing

The base should be smooth, level and without gaps, Good quality resilient underlays, either separate or integral, add considerably to the lives of carpets and reduce the downward transmission of impact noise.

After being well stretched, carpets should be fixed at their edges by tacks or by angled pins on *gripper strips.* Carpet to carpet joins can be made by sewing, or by adhesive strips.

Some felts are stuck to subfloors, but animal hair carpet tiles bind together at their contacting edges and do not require to be stuck down.

Aluminium or brass extrusions are used to protect the edges of carpets at junctions with other floorings.

Maintenance

Stains should be removed immediately. Vacuum cleaning is necessary at intervals varying widely with use, and less frequently, dry cleaning or shampooing, which are best done *in-situ*, are required.

Material, form and references[1]	Base	Properties	Appearances
1 Linoleum Powdered cork, fillers, pigments, oxidized linseed oil and resins pressed on jute canvas or cork Also on bitumen felt in 2·5 and 3·2 mm thicknesses only Available sealed with polyurethane and butadiene copolymers BS 810 : 1966 *Sheet linoleum (calendered type) and cork carpet* BS 1863 : 1952 *Felt backed linoleum*	1 *Concrete screed* - with steel trowelled finish and levelling compound if required *hardboard* (with rebated edges on polythene film, on sand) A dpm is essential in solid ground floors 2 *Wood boards* (at ground level protected by dpcs and ventilated below) *existing boards* – if sanded and filled lay flooring on paper felt, or preferably treat as: *new boards* – should be t and g preferably strip	Wear – low to high resistance, increases with thickness. *Hardened grades* have good resistance to sharp point loads and to burns Resilience: high for thicker grades Cannot be bent to small radii Quiet and warm Slippery if highly polished Resists oils and weak acids but deteriorates in damp conditions Attacked by alkalis	Colours – large range Patterns – plain, jaspé, moiré, granite, marble, geometrical Textures – semi-matt
2 Cork carpet Granulated cork, pigments, oxidized linseed oil and resins pressed on jute canvas BS 810 : 1966 *Sheet linoleum (calendered type) and cork carpet*	width. Cover with 4·8 mm standard hardboard or 4 mm resin-bonded plywood in sheets not larger than 1 m² laid breaking joint and fixed with ring nails or self-clinching staples at 150 mm centres over the whole area. Paper felt may prevent nails or staples 'grinning' through flooring	Wear – moderate if well maintained in light domestic use Not suitable where excessive soiling is likely Softer, more resilient, quieter and warmer than linoleum Non-slip even when wet or polished Resists occasional water and weak acids Low resistance to alkalis and burns	Colours – medium to dark cork colour and shades of green, red and brown Texture – open
3 Felt base or **printed 'linoleum'** Paint finish or thin vinyl film on bituminous felt	3 *Chipboards* – as floor finish See table 14 4 *Mastic asphalt* – as floor finish See table 9 ·5 *Clay and concrete tiles, stone slabs etc* – If in contact with the ground	Wear – low resistance but sufficient for very light duty or temporary work Cracks at low temperatures Not suitable over underfloor warming	Colours – various Patterns – various Texture – glossy
4 Flexible vinyl – homogeneous Mainly PVC binder with varying contents of fillers, plasticizers and pigments	and there is no dpm, surface with 13 mm mastic asphalt. If dry but irregular, apply levelling compound	Wear – moderate to high. Resistance varies with vinyl content and thickness Resilience – varies similarly	Colours – very wide range Patterns – very wide range including vinyl chips in clear vinyl

Table 13   B I Sheet supplied rolled

TABLE 13

Typical sizes			Laying	Surface treatment		Average cost factors[2]
Thickness mm	Width mm	Length m		Initial	Maintenance	
1·6 jaspé and moiré only			Lay flat and keep at room temperature at least 48 hours before fixing	If not factory-finished with a hard seal, clean with mild soap or detergent (not with abrasives or strongly alkaline soap or detergent). Rinse and dry	Sweep Damp mop with mild soap or neutral detergent Burnish polish and only occasionally renew sparingly, or maintain seal	21 (3·2 mm)
2·0	1830	9	Lay on adhesive and roll			28 (4·5 mm)
2·5 plain and marbled only		27	For cheap work on boards, lay loose with edges lapped. Trim edges and tack down after sheet has expanded	Apply suitable seal (later removing any factory dressing) Apply wax or emulsion polish on unhardened, or emulsion polish on prehardened linoleum		
3·2 4·5 6·0 plain only 6·7	2000					
3·2 4·5 6·0	1830	15	Keep at room temperature for at least 48 hours Must be bonded to base and rolled	Wash, rinse and dry as linoleum Suitable seals reduce dirt being ingrained Wax polishes on unsealed and emulsion polishes on sealed material	Generally as for linoleum but removal of grit is very important. Apply polish lightly – 'build-up' is difficult to remove	23 (4·5 mm)
1·0			Normally laid loose	None required	Damp mop	2
			Keep at not less than 18°C for at least 24 hours. Must be bonded to base and rolled	Water-wax emulsion polish (non-solvent type)	Damp mop Burnish polish and renew sparingly, only occasionally	24 – 33 (2 mm)

– continued

39

Material, form and references[1]	Base	Properties	Appearances
Non-slip grade contains aluminium oxide grains	6 *Metal decking*	Moderately warm and quiet High resistance to surface water Tends to shrink More resistant to chemicals, oils, alcohols etc and less easily stained than linoleum and vinyl-asbestos tiles Cigarettes may char	Texture – matt to glossy and embossed simulations of travertine, marble, mosaic, timber, etc
BS 3261 : *Unbacked flexible PVC flooring*: Part 1 : 1973 *Homogeneous flooring*			
Flexible vinyl – backed Cork, foamed plastics, needled felt or inorganic backings *'Cushion vinyl'* has a thin foam interlayer *'Foam-backed vinyl'* has a thick foam backing		Very quiet with resilient backings but surface may be punctured and backings may lose resilience with age Inorganic fibre felt improves dimensional stability	
5 Rubber Natural or synthetic rubber vulcanized, with fillers and pigments, in some cases on fabric backing Available with foamed-rubber base		Wear – good resistance increases with thickness. Heavy duty quality (black) Very resilient and quiet especially with foamed-rubber base Smooth types slippery when wet Warm Good resistance to water, weak acids but natural rubber is damaged by oils, fats and solvents Damaged by ultra-violet radiation	Colours – very wide range and black and white Patterns – plain, marbled, mottled etc Textures – matt to glossy, studded, grooved, rough texture
BS 1711 : 1951 *Solid rubber flooring* BS 3187 : 1959 *Electrically conducting rubber flooring* BS 3398 : 1961 *Anti-static rubber flooring*		Emits rubber odour, particularly over underfloor heating Special grade required over underfloor heating	

General considerations in selecting, laying and maintaining sheet floorings are discussed on page 32

Table 13   B I Sheet supplied rolled

TABLE 13

Typical sizes			Laying	Surface treatment		Average cost factors[2]
Thickness mm	Width mm	Length m		Initial	Maintenance	
1·5	1200	11	Joints can be welded in-situ	Do not seal		
	1500	27				
2·0	1800					
2·5	2000					
3·0	2100					
*{ 3·0						
3·9						
4·5						
* with resilient backings			As above seams should be welded			44 (foam backed)
3·8 light domestic floors 4·8 6·4	910 1370 1830	15 — 30	Must be bonded to minimize creep caused by wheeled traffic Press down	Water-wax emulsion polish applied sparingly (non-solvent type only)	Damp (not wet) mop with mild soap (Not with alkaline or abrasive soap, detergents not having a soap base or 'cleaning agents') Burnish polish and renew sparingly occasionally only Strip polish when 'build-up' becomes excessive	45 (4·8 mm) 56 (6 mm wide-ribbed surface)
12·7 to order						
4·5 with foamed backing						

[1] General reference : CP 203 : 1972 Sheet and tile flooring
[2] Approximate cost relationship for typical floorings 'as laid', based on granolithic = 10

Material, form and references[1]	Base	Properties	Appearance
1 Plywood Resin bonded plies Face-ply at least 3 mm thick T and g boards available BS 1455 : 1972 *Plywood manufactured from tropical hardwoods*	*Full support* Boarded floor Sand bed Expanded plastics boards *Partial support* thicker boards only on:	Wear – moderate, resistance varies with timber and life is determined by thickness of the top ply Moderately warm and quiet – but thin boards 'drum' if not fixed overall to base	Pattern – Normally rotary cut timber
2 Chipboard Wood chips bonded with synthetic resin and compressed Density not less than 640 kg/m^2 Sanded or sealed finish Available with edges t and g or grooved for loose tongues BS 5669: 1979 *Resin-bonded wood chipboard*	Joists or battens with noggings to support ends of boards without tongues Compressible quilt and t and g boards (only) laid loose as floating floor	Wear – Moderate to good resistance Low resistance to water	Colour – warm yellow Pattern – as wood chips
3 Hardboard Wood fibres compressed Preferably *tempered hardboard* BS 1142 : Part 2 : 1971 *Fibre building boards*	Sub-floors must be dry	Wear – moderate resistance Properties of tempered hardboard similar to plywood	Colours – natural browns and integrally coloured yellow, green or red

Table 14   B II Boards (Timber boards see table 15)

TABLE 14

Typical sizes[2]			Laying[3]	Surface treatment		Average cost factors[4]
Thickness mm	Width mm	Length mm		Initial	Maintenance	
4 fully supported	1220	2440	Panel pins where appropriate Face grain must be at right angles to main supporting members 50 mm nails should be inserted at 150 mm centres	As wood blocks See page 44		19 (6 mm) 28 (13 mm)
13 supported at 460 mm centres	1220	2440				
16 supported at 610 mm centres	1220	2440				
12 fully supported	1220	2440	*On sanded boards* Lost head nails at 400 mm centres punched home and holes filled *On joists or battens* Lost head nails at 400 mm centres punched home or can be glued Fill holes Leave expansion gap below skirtings	Fill open texture of untreated boards and apply plastics seal	Damp mop Renew seal when necessary	21 (12 mm) 23 (18 mm)
18 supported at 400 mm centres	1220	2440				
22 supported at 600 mm centres	1220	2440				
4·8 fully supported	1220	1220	Wet backs of boards and store flat for 48 h (72 h for tempered hardboard) *On sanded boards*: nail with 25 mm lost head panel pins at 150 mm centres at edges and at 200 mm centres on lines 400 mm apart *On smooth concrete*: bond with adhesive	Can be sealed	Damp mop Polish regularly (must be non-slip type) Renew seal when necessary	14

[1] General reference: *MBS Materials*, chapter 3
[2] Thicknesses and spans between supports relate to domestic loadings
[3] Edges of boards must be protected. Boards can, in suitable qualities, be used as bases for thin floor finishes, but they are considered here as floorings in their own right
[4] Approximate cost relationships for typical floorings 'as laid', based on granolithic = 10

Form of unit and references[1]	Base	Properties	Appearance
1 Blocks Hardwood and softwood units tongued and grooved or dowelled BS 1187:1959 Amd 1968 *Wood blocks for floors (interlocking)*	Floated screed on dry concrete slab	Moderately resilient, warm and quiet Not suitable in damp conditions or where wide variations in atmospheric humidity occur The greater moisture movement of timber across the grain than that along the grain is balanced by alternating lengths and widths of blocks thereby avoiding accumulated movement across a floor	Colours – as timbers; some timbers darken and others fade with age Joint patterns *basket* – square and open *herringbone* – square, single and double *brick bonds*
2 Blocks – end grain Usually softwood, impregnated with preservative for wet conditions of use	Level concrete	Exceptional resistance to wear and impact Brittle objects if dropped are less likely to break than on other industrial floorings	Utilitarian
3 Boards Usually softwood Should be tongued and grooved to increase strength and fire-resistance and for draught proofing BS 1297:1970 *Grading and sizing of softwood flooring*	Joists or battens Maximum spans for t and g softwood boards or strip for domestic loadings (1·44 kN/m²) are: 	Finished thickness mm	Maximum span (c–c) mm
---	---
16	505
19	600
21	635
28	790 | Building Regulations 1976	More resilient than blocks At the BS 1297 'normal range' of m.c. (16–22%) marked cupping of and gaps between sawn boards – particularly wide boards – will occur. Kiln dried m.c. 12–15%	Good appearance requires first-class material, laying techniques and maintenance
4 Strip Hardwoods and softwoods. Up to 102 mm wide with tongued and grooved edges and ends – long lengths		As t and g boards	Joint pattern – Narrow widths (sometimes random) and long random lengths

Table 15   B III Timber floorings

TABLE 15

Typical sizes			Laying	Surface treatment[2]		Average cost factors[3]
Thickness mm	Width mm	Length mm		Initial	Maintenance	
21	75	229 305	(1) Screed primed and blocks laid in hot bitumen, or (2) blocks laid in cold adhesive 13 mm gaps or cork strips under skirtings 13 mm cork strips sometimes recommended to divide floor into bays	Stop if required, sand, stain or dye if required and seal with oleoresinous solvent-based seal (eg polyurethane) or apply wax polish Floor seal or plastics polish is necessary to protect softwoods Non-slip gymnasium oil for gymnasia (only)	Wipe seal with damp (not wet) cloth or apply wax polish Renew seal (surface must be wax-free). Polyurethane seals can be patch repaired Renew wax polish When badly worn resurface by sanding (Effective wearing surface is determined by depth of tongues or dowels below the surface)	40 (softwood) 43 – 79 (hardwood)
63 — 114	 76	102 127 229	Blocks dipped in hot soft pitch and laid with close joints or laid dry and grouted	Usually none but hard grit can be rolled into bituminous dressing	Sweep	33 (63 mm)
min 16 19 21 28 BS 1297 t and g flooring	± 1 65 90 113 137	Random 1800 min 3000 min average in any one delivery	Boards cramped Header joints to bear on joists or battens and be staggered at least two boards' width in both directions Softwood boards Fix with brads, punch in and stop one brad per bearer for 65 and 90 mm, two for 113–178 and three for wider boards Hardwood boards Secret nail through tongue and nail or screw through face and stop or pellet	As 1 Blocks	As 1 Blocks	22 (25 mm ordinary softwood t and g)
19 25	51 63 76 89 102 less 13 mm as laid	Random	Strips cramped Secret nail at 50° just above tongues to all bearers T and g header joints need be supported by noggings only for heavy duty floor			50 – 80 (25 mm hardwood t and g)

– continued

Form of unit and reference[1]	Base	Properties	Appearance
– short lengths – (reduce price slightly) BS 1297 : 1970 *Grading and sizing of softwood flooring*	Floated concrete	Resilience etc as for blocks	Narrow widths and short random lengths

5 **Overlay strip**
    Hardwood
    Tongued and grooved edges, ends may be tongued and grooved
	Sound, sanded, softwood flooring or softwood flooring with underlay	Suitable for light duty	Joint pattern – as end-matched hardwood strip

6 **Parquet**
    Selected hardwoods square or t and g edges
    Units for laying may comprise components glued together at their edges
	Thoroughly seasoned and level boards – preferably overlaid with 4 mm resin-bonded plywood or 4·8 mm hardboard	Suitable for light domestic duty only	Exotic and costly woods can be used in parquet thickness Patterns, including elaborate marquetry, are independent of base

7 **Parquet panels**
    6 mm hardwood parquet mounted on laminated softwood
    Tongued and grooved on all edges
	1 Joists or battens
	
	2 Screed
		Composite construction gives wear properties equivalent to strip	As end-matched hardwood strip

8 **Mosaic** Hardwood butt-edged 'fingers' bonded to a base of scrim, felt or perforated aluminium foil or overlaid with membrane which is stripped off after laying BS 4050 : 1966 *Wood mosaic flooring*	Floated screed, 4 mm resin-bonded plywood or 4·8 mm hardboard	Similar to blocks Smaller units and basket pattern localize moisture movement	Generally supplied in less exotic hardwoods than parquet Joint pattern – Usually basket weave in 114 or 150 mm square units each comprising five or six 'fingers' respectively

Plywood, chipboard and **hardboard** see page 42

General considerations in selecting, laying and maintaining timber floorings are discussed on page 32.

Table 15 B III Timber floorings

TABLE 15

Typical sizes			Laying	Surface treatment[2]		Average cost factor[3]
Thickness mm	Width mm	Length mm		Initial	Maintenance	
25	76 less 13 mm as laid	Random 230 — 610	As 1 Blocks	As 1 Blocks	As 1 Blocks	
9 — 16	up to 76	Random	Glued and secret pinned along tongued edges Laid at an angle with boards if no underlay is used			46 – 55
5 — 10	51 76 89	Various	Glued and pinned Pins punched home and holes filled	As 1 Blocks or can be french polished for light duty	As 1 Blocks or revise french polish	90 (6 mm)
25 — 32	305 and 610 squares for laying		1 Glue tongues and nail through tongues if necessary 2 Bedded in hot bitumen 3 Some interlocking products can be laid loose, eg as removable dance floor on carpet	Products without-shop finishes treated as *blocks*	As 1 Blocks	
10 — 16	305 and 457 squares for laying		Bonded with cold adhesive and rolled Any surface overlay removed Gaps below skirtings and cork expansion strips as for wood blocks			34 – 60 (10 mm)

[1] *General reference*: CP 201: Part 2: 1972 *Flooring of wood and wood products*
[2] See CP 209: 1963 *Care and maintenance of floor surfaces* Part I: Wooden flooring
[3] Approximate cost relationships for typical floorings 'as laid', based on granolithic = 10

– continued

Material, form and references[1]	Base	Properties	Appearance

1 **Bricks**
    Manufactured from un-refined clays, pressed and burnt
    Intended primarily for walling
    BS 3921 : 1969 *Bricks and blocks of fired brickearth, clay or shale*
    BS 3679 : 1963 *Acid resisting bricks and tiles*
	Internally – concrete
	
	Externally –
	    (i) for vehicular traffic – concrete
	    (ii) for pedestrian traffic – rammed earth or hard-core
		Best products (eg *Engineering bricks Classes A and B* (BS 3921) have excellent resist-ance to wear, impact, chemicals and frost)
		For external use '*Special quality*' (BS 3921) bricks must be specified
			Colours – wide range
			
			Joint patterns – brick bonds and unbond-ed, with wide joints
			Texture – usually plain

2 **Paviors (or Pavers)** (i) Manufactured as for *Engineering bricks*	Concrete or screed finished to suit method of laying	As *Engineering bricks* but without frogs	
(ii) Manufactured from refined clay and fired at very high temperature		Most paviors have resistance to chemicals and wear sup-erior to that of quarries	Colours – red, buff, cream, brown Texture – plain, rib-bed, chequered and roughened

3 **Quarries**
    Manufactured from un-refined clays, pressed and burnt
 	
    BS 1286 : 1974 *Clay tiles for flooring*
	A damp-proof mem-brane may be need-ed to prevent water vapour passing through joints and through porous units and to prevent water evapora-ting from the sur-face leaving salt deposits	Similar to equivalent bricks. Some have harder surfaces than interiors
		Wear resistance good to ex-cellent, especially for red and blue quarries
		Slipperiness: moderate to good
		Maximum water absorption (BS 1286):
		    Class 1 6 per cent
		    Class 2 10 per cent
		Size tolerance (BS 1286):
		    4 (±2) per 95 mm
		    8 (±4) per 193 mm
			Colours – natural clay colours, ie red and in certain sizes, brown, blue and buff. Slight vari-ations are charac-teristic
			Texture – slightly ir-regular
			Joint patterns – usu-ally square bond. Wide joints are necessary for less accurate quarries

4 **Vitrified ceramic floor tiles**[2] Manufactured from re-fined clays, of more uni-form composition than used for quarries and which include fluxes to increase vitrifica-tion		More accurate size and shape and more uniform colours than above units Smooth surface Greater resistance to wear, oils, fats and chemicals in-cluding alkalis and to frost than quarries	Colours – black, white and wide range of mono-chromes and min-gled colours Textures – *Matt* de-velops sheen with wear. Available

Table 16   B IV Clay and precast concrete floorings

TABLE 16

Sizes[4]			Laying	Surface treatment		Average cost factor[5]
Thickness mm	Width mm	Length mm		Initial	Maintenance	
65 or can be laid *brick-on edge* or *brick-on-end*	102·5	215	*Externally*: pedestrian traffic – units may be bedded in sand or weak mortar heavy traffic – units bedded on 16–19 mm cement : sand mortar on concrete base	Clean off and protect as for quarries	Sweep	30 – 60
19 — 51	95 108 114 124	190 216 241 251	*Internally*: See page 34 Remove cement stains with proprietary fluid	As *Bricks*		60
				Externally as *Bricks* *Internally* as *Vitrified tiles*		70
Preferred Modular co-ordinating sizes: 19 | 100 | {100, 200} *Modular work sizes* 19 | 95 | {95, 193} *Non-modular work sizes* 15 | 150 | 150 16 | {76 | 152} | 152 19 22 | {114 | 229} | 229 32 *Other BS thicknesses* 12·5 | — | — 19·0 | — | — also diagonal halves, sills, stairtreads, etc			Methods of laying See page 34 *Thickness of bedding mm* *Mortar* on – concrete 15–20 – separating layer 15–25 *Semi-dry mix* 25 min *Cement-based adhesive* 5 max	Clean immediately with sand or sawdust Wash repeatedly with water until any efflorescence ceases Protect with whitewood sawdust during works	Wash with warm water and neutral sulphate-free detergent (Soap residues cause slipperiness and hold dirt) Rinse thoroughly with clean water (Do not use oiled sweeping compounds)	30 – 50
Preferred Modular co-ordinating sizes 9·5 | 100 | {100, 200} *Modular work sizes* 9·5 | 95·5 | {95·5, 194·0}				Polishes, linseed oils and other seals are not absorbed. Use polish sparingly and remove occasionally – a build-up becomes slippery and holds dirt		60

– continued

Material, form and references[1]	Base	Properties	Appearance
Non-slip tiles contain silicon carbide The clay is ground, pressed and fired at high temperatures BS 1286: 1974	As previous page	Electrically conductive grades are available *Slipperiness*: moderate when dry and oil, grease and wax free *Water absorption*: (*BS 1286*) 4 per cent max (Typical products 1–2 per cent) *Size tolerance* (BS 1286): 3 ($\pm$1·5) per 95·5 mm 6 ($\pm$3·0) per 194 mm	with non-slip silicon carbide surface and a glazed tile is textured with sand *Ribbed, studded, panelled and granulated* *Glazed* – not suitable for heavy duty Joint patterns – geometrical. Accurate size and shape of tiles permits narrower joints than quarries
5 Fully vitrified ceramic tiles[2] Manufactured to give a higher degree of vitrification than *vitrified ceramic floor tiles Class 2* BS 1286: 1974		Similar to vitrified ceramic tiles but are virtually impervious and have excellent resistance to chemicals and staining *Water absorption:* (BS 1286) 0·3 per cent max (Typical products absorb appreciably less)	Colours – wider range than for vitrified ceramic tiles Textures and joint patterns – as for vitrified ceramic tiles
6 Mosaic Tesserae, usually of vitrified or fully vitrified ceramic are supplied bonded to paper in sheets up to 800 mm square. (Also available in glass and marble)		Similar to equivalent tiles of equal thickness *Slipperiness:* Rice grain clay tesserae and recessed joints reduce slipperiness for bare feet. Flush joints can be dusted with silicon carbide abrasive Glass suitable only for light pedestrian traffic	Colours – as tiles Texture of tesserae – Glazed, matt rice grain and incorporating abrasive. (The latter can be used as non-slip insets in terrazzo or marble stair treads Joint patterns – Normally regular but special patterns can be ordered
7 Concrete – precast Ordinary or coloured cement and aggregate hydraulically pressed Heavy duty tiles have hard stone or metal aggregate and/or abrasive included in surface		Properties vary widely Better products benefit by quality control, hydraulic pressing etc, are 'pre-shrunk' and have high resistance to wear, but inferior products may craze and 'dust' Resistance to chemicals varies with density	Colours – given by natural grey, white and pigmented cements and by aggregates when exposed in manufacture, by wear or by weathering Textures – plain, rib-

Table 16   B IV Clay and precast concrete floorings

TABLE 16

Sizes[4]			Laying	Surface treatment		Average cost factors[5]
Thickness mm	Width mm	Length mm		Initial	Maintenance	
Non-modular work sizes 9·5 12·5	76 152	152	After bedding mortar has set, completely fill joints with 1 cement: 1 fine sand grout[3] and point joints wider than 6 mm with 1 cement: 3 fine sand[3]. Remove surplus with dry cement (not sawdust) Joints See page 35 Damp-cure and do not allow even light foot traffic for at least 4 days	As previous page	As previous page	
Other BS thicknesses 16·0 19·0	— —	— —				
Some non-BS sizes 8·5 10·0 11·0 12·7 13·0 15·0 17·5 18·0 22·2 32·0	76 100 102 150 60 250	67 100* 102 150* 200* 240 250* 254				80
* imported tiles also diagonal halves, hexagonal and other shapes, sills, stairtread tiles etc						
4 — 10	5 – 13 sided squares, hexagons etc		Bed as for ceramic tiles. When the bedding is hard, the paper is stripped and joints are grouted with neat cement Joints See page 35			100
15 20 20 30 35 40	150 200 225 300 400 500	150 200 225 300 400 500	As for similar clay products see above and page 34 but the backs of concrete tiles or slabs are brushed with neat cement slurry immediately before they are laid	May be sealed to prevent oil stains – see Concrete Finishes page 31	Scrub with detergent in hot water and with mild scouring powder if dirt is engrained (Avoid acidic cleaning agents on Portland cement, and strong alkaline	30 – 50
also hexagons and other shaped *tiles*						60 (indusrial)

– *continued*

Material, form and references[1]	Base	Properties	Appearance
		Not suitable for chemical-resisting floors Accurate size tolerances: tiles ± 1 mm flags ± 2 mm on length and breadth	bed and containir abrasives
BS 1217 : 1945 *Cast stone* BS 1197 : 1973 *Concrete flooring tiles and fittings* BS 368 : 1971 *Precast concrete flags*	Flags for pedestrian traffic may be laid on rammed earth or hardcore		
8 **Terrazzo – precast tiles** Hydraulically pressed concrete tiles, faced with marble aggregate in white or coloured cement matrix about 10 mm thick (abrasive may be incorporated) Surface ground BS 4131 : 1973 *Terrazzo tiles* BS 4357 : 1968 *Precast terrazzo units* (*other than tiles*) eg stair treads and risers	Concrete	Properties generally as for high quality precast concrete units Similar to in-situ terrazzo, but tiles benefit from factory production as above Should not be laid for 21–28 days after pressing *Size tolerance* (BS 4131) ± 1 mm	Colours – wide ran; Joint pattern – can l inconspicuous colours of tiles ca be alternated Appearance similar i in-situ terrazzo b very large aggre ate is sometim used in a matr of smaller particl and cement Liable to staining l some timbers, ro] and straw

General considerations in selecting, laying and maintenance are discussed on page 34
[1] *General references*: CP 202 : 1972 *Tile flooring and slab flooring*; BRE Digest 79 *Clay tile flooring, MBS Materia Ceramics* chapter 5, *Bricks* chapter 6, *Concrete* chapter 8

Table 16   B IV Clay and precast concrete floorings

Composition blocks	Concrete or screed	Properties	Appearance
Composition blocks Various combinations of cement and drying oil or PVC binder, chalk, sawdust, wood flour, inert aggregate, and pigments pressed into blocks and cured Blocks have dovetailed keys on underside CP 202 : 1972 *Tile flooring and slab flooring*	Concrete or screed A dpm is recommended on wet sites and is essential below floor warming	Good resistance to wear Heavy duty blocks incorporate white spar chippings Resilience low. Very good resistance to indentation Moderately warm Slippery only if highly polished Very good resistance to vegetable oils Good resistance to water, alkalis, acids, animal and mineral oils	Colours – rather da Black and four co ours on grey ceme base Seven colours on white cement bas Patterns – basket, herringbone and brick bond

Table 17   B V Composition blocks

TABLE 16 AND 17

Typical sizes[4]			Laying	Surface treatment		Average cost factors[5]
Thickness mm	Width mm	Length mm		Initial	Maintenance	
50⎫ ⎬ 63⎭ work sizes for *flags*	598	⎧448 ⎪598 ⎨748 ⎪898 ⎩	Mortar for flags from 1 lime : 3–4 sand (slow setting, not frost proof), PC lime : sand mixes, to 1 Portland cement : 6 sand (strongest) Joints See page 35		cleaners on high alumina cement products) Phenols and cresols in some disinfectants cause indelible pink stains	17 (flags)
15 20 20 30 35 40 300 and 500 max width hexagons	150 200 225 300 400 500	150 200 225 300 400 500	As for clay tiles see page 282 but backs of tiles are brushed with neat cement slurry immediately before they are laid. Dividing strips (see in-situ terrazzo) between groups of tiles	Usually ground after laying to remove any lipping edges Protect with non-staining sawdust Scrub with non-alkaline non-acid soap and allow to stand overnight Rinse with hot water Can be protected against staining with suitable water-based seal	Wash with warm water and occasionally fine abrasive powder. Use soap only if it is thoroughly rinsed off Do not apply polish or allow to become contaminated with soap or wax Do not use oiled sweeping compounds or disinfectants containing phenols and cresols	70

[2] Geometrical shapes sometimes called tessellated tiles
[3] Mixes by volume
[4] Subject to specified tolerances
[5] Approximate cost relationships for typical floorings 'as laid', based on granolithic = 10

10 and 16 Also accessories	52 63	157 190	Bed on 13 mm 1 cement : 3 sand Joints grouted with proprietary mortar Cure with wet sawdust	Sand Seal	Sweep with damp sawdust Wash with soap and water Rinse Apply proprietary polish Can be resurfaced by sanding	36 (10 mm) 43 (16 mm)

Material, form and references[1]	Base	Properties	Appearance
1 **Granites** eg Cornish BS 435 : 1931 *Granite and whinstone kerbs, channels, quadrants and setts*	1 *Internally* and for heavy-duty externally – concrete	Excellent resistance to wear, impact, frost and chemicals Slippery when polished, eg by wear Impervious to water and water vapour Resistant to staining	Colours – grey, red, pink, blue, black Pattern – mosaic of crystals Texture – from rock face to glossy
2 **Sandstones** eg 'York stone' type (usually riven) Darley Dale Forest of Dean BS 706 : 1936 Amd PD 3670 : 1960 *Sandstone kerbs, channels, quadrants and setts*	2 *Externally* for pedestrian traffic only: Sound hardcore or compacted soil	Wide range of density and hardness Some varieties eg 'York stones' have very high resistance to wear and frost and are 'non-slip' More absorbent stones readily stained Sandstones are attacked by sulphates washed from limestones in towns	Colours – grey, buff, brown, pink, red Texture – from rough sawn to smooth. Riven surfaces may have mica particles
3 **Limestones** eg Portland Hopton Wood Kotah		Some varieties have high resistance to wear and frost Resistant to alkalis but not acids More absorbent varieties readily stained Hard varieties slippery when worn Best laid joint bedded	Colours – grey, buff, white Texture – from sawn to high (integral) polish
4 **Marbles** eg Swedish green Dove Sicilian Travertine and hard limestones commonly called *marbles*	Granite, slate and quartzite are impervious but a dpm in bases at ground level may be needed to prevent salt deposits on joints	Many varieties are very hard but superficial scratching by footwear tends to obscure bright colours and markings Generally darker marbles are harder than lighter ones	Colours and Markings – very wide range Texture – from sanded to very high (integral polish Pattern – slabs or mosaic
5 **Slates** usually riven and edges sawn eg North Wales Westmorland Lancashire BS 680 : 1971 *Roofing slates*		Very good resistance to abrasion Riven surfaces of coarser slates are non-slip but polished smooth surfaces are slippery when wet Impervious to water and water vapour Stained by oils and greases if not sealed	Colours – green, blue, purple, black, grey (seals intensify colour) Texture – riven, sawn, sanded, rubbed or finely polished

General considerations in selecting, laying and maintenance are discussed on page 36

Table 18   B VI Stones (Cast stone—see Concrete-precast page 50)

TABLE 18

Typical sizes		Laying	Surface treatment		Average cost factors[2]
Thickness mm	Length and width mm		Initial	Maintenance	
40 and setts	up to about 1830 × 910	*Internally* and for heavy-duty externally *Granites* Bed on 1 cement : 1 lime : 3 sand	Clean	Scrub with water and neutral sulphate-free detergent Rinse Surface may need to be roughened after many years	310–560
40–75 and setts	up to about 3050 × 1220	*Limestones and sandstones* Bed on 13–76 mm 1 Portland cement : 1 lime : 5–6 sand on concrete base	Clean Seals prevent staining but are not recommended by CP 202 Polish can make smooth surfaces dangerously slippery	Scrub with water and where necessary, a suitable neutral, sulphate-free pumice powder or detergent Rinse	110
15–40	300–600 squares				110
50	up to about 1500 × 600	*Externally*: for light pedestrian traffic only: bed on 1 lime : 3–4 sand to 1 Portland cement : 1 lime : 5–6 sand on compacted subsoil hardcore. If base is impervious, bed should be drained to prevent frost heave. Hollow bedding may cause cracking of slabs			
15–30	up to about 1500 × 900			Scrub with warm water and sulphate-free non-caustic detergent Rinse Do not use soap (causes slipperiness), or oiled sweeping compounds	270 – 370 (19 mm)
and mosaic – see table 15					
6–13 19–25 32–40	457 × 229 381 × 381 1500 × 900	*Marbles, slates and quartzites* Bed on 1 cement : 1 lime : 3 sand. Brush backs of slate and quartzite with neat cement slurry			250 – 270 (19 mm)
Due to natural camber, riven slates require to be thicker than sawn slates, and may not be suitable in large sizes					

[1] *General references*: CP 202 : 1972 *Tile flooring and slab flooring*, *MBS Materials*, chapter 4
[2] Approximate cost relationships for typical floorings 'as laid', based on granolithic = 10

– continued

Material, form and references	Base	Properties	Appearance
6 **Quartzite** eg Norwegian		Excellent resistance to abrasion and chemicals Riven surfaces are non-slip wet or dry Resistant to staining Dirt is not absorbed but riven surface holds dirt	Colours – grey, green, buff, yellow Texture – riven

Table 18   B VI Stones

Material, form and references	Base	Properties	Appearance
1 **Linoleum**	As sheet linoleum page 38		Pattern can be provided by varying sizes and direction of tiles

2 **Cork**
   Granulated cork (no fillers) bonded by natural or artificial resins under heat and pressure
   Square, or tongued and grooved edges for tiles 8 mm thick and upwards
   Available with thin vinyl film surface
   Common densities: 480 and 560 kg/m^3
 	
   CP 203 : 1972 *Sheet and tile flooring*
	Trowelled screed
	
	Paper felt underlay on boarding
	
	A dpm is essential in solid ground floors
		Wear – good resistance especially high density grade tiles, but damaged by stiletto heels or badly designed furniture. Dirt becomes ingrained and cork is readily stained if not protected
		Resilient
		Very quiet and warm
		Non-slip – even when wet or polished
		Moderate resistance to acids
		Low resistance to alkalis
		Not suitable in damp conditions
			Colour – honey to dark brown and dyed colours
			
			Pattern – cork granules
			
			Appearance deteriorates if maintenance is neglected

3 **Rubber**
   (i) Cut from sheet
   Some tiles contain fibre reinforcement
	As sheet rubber
	page 40
			Colours – as sheet but heavy duty tiles usually black
			
			Pattern – can be provided by varying direction and sizes of tiles
			
			Texture – smooth, studded bold ribbed, and other anti-slip grooved textures

(ii) Moulded with dovetailed grooves on underside and bold grooves or ribs on upper surface
   Interlocking or plain edges
 	
   BS 1711 : 1951 *Solid rubber flooring*
   CP 203 : 1972 *Sheet and tile flooring*
	Tiles laid into screed or mastic asphalt on concrete – a dpm is not required	As sheet but non-slip
		Suitable for heavy duty public circulation areas
		Grease resistant grade available	

Table 19   B VII Other tile and slab floorings

Typical sizes[1]		Laying[2]	Surface treatment		Average cost factors[3]
Thickness mm	Width and length mm		Initial	Maintenance	
10–20	152–229-mm sided squares and ob-longs Random sizes up to 900 mm long	Movement joints as *concrete units* page 35			135 (19 mm)
As sheet	229 305 up to 914	As sheet linoleum but must be bonded to base	As sheet linoleum page 39		21 (3·2 mm)
3 5 8 25 stair treads	229 305 —	Keep tiles at room temperature for at least 48 hours Fix with adhesive and headless steel pins If pinning is not practicable 'load' tiles until adhesive has set	After fine sanding ordinary tiles, apply flexible seal or heavy grade solvent wax polish If great care has been taken in laying, sanding of prefinished tiles may not be necessary Water emulsion polish can be applied on sealed tiles, and wax polishes on unsealed tiles	Sweep frequently Damp (not wet) mop with detergent or mild (non-alkaline) soap Revive polish or seal periodically Smooth surface and colour can be restored by sanding	32 (6 mm)
As page 289 6 13 ribbed	229 – 914 914 × 1829	As sheet rubber page 41			44 (5 mm)
10 20	457 914	*On fresh screed:* Sand/cement applied to backs *On old screed or mastic asphalt:* tiles bedded in latex/ cement	—	Sweep and vacuum Wash occasionally Can be polished (non-solvent type)	50

– continued

Material, form and references	Base	Properties	Appearance
4 **Thermoplastic 'asphalt tiles' standard** (not to be confused with 'vinyl' tiles which are also thermoplastic, or with mastic asphalt tiles) Bitumen or non-vinyl resin binder, mineral fillers, asbestos fibres and pigments BS 2592: 1973 *Thermoplastic flooring tiles, sometimes known as asphalt tiles* CP 203 : 1972 *Sheet and tile flooring*	As for 'Sheets supplied in rolls' – but not wood boards	Wear – moderate resistance Rather noisy Hard at lower temperatures and crack if not uniformly bedded Surface temperature with floor warming must not exceed 27°C (they soften at higher temperatures) Resistant to alcohol and water Moderate resistance to alkalis May be attacked by dissolved salts Poor resistance to solvents, acids, oils and greases Slippery if highly polished	Colours – limited range of dark colours (darker colours are cheapest) Patterns – plain or marbled
5 **Thermoplastic – 'Vinylized'** thermoplastic tiles with vinyl content BS 2592 : 1973 CP 203 : 1972 *Sheet and tile flooring*	A dpm is essential where rising moisture is severe	Slightly flexible and more resistant to wear, oils and greases than ordinary thermoplastic tiles	Colours – wider range than ordinary thermoplastic tiles
6 **Vinyl asbestos** vinyl (usually PVC) binder, asbestos fibres, fillers and pigments BS 3260 : 1969 *PVC (vinyl) asbestos floor tiles* CP 203 : 1972 *Sheet and tile flooring*		Properties intermediate between thermoplastic tiles and flexible vinyl tiles	Colours – brighter than thermoplastic tiles Textures – include 'travertine'
7 **Flexible vinyl** material as flexible vinyl sheet Tiles are not suitable where welded joints are required BS 3261 : 1973 *Unbacked flexible PVC flooring* CP 203 : 1972 *Sheet and tile flooring*	As for flexible vinyl sheet page 38		Colours – as sheet material Pattern – can be provided by varying direction and size of tiles

Table 19   B VII *Other tile and slab floorings*

TABLE 19

Typical sizes[1]		Laying[2]	Surface treatment		Average cost factors[3]
Thickness mm	Width and length mm		Initial	Maintenance	
2·5 or 3·0	250 or 300	Usually warmed to make them more flexible before laying on a suitable adhesive Thermoplastic tiles may crack at low temperatures if not uniformly bedded	Water-wax emulsion polish only (not polish containing solvents) Seals should not be used	After at least two weeks wash with mild soap or neutral detergent (not alkaline cleaners) Remove stains with fine steel wool and cleaning powder Burnish and apply polish sparingly	9 – 14 (3·2 mm)
2·5 3·0	229				21 (3·0 mm)
1·6 2·0 2·5 3·0 or 3·2	225 or 300				24 (3·2 mm)
1·5 2·0 2·5 3·0	225 250 300 457–914 non-BS				24 – 33 (2 mm)

– continued

Material, form and references	Base	Properties	Appearance
8 **Asbestos-cement** Portland cement and asbestos fibres *Semi-compressed tiles* (BS 690 : 1971) – suitable for roof terraces *Fully-compressed tiles* (BS 4036 : 1966) – suitable for roller skating rinks etc	Floated concrete or screed on concrete	Wear resistance moderate to good High resistance to water and alkalis Moderate resistance to acids Low resistance to animal and vegetable oils	Light grey – standard
9 **Mastic-asphalt – preformed** as in-situ material but tiles are pressed		Generally as for in-situ flooring but preformed tiles are denser Acid resisting grade available	Colours – black, brown, dark red Texture – plain or chequered
10 **Cast iron** plates and grids	Concrete	Hard, cold and noisy Extremely resistant to metal tyred trucks, impact and molten metal spillage High resistance to acids and alkalis Suitable for heavy duty industrial floors	*Plates* – plain, studded, ribbed *Grids* – with hexagonal holes
11 **Steel** *'Anchor plates'* – trays pressed from 10 swg (3 mm) sheet. Tongues turned down from slots in face form 'anchors'. Available unfilled or filled with concrete	Concrete	As cast iron	Steel plates with bedding mortar exposed in slots

Table 19   B VII Other tile and slab floorings

TABLE 19

Typical sizes[1]		Laying[2]	Surface treatment		Average cost factors[3]
Thickness mm	Width and length mm		Initial	Maintenance	
8 25	305	Flexible bedding com-·pound	Fully compressed tiles can be sealed or polished	Wash and sweep	15
16–51	114 × 229 203 254	Bedded in screed, 13 mm mortar or bitumen Often laid with tight joints	As in-situ mastic asphalt page 25		21
6·3 25·4 over flange *Squares* 22·2–25·4 *Triangles*	229 × 229 305 × 152 and 305 mm 305 mm sides	Bedded in 19–76 mm 1 cement : 1½ sand : 3 gravel, 6·3–3·2 mm Damp cure for at least 3 days and delay use for 5 days	—	Sweep and scrub	50
12·7	305 × 152 and 305 mm	Holes filled with 1 ce-ment : 1 granite, 3·2 mm Cure as above			
22–50	305 × 152, 305 and 457 mm	Plates 'buttered' on un-derside and laid, with anchors downwards in 38 mm bed of stiff 1 cement : 2 sand : 1½ gravel Cure as above	—	Sweep and scrub	74

[1] Preformed skirtings and other fittings are available in some materials
[2] Adhesives should be those recommended by the manufacturer of the flooring and should be used as they advise. (No adhesive is effective as a damp-proof membrane)
[3] Approximate cost relationships for typical floorings 'as laid' based on granolithic = 10

2 Plastering

The term *plastering* is usually applied to internal wall and ceiling finishes which give jointless, hygienic, easily decorated, and usually smooth surfaces, often on uneven backgrounds (external plastering is usually called *external rendering* – see chapter 3). Plasterwork may also be required to provide thermal insulation, fire resistance, and to contribute to sound insulation by sealing porous materials such as no-fines concrete. Special plasters are used to absorb sound within rooms and others to insulate against the passage of X-rays.

This chapter deals with *In-situ plasterwork* and with *Precast plasterwork* including *fibrous plaster* and *glass-fibre reinforced plaster*. See page 79.

In–situ plasterwork

References include: BS 4049: 1966 *Glossary of terms applicable to internal plastering, external rendering and floor screeding.*
BS 5492: 1977 *Code of practice for Internal Plastering* BRE Digest 213 Choosing specifications for plastering.

In-situ plastering is a wet messy process and today, brickwork, blockwork and concrete are often left unplastered, or lined with preformed boards which, however, present problems in concealing joints, or in making them aesthetically and hygienically acceptable.

In-situ plasterwork is considered under the following headings:

1 Properties of plaster finishes
2 Materials for plastering
3 Backgrounds
4 Mixes and application of plasters.

1 PROPERTIES OF PLASTER FINISHES

Thermal insulation

Plaster finishes are relatively thin and make a correspondingly small contribution to the thermal insulation of ordinary buildings.

Condensation

Gypsum lightweight plasters, lime plasters and to a lesser extent sanded gypsum plasters with permeable decorative treatments absorb temporary condensation, but in conditions which give rise to permanent condensation all plasters may become saturated and lose their thermal insulation value. Gypsum lightweight plaster having a low thermal capacity, warms up quickly and having superior thermal resistance tends to keep the surface temperature above the dew point of the air so that condensation does not occur.

Sound absorption

This is a property of surface which affects the volume and character of sound in a room. See *MBC: Environment and Services* and *Materials* volumes. It is most important to understand that although sound absorbent finishes reduce the level of sound in transmitting rooms their effect on sound insulation between rooms is negligible. Ordinary plasters have values for sound absorption – from 1 to 3 per cent, but special *acoustic plasters* have values up to 25 per cent (see page 315).

Sound insulation

The effectiveness of a solid and airtight sound barrier increases with its mass but, being thin, plaster finishes contribute significant mass only to lightweight elements. Plaster can also improve sound insulation by sealing the surface to porous barriers, in particular no-fines concrete, the result usually being most favourable when plaster is applied directly rather than being separated from the surface by battens.

Fire protection

Normal plasters are *non-combustible*[1], have no

[1] BS 476 see *MBS: Materials*, chapter 1.

spread of flame[1], do not evolve smoke, and where adhesion to surfaces is good they contribute to the fire resistance of elements. Gypsum plaster is particularly effective and lightweight aggregates provide better fire resistance than sand. See page 67.

Resistance to heat

Gypsum plaster work should not be subjected to temperatures above about 43°C.

Corrosion of metals

Lime and Portland cement mixes which contain uncarbonated lime, or gypsum plaster mixes to which substantial proportions of lime have been added afford protection to ferrous metals, but when they are persistently damp they corrode lead and aluminium. Some *anhydrous Class C* and *Keene's Class D*[2] gypsum plasters containing a salt accelerator have an acid reaction and when they are damp tend to corrode metals. Salts resulting from the use of sea sand or from frost-proofing admixtures such as calcium chloride mixed with Portland cement, also tend to increase the corrosion of metals.

Hardness

In housing a fairly soft finish may be preferred, but in public buildings, and more so in factories, plaster finishes on walls and in particular dados and arrises must often be very hard. Arrises were formerly often plastered for about 76 mm on each return in *Keene's plaster*[2] where the main surfaces were in soft lime plaster. Today, the metal angle beads often used to protect vunerable corners also provide a line for the plaster to work to. Finishing coats are given on page 77 in ascending order of hardness.

Texture

Smooth trowelled surfaces comprising either neat gypsum or gypsum including a fine grade of exfoliated vermiculite are the most common, but texture can be provided by manipulation of a trowel or other tools or by including sand in the finish.

Suitability for decoration

Mixes containing lime or cement are alkaline and

unless they are dry and likely to remain so an alkali resisting sealer or primer is necessary, see page 114. Gypsum plasters are not chemically aggressive to decorative or protective treatments, and in particular *Classes C* and *D* can give smooth finishes suitable for high gloss paint.

Gloss, semi-impervious finishes and wallpapers should not be applied on surfaces which are not dry (see page 108) but although newly applied *Class B* plaster can be safely dried by moderate artificial heat if there is through-ventilation, or by the use of a dehumidifier, *Classes C* and *D* must not dry quickly.

2 MATERIALS FOR PLASTERING

These comprise binding materials, workability agents, described here, aggregates and water, page 66: ancillary materials and premixed plasters, page 67

Binding materials.

The main materials and their more common uses are:

1 *Gypsum plasters* (calcium sulphate) for undercoats and finishing coats.
2 *Portland cement*[3] – for undercoats and very hard and water resistant finishing coats.
3 *Organic binders* – for single coats on true backgrounds
4 *Limes*[3] – for undercoats and finishing coats but rarely used as binders today.

1 *Gypsum plasters*

Gypsum (calcium sulphate) plasters which have been in general use in this country during this century are made by pulverizing and driving off more or less of the chemically combined water from natural gypsum rock which is essentially $CaSO_4 \cdot 2H_2O$. The resulting powder is white, or coloured pink or grey by impurities which do not affect the properties of the product. BS 1191: 1973 – Part 1 *Gypsum Building Plasters* describes four classes.

When water is added to gypsum plaster it sets and hardens into a crystalline solid, heat being evolved as it recombines with water and reverts to the dehydrate form of calcium sulphate. The reaction is *hyfraulic, ie* it does not require air.

Gypsum plasters expand slightly in setting, and

---

[1] BS 476 see *MBC: Materials*, chapter 1.
[2] BS 1191: 1973 *Gypsum building plasters*, see page 65

[3] See *MBS: Materials*, chapter 7.

while this is beneficial in forming castings from moulds and in filling cracks, the movement can cause failure in adhesion on non-rigid backgrounds such as concrete on which it is important to use *Class B* (BS 1191) *Board plaster* which has *low setting expansion.* Premature drying out of *Class C – Anhydrous plaster* and *Class D – Keene's Plaster* sometimes leads to *delayed expansion* with consequent disruption of plaster. Unlike Portland cement and limes, gypsum plasters undergo negligible drying shrinkage. It is not necessary to wait for one coat to dry and crack before applying the following coat and surfaces can be trowelled to a very smooth finish without crazing. Gypsum plasters are not strongly alkaline and 'the provisions of BS 1191 virtually exclude from most types of calcium sulphate plaster those salts which are likely to lead to appreciable efflorescence' (National Building Study 2 *Painting new plaster and cement* HMSO)' The rate of early strength development is superior to that of Portland cement and the final strength of a 1 plaster: 1 sand mix is about the same as a 1 Portland cement: 3 sand mix. Gypsum is slightly soluble in water and break down in persistently damp conditions so that it is not suitable for use externally.

Lime, particularly site-slaked, non-hydraulic, high calcium (fat) lime, improves the workability of gypsum plasters and may be added to all *Class A, B* and some *Class C* plasters. The factory-made *dry hydrate* which is usually employed should be *soaked overnight,* i.e. steeped in water for at least 24 hours to improve its *fatness* before use. Lime also counteracts any acidity and tendency to corrode metals by soluble salt or acid accelerators in *Class C* plasters.

Gypsum plaster which has already set, seriously accelerates the setting of fresh gypsum plasters. and plasterer's tools and equipment should be kept free of set material. Setting is also accelerated by organic matter, and sand should comply with BS 1198 to ensure cleanliness. *Class B* plasters are accelerated by lime.

Gypsum plaster can be safely applied to dry backgrounds containing Portland cement but the two materials must never be mixed as the formation of sulpho-aluminates disrupts the plaster.

In fires, gypsum containing only inorganic matter is *non-combustible* and does not evolve smoke or spread flame. The outer surface dehydrates first but provides an insulating layer until all the water

or crystallization (about 21 per cent) is expelled. Disintegration occurs at a temperature above 110° C. Adhesion is good and various combinations of gypsum products protect steel members for ½ to 4 hours (see page 72).

The choice of a suitable type of gypsum plaster from BS 1191: 1973 *Gypsum building plasters* is determined by the nature of the background and by the smoothness and hardness required of the finish. (Hardness increases from *Class A* to *Class D*.)

Class A   Hemi-Hydrate calcium sulphate plaster (commonly called *Plaster of Paris*) results when three-quarters of the water of crystallization contained in the mineral gypsum is driven off in manufacture. Because *Class A* sets quickly its uses are limited to small areas of stopping and filling and to casting in moulds, eg as *fibrous plaster* (see page 79). Formerly non-hydraulic lime plaster was gauged with Plaster of Paris to give the lime early strength and hardness.

Trade names include:
> CB Stucco pink or grey
> SNB and CBD casting plasters
> Fine and superfine casting plasters

Class B   Retarded Hemi-hydrate plaster in which retarders have been added to Plaster of Paris to delay the set is the most generally useful gypsum plaster. Setting times are adjusted in manufacture to give relatively slow setting for undercoats and a more rapid set for finishing coats. Non-hydraulic (*fat*) limes added to *Class B* finish coats accelerate setting but improve working qualities and reduce the hardness of the surface. Mixes should never be retempered after the initial stiffening has taken place.

BS 1191: Part 1 specifies:

Type a   *Browning* and *Metal lathing* grades including haired plasters suitable for sanded undercoats.

Type b   *Wall finish* or *Finish* plaster for final coats to be used neat or gauged with up to 25 per cent lime by volume *Board finish* plaster which is intended for use neat as a one coat finish on boards.

Trade names of *Class B* plasters include: *Thistle.*

Class C   Anhydrous gypsum plaster

In this case gypsum is calcined at a higher temperature so that all the water of crystallization is driven off leaving *Anhydrous calcium sulphate* ($CaSO_4$) the set of which is accelerated. Due to the presence of a small proportion of calcium sulphate hemihydrate, setting is in two stages. The initial set is rapid and it may not be possible to apply fresh plaster before it has taken place. However, within one hour of mixing the plaster it can be *retempered (knocked back)*, and the relatively slow final set of *Class C* plasters gives the plasterer adequate time to obtain a good flat finish, or if required, textural effects by the manipulation of special floats, sponges, brushes and other tools. On the other hand, slow setting means that care must be taken to avoid drying out before hydration of the plaster is complete, with the danger of *delayed expansion* later.

Class C plasters are not suitable on plasterboards or other boards but are used as a final coat on most gypsum or Portland cement sanded undercoats. They are applied neat, or with the addition of up to 25 per cent thoroughly slaked lime putty (by volume), or of sand if a rough texture is required.

Trade names include: *Sirapite*

Projection plaster (British Gypsum Ltd) is a mixture of *Classes B* and *C* plasters which is suitable for machine application. It is made in types suitable for normal and high suction backgrounds. Lime must not be added.

Class D   Keene's plaster (or 'cement')

As with *Class C* all the water of crystallization is driven off in manufacture so that the product is anhydrous. The slow continuous set and working properties allow it to be scoured with a cross-grained float and brought to a surface smooth enough for a high quality gloss paint finish. Even greater hardness makes Keene's plaster suitable for dados and it was used for exposed arrises where the general surfaces were plastered with a softer plaster. Today metal trim (see page 67) is commonly used to strengthen arrises. Important uses of Keene's plaster are for squash rackets courts and refrigerated stores.

The plaster is sold only as a finishing coat type for use neat, preferably on strong cement/sand

undercoats and never on backgrounds such as plasterboards or insulating fibreboards. It should not be mixed with lime, or normally be retempered after one hour from the time of adding water to the plaster.

Trade names include: *Fine Keene's cement, White Keene's cement, Standard and fine Polar white gypsum cements.*

2 Portland cement

Portland cement is sometimes used as a binder in undercoats and in finishing coats where an exceptionally hard surface is required. Too rapid drying increases the likelihood of cracking and of efflorescent salts penetrating, but shrinkage must be substantially complete before a further coat is applied. See *MBS: Materials.* page 142.

3 Organic binders

These are used in *Scandinavian thin-wall or veneer type* single coat plasters, see page 76.

4 Limes

Plasters in which limes are the only binders are rarely used today. Fat lime (BS 890: 1966) is non-hydraulic and it hardens very slowly in moist conditions. Any surfaces in contact with air harden first and retard the hardening of the interior. Final strength is very low. Sand reduces the tendency for shrinkage cracks to appear on surfaces, but fat lime plaster must be applied in several coats each being allowed to dry slowly so that shrinkage movement is divided into stages. Hydraulic lime/sand mixes are similar to Portland cement/lime/sand mixes, but weaker. See *MBS: Materials,* page 141.

Workability agents

Workability agents comprise non-hydraulic lime and plasticizers based on organic materials.

Non-hydraulic (fat) lime is most plastic in the form of well matured site-slaked lime, but factory produced *dry hydrate* which is usually employed is improved by *soaking overnight.* Fat lime also reduces the strength of Portland cement and gypsum mixes. In the former it distributes shrinkage stresses by *creep*, reducing the tendency for visible cracks to form, and it retains the water which is essential for thorough hydration.

Organic based plasticizers, available in liquid and powder forms, entrain air which improves the workability of mixes.

Aggregates

The usual aggregates for plastering are *sand*, or lightweight *expanded perlite* and/or *exfoliated vermiculite* (see premixed plasters, opposite page).

Sand

BSs 1198 and 1199: 1955 describe *Building sands from natural sources.* Sand obtained from a river or sandpit or by crushing sand, gravel or other stones is used in plaster undercoats, and sometimes in finishing coats for textural effect. It reduces the shrinkage of plasters containing Portland cement and lime.

Impurities – may adversley affect the rates of setting and hardening, reduce strength and cause *cracking, flaking, blowing, popping* and *pitting* of plaster. *Iron* which is present in most sands, in some forms affects the set of gypsum plasters. If sand is dark or reddish a trial mix should be made up. *Iron pyrites* expands in taking up oxygen and may cause stains. *Coal dust* may cause popping, pitting or blowing and excessive proportions of *flaky material* reduce strength. *Calcium carbonate* may retard the set of *Class C* and *D* gypsum plasters which contain accelerators. *Salts,* in particular *sea salt,* may affect the setting of Portland cement and gypsum plasters, lead to dampness and corrosion of metals and to efflorescence in the completed work. *Animal and vegetable matter* may retard or even prevent setting especially of Portland cement. If the colour of liquid tested as laid down in BS 812 clause 22 is darker than the standard colour 'the purchaser should request satisfactory evidence of the general performance of the material'. *Clay* (as distinct from *silt* which is very finely divided sand), increases drying shrinkage, reduces adhesion and final strength. It may accelerate the setting of *Class B* gypsum plaster but retards the setting of Portland cement and counteracts the action of accelerators used in the manufacture of *Class C* and *D* gypsum plasters, BS 1198 limits the content by weight of clay, fine silt and fine dust to 5 per cent for natural sand or crushed gravel sand and 10 per cent for crushed stone sand.

With experience, a fair idea of the quality of a sand can be obtained by simple site tests. For example, when rubbed between the fingers sand should not ball too readily or leave stains or show impurities under a magnifying glass. A layer of silt will form after about 15 minutes on top of sand shaken with water in a glass bottle; clay takes much longer to settle. Too much iron oxide is indicated by persistent red cloudiness.

Grading   A well graded sand in which the voids between the larger particles are filled by smaller particles makes for easy working and reduces the shrinkage of Portland cement and lime mixes. BS 1198 gives percentages by weight passing BS sieves for two types of sand suitable for gypsum undercoats, and a third grade for internal finishing coats of gypsum as follows:

BS Sieve	Gypsum undercoats		Gypsum finishing coats
	Type 1	Type 2	Type 3
5 mm	100	100	100
no. 7	90 – 100	90 – 100	100
no. 14	70 – 100	70 – 100	90 – 100
no. 25	40 – 80	40 – 100	55 – 100
no. 52	5 – 40	5 – 50	5 – 50
no. 100	0 – 10[1]	0 – 10[1]	0 – 10[1]

[1] Higher proportions of certain crushed stone material may be satisfactory.

A 5 per cent total tolerance, which can be split up between the sieves, is allowed for each type. Samples of about 0.5 kg must be carefully taken from the bulk and dried before sieving. The undercoat mixes given in table 21 page 78 are for BS 1198 *Type 1 sands. Type 2 sands* being finer, require more water to obtain a workable mix and as this reduces the strength of plaster, one third less sand should be used. For *Portland cement based plasters* BS 1199 gives a grading for cement/lime external renderings, internal cement plastering and lime plaster undercoats, see page 84. It shows the BS 1198 grading, *Type 3,* as being suitable for lime finishing coats.

Water

Water must be free from excessive proportions of salts and other impurities and if not suitable for drinking its suitability for plastering should be checked by analysis.

Ancillary materials

Fibres BS 5492 states that goat hair is the most suitable animal hair for reinforcing plaster undercoats at the rate of 5 kg/m^3, but 'at works' clean vegetable or synthetic fibres are usually incorporated in so-called *'haired' plasters.*

Bonding agents – applied to 'difficult' backgrounds give improved adhesion for plaster.

Scrim – with a mesh just large enough for plaster to pass through is an open weave fabric of hessian, cotton or corrosion-resistant metal which is used to reinforce plaster at joints between boards and slabs and in other positions where local stresses occur.

Metal beads Metal angle and casing beads.

Galvanized wire netting – for use in plaster which is described by BS 1485: 1971 should be 22 swg (0.71 mm) with a mesh not exceeding 51 mm.

Plasterboards see page 70

Metal lathing see page 75

Premixed plasters

We consider under this heading:
1 Premixed gypsum/lightweight aggregate plasters
2 Thin-wall (thin-coat) plasters
3 Acoustic plasters
4 X-ray resistant plasters

1 *Premixed gypsum/lightweight aggregate plasters*

These plasters described by BS 1191: Part 2: 1973 *Premixed lightweight plasters* contain *exfoliated vermiculite* produced by heating a form of mica, and/or *expanded perlite* which is produced by heating a siliceous volcanic glass.

Compared with sanded plaster mixes, premixed lightweight plasters have the advantage of being clean and accurately proportioned. The wet mix is only about half the weight of sanded plaster and the dry weight about one third. Also the thermal insulation provided by premixed lightweight plasters is better than that of sanded mixes. (See column 2)

It follows that pattern staining and condensation are less likely to occur, and lightweight plasters being more absorptive than sanded plasters, con-

Plaster	Density kg/m^3	Thermal conductivity (k) W/m deg C
Gypsum/perlite *browning grade*	572	0·162
Gypsum/perlite/vermiculite *metal lathing grade*	675	0·188
Gypsum/vermiculite *bonding grade*	658	0·218
Gypsum/sand	1826	0·577

densation is less likely to show on surfaces in conditions of temporary condensation. Gypsum/vermiculite plasters adhere particularly well even to difficult backgrounds such as smooth concrete. Lightweight plaster is softer than sanded plaster but being more resilient it can accept light blows without damage and absorb movements of the background where sanded mixes would crack or lose adhesion to the background.

Lightweight aggregates also improve the *fire resistance* of gypsum plaster. For example, 2 hours fire resistance is provided to a steel column by steel lathing with 38 mm thick sanded plaster or 19 mm thick lightweight plaster.

British Gypsum Ltd make *Carlite plasters* and *Welterweight bonding* plasters. The latter have easier working qualities than *Carlite bonding plasters.*

2 *Thin-wall (thin-coat) plasters*

See *single coat finishes,* page 76

3 *X-ray resistant plasters*

These pre-mixed gypsum plasters supplied *rough* or *haired* for undercoats and as a finish, contain a barytes aggregate. Backgrounds must be prepared and the plaster mixed and applied in very strict accordance with the manufacturers' recommendations to ensure the calculated minimum thickness and freedom from cracking.

A trade name is *Barytite X-ray plaster.*

4 *'Acoustic' plaster*

These proprietary plasters, comprising *Class B* retarded hemi-hydrate plaster ready-mixed with a porous aggregate, should be applied 13 mm thick on a *Class B* undercoat suitable for the background. For maximum sound absorption acoustic plaster should be finished with a cork or carpet surfaced float to give a rough open texture. Poor suction of backgrounds, too much water in a mix, over trowelling and thick paint coatings all reduce surface porosity and the resulting sound absorption. Decoration should consist of two thin sprayed coats of diluted emulsion paint or water-bound distemper.

Average coefficients of sound absorption for ordinary and *acoustic* plasters are:

	Frequency, cycles per second (Hz)		
	125	500	2000
Gypsum, cement or lime plasters on a solid background	0·02	0·02	0·04
12·7 mm thick acoustic plaster on haired retarded hemi-hydrate plaster	0·10	0·20	0·30

Unlike most other sound absorbent finishes *acoustic plaster* is jointless, non-combustible and can be applied to irregularly shaped surfaces. It is not suitable where knocks and abrasions are likely to occur, eg low soffits and on walls up to a height of about 2 m. A trade name is *Deekoosto*.

3 BACKGROUNDS

Properties

Backgrounds are considered under the following headings: movements, key, strength, suction, efflorescence and accuracy.

Movements

Differences in the movement of plaster and background arising from structural settlements or from changes in temperature[1] or moisture content[1] of backgrounds particularly at junctions between dis-

[1] See *MBS: Materials*, chapter 1.

similar backgrounds can be considerable and often cause cracking and loss of adhesion of plaster. The unrestrained thermal movement of gypsum plaster is greater than that of most backgrounds, and about twice that of brickwork and concrete.

A straight cut through plaster is the simplest way to avoid irregular and disfiguring cracks due to differences in movement at changes in background or plane, e.g. at junctions between blockwork and concrete and between walls and ceilings. Alternatively, metal *plaster stop beads* provide an efficient and inconspicuous controlled joint. Where the expected movement is very small the plaster undercoat can be reinforced with 90 mm wide jute scrim or with a 76 mm wide strip of expanded metal. Narrow widths of different backgrounds can be bridged by expanded metal, fixed for example to blockwork on each side of a concrete column. Spacers should be used to ensure a good key for the plaster, and building paper should be interposed to prevent the plaster bonding to the background being bridged.

Key

Voids in surfaces into which plaster can penetrate and interlock provide the most effective means of supporting the weight of plaster and resisting the effects of thermal and drying movements,[1] and for strong undercoats an effective mechanical key is essential. Wood-wool slabs, porous bricks, no-fines concrete and metal lathing provide good mechanical keys. *Bonding agents* consisting of emulsions of polyvinyl acetate (PVA), and other polymers provide good adhesion for plaster on dense and smooth concrete, glazed bricks and tiles and firm and clean painted surfaces if applied strictly in accordance with the manufacturers' instructions.

Bituminous bonding agents resist damp penetration, but they are not recommended to be used on soffits.

Strength

A background should be at least as strong and not less rigid than the plaster which is to be applied to it. It must be strong enough to restrain the drying shrinkage of Portland cement[2] and any setting expansions of gypsum plasters.

[2] See *MBS: Materials*, chapters 1 and 7.

Suction

Absorptive backgrounds reduce the water:plaster ratio, which, as in the case of Portland cement mixes, increases the density and therefore the strength of the products. Thus, a 1 gypsum plaster :3 sand mix on a high suction background has about the same strength as a 1:1½ mix on a low suction background. However, an excessively absorptive background such as aerated concrete may remove water from plaster so rapidly that there is insufficient time to compact and level a surface, so the adhesion is permanently weakened. Prevention of loss of water by excessive wetting of backgrounds such as aerated concrete may lead to drying-shrinkage of the concrete with consequent cracking, or to efflorescence. To reduce suction while avoiding these defects, a polyvinyl acetate emulsion bonding agent may be applied to the surfaces, or a water-retaining ingredient added to the plaster, ie either fat lime putty (BS 890) on the site, or cellulostic material as included in some proprietary plasters.

Efflorescence

Clay bricks and blocks contain efflorescent salts (see *MBS: Materials,* chapter 1 and 6), which may be brought forward to the surface of the wall when any water contained in them dries out. If the background is dry before plastering, and any efflorescence on plaster surfaces is brushed off before decorations are applied, there is little likelihood of trouble, but if clay brickwork or blockwork is not dry it is advisable to use an undercoat which will provide a barrier to salts. Cement based undercoats, in particular aerated cement/sand mixes, are more effective barriers than undercoats based on gypsum plaster.

Accuracy of backgrounds

On dimensionally true backgrounds one coat is usually sufficient but to obtain a true surface on an irregular background a greater thickness and hence number of coats of plaster are applied. Thus on well fixed plasterboards one *set* coat, and on ordinary brickwork and blockwork two coats (*render* and *set coats*) are normally required. On backgrounds which are irregular and out of plumb and line, *dubbing out* of depressions and three coats (ie: *render, float* and *set* coats) are necessary.

Types of backgrounds

The more common backgrounds and their preparation for plastering are discussed here:
1 Clay brickwork and blockwork
2 Concretes
3 Boards
4 Wood-wool slabs
5 Compressed straw building slabs
6 Cork slabs
7 Metal lathing
8 Dovetailed bitumen-impregnated fibre sheets
9 Wood laths

1 *Clay brickwork and blockwork*

The more porous clay bricks and blocks usually give a good 'natural' key, and raking out mortar joints gives a valuable key. Some bricks and blocks are manufactured with a mechanical key but dense bricks such as clay *engineering bricks* (BS 3921: 1969) are usually smooth and should be treated generally as dense concrete. (*Bricks and blocks* are described in *MBS: Materials,* chapter 6 and *Mortars* in chapter 15).

Before plastering, local projections should be trimmed off, dust and loose particles removed and deep impressions *dubbed out.* Bricks and blocks and any Portland cement/lime dubbing out should be allowed to dry and shrink and salts should be brushed off without the use of water, which would bring further salts forward when it dried out.

2 *Concretes*

The properties of concrete backgrounds vary widely. (Concretes are described in *MBS: Materials,* chapter 8). Problems in plastering are concerned with drying shrinkage, lack of key or suction and differences between thermal movements of concrete and plaster. We now consider (i) dense, (ii) lightweight and (iii) no-fines concrete backgrounds.

(i) *Dense concretes*

The drying shrinkage of dense concretes varies from low to high according to quality. Any traces of mould oil reduce suction and should be removed with a suitable detergent and washed off with clean water. Where the suction of concrete surfaces is pronounced a clean water brush should be applied before plastering commences. A mechanical key can be obtained by the use of surface retarders on the formwork followed by brushing, or by special linings which provide dovetailed grooves and this is essential for cement: sand undercoats with high drying shrinkage. Hacking, even if done thoroughly over the whole surface and from two directions, is of limited value. Other pretreatments which are sometimes recommended are *bonding agents* and *spatter-dash coats* (thrown on) of 1 Portland cement: 2-3 coarse sand or proprietary mixtures which should be allowed to harden before plastering.

In most cases, *an undercoat of premixed lightweight bonding plaster* followed by a coat of premixed *lightweight finish plaster* adheres well. If the accuracy of a surface permits, one coat of neat *Class B Board finish plaster* can be applied even on smooth concrete, while *thin-wall plasters* can be used on very accurate surfaces. In damp situations, or where plaster will be subject to rough use Portland cement undercoats should be applied on an additional bonding coat usually based on PVA or other polymers, having the manufacturers' assurance as to suitability.

(ii)   *Lightweight concretes*

Aerated (cellular) concretes and those containing lightweight aggregates have high drying shrinkage and should be allowed to shrink before being plastered. Suction of products varies widely and specifications should always be obtained from the manufacturers of blocks, or for in-situ concrete from the manufacturers of the aggregate.

(iii)   *No-fines concrete*

No-fines concrete provides a good mechanical key but has low to moderate drying shrinkage and suction according to the aggregate employed. Where lightweight aggregates are used, specifications for plastering should be obtained from the manufacturers of the aggregate.

3   *Boards*

Boards suitable for plastering are: (a) *plasterboards* (b) *asbestos boards,* (c) *plastics boards* and (d) *insulating fibre building boards.*

Boards must be evenly supported and stored flat in dry conditions. Fixing methods, including details such as the widths of gaps between boards, should accord with the manufacturers' recommendations. Boards must be fixed at all edges and intermediately, to give a firm and level surface, particularly where single coat plastering is intended. Boards should be staggered to break the joints, and to avoid unsightly cracks the latter should be reinforced, except joints between *gypsum laths* which are fixed in one plane (or alternatively a straight cut can be made in the plaster). Joint reinforcement should preferably be jute scrim, not less than 90 mm wide. If galvanized wire scrim is used cut ends should be painted. Joints are covered with the same plaster which will be used directly on the boards, the reinforcement is pressed into it, avoiding overlapping, and the plaster trowelled as flat as possible. Plastering should follow when the joints have set, but before they have dried out, and before boards become dirty or damaged. Boards having excessive suction should be sealed with one or two coats of suitable PVA emulsion. Mixes containing lime are unsuitable for direct application on boards and mixes containing Portland cement must never be used. See table 21.

3a   *Plasterboards*

These boards, described in BS 1230: 1970 *Gypsum plasterboard* comprise a solid or cellular gypsum plaster core which sometimes contains a small proportion of fibres, surfaced with heavy paper. Plasterboards are a low cost and very common form of internal wall and ceiling lining which can either be plastered or decorated direct. A proprietary partition unit comprises two plasterboards separated by an 'egg crate' cellular core and another product consists of two thick plaster boards (*gypsum planks*) stuck back to back.

The long edges of boards are bound, and shaped as shown in figure 2, but ends of boards are cut exposing the plaster core.

Properties Plasterboard is a *stressed skin* construction. As the *strength* lies mainly in the paper liners and as the strength of the paper in the machine direction is about twice that across it, it is important that plasterboard should be fixed with the bound edges running across joists or other supports. Boards have a *density* of about 849 Kg/m^3. *Moisture movement* is low.

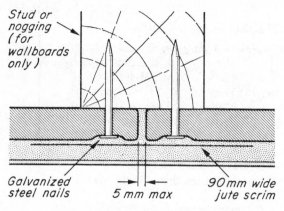

Stud or nogging (for wallboards only)

Galvanized steel nails

5 mm max

90 mm wide jute scrim

Baseboards and wallboards

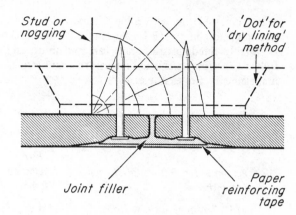

Stud or nogging

'Dot' for 'dry lining' method

Joint filler

Paper reinforcing tape

Wallboards with tapered edges

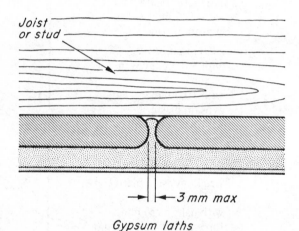

Joist or stud

3 mm max

Gypsum laths

BOARDS FOR PLASTERING
–on grey paper surfaces

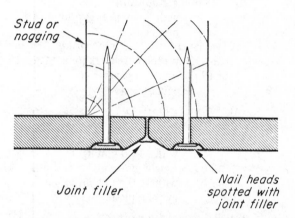

Stud or nogging

Joint filler

Nail heads spotted with joint filler

Wallboards with bevelled edges.

BOARDS FOR DECORATION DIRECT
– on ivory paper surfaces

The plasterboards are shown 12·7 mm thick which is suitable for support by joists, studs or dots and dabs at 610 mm maximum centres. Supports should be at least 50 mm wide.

Boards for plastering Two-coat plaster is shown. (If one coat only is used it should be at least 5 mm thick.) Joints in gypsum laths require scrim at all wall/wall and wall/ceiling junctions.

Boards for decoration direct The tapered edges (exaggerated for clarity) are finished with *paper joint tape* firmly embedded in *joint finish* (not shown), followed by a wider band each having the edges feathered out. A thin slurry of *finisher* is then applied over the whole surface to equalize suction between the joints and boards. For ceilings a very common and simple method is to butt square edge boards closely together and smooth joints with a filler. A proprietary, flexible, textured paint is then applied over the whole surface (not shown).

2   Plasterboard edge joints

Although the paper liners are *combustible,* plasterboards satisfy the requirements of the *Building* *Regulations* 1976 for *Class O surfaces* because the paper bonded to the plaster core have a fire propagation index (I) not exceeding 12 and a sub-index (i_1) not exceeding 6 (BS 476: Part 6: 1968 test). If suitably fixed, plasterborads can contribute usefully to the *fire resistance* of separating and structural elements. For example:

Non-loadbearing partitions

	Fire resistance hours
1 *Steel or timber frames faced each side with:*	
(a) 12.7 mm *gypsum wallboard* — unplastered	½
(b) 9.5 mm *gypsum lath* — with 5 mm neat gypsum plaster	
(c) Two layers of 10.0 mm *gypsum plasterboard* fixed to break joint or 19 mm *gypsum plank* – unplastered	1
(d) 9.5 mm *gypsum lath:* — with 12.7 mm sanded gypsum plaster — with 10.0 mm lightweight gypsum plaster	1
— with 16.0 mm lightweight gypsum plaster	
(e) 19.0 mm *gypsum plank:* — with 10.0 mm lightweight gypsum plaster	1½
— with 16.0 mm lightweight gypsum plaster	
(f) 9.5 mm *gypsum lath:* — with 25 mm lightweight gypsum plaster	2

	Fire resistance hours
2 *Cellular core plasterboard partitions*	
(a) 57.0mm thick comprising two 9.5 mm *gypsum plasterboards* – unplastered	½
(b) 63 mm thick comprising two 12.7 mm *gypsum plasterboards:* — with 12.7 mm sanded gypsum plaster each side	1
— with 15.9 mm lightweight plaster each side	2

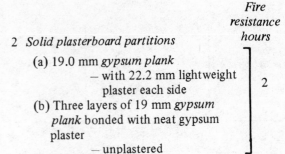

	Fire resistance hours
2 *Solid plasterboard partitions*	
(a) 19.0 mm *gypsum plank* — with 22.2 mm lightweight plaster each side	2
(b) Three layers of 19 mm *gypsum plank* bonded with neat gypsum plaster — unplastered	

Encasures to steel stanchions
(weight not less than 45.0 kg/m)

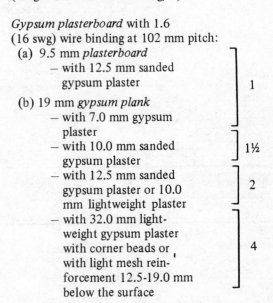

Gypsum plasterboard with 1.6 (16 swg) wire binding at 102 mm pitch:	*Fire resistance hours*
(a) 9.5 mm *plasterboard* — with 12.5 mm sanded gypsum plaster	1
(b) 19 mm *gypsum plank* — with 7.0 mm gypsum plaster	
— with 10.0 mm sanded gypsum plaster	1½
— with 12.5 mm sanded gypsum plaster or 10.0 mm lightweight plaster	2
— with 32.0 mm lightweight gypsum plaster with corner beads or with light mesh reinforcement 12.5-19.0 mm below the surface	4

Types of plasterboards The types of plasterboards contained in BS 1230 are described here with the sizes which were available from 1 April 1970 (figures in bold type are dimensionally coordinated basic sizes. The other lengths will be progressively withdrawn).

Gypsum wallboard This has one side with a cream or ivory finish ready for decoration direct with paint. The back, recognized by the double thickness of paper along the longitudinal edges, has a grey paper suitable to receive an appropriate gypsum plaster. The edges are square, rounded, tapered or bevelled. The shallow depressions formed by adjacent tapered edges are intended to be filled with plaster reinforced with *wallboard joint tape* and brought to a flush finish. See figure 2.

Dimensions
Thicknesses: 9.5   (except bevelled) 12.7 mm
Widths: **600   900 1200** mm
Lengths: **1800** 2350 **2400** 2700 **3000** mm

Gypsum lath is a narrow plasterboard with rounded edges which is designed to receive gypsum plaster on one side only. The small size makes for easy handling and when correctly fixed movement is distributed over a larger number of longitudinal joints. Also the extra thickness of plaster at joints makes cracking less likely so they require to be reinforced with scrim only at internal and external angles.

Dimensions
Thicknesses: 9.5 mm   12.7 mm
Widths: 406 mm
Lengths: **1200** mm

Gypsum baseboard is designed to receive gypsum plaster on either side. The edges are usually square but rounded edges are available.

Dimensions
Thickness: 9.5 mm
Width: 914 mm
Lengths: **1200** mm

Gypsum plank is a narrow board with surfaces suitable for plaster or decoration direct. Its greater thickness is useful where additional strength, sound insulation or fire protection is required.

Dimensions
Thickness: 19 mm
Width: **600** mm
Lengths: 2350 **2400 2700 3000**mm

Insulating gypsum plasterboards All types of plasterboards are available with a sheet of bright aluminium foil on one side. If the foil is fixed facing an enclosed cavity it provides thermal insulation by reflection so that the thermal conductance of the board with an adjacent cavity is 12.3 W/m^2 deg C for 9.5 mm boards and 13.9 W/m^2 deg C for 12.7 mm boards.

PVC faced plasterboards Plasterboards (not described in BS 1230) are available with both heavy and light gauge PVC veneers in plain colours and printed designs with smooth or textured surface. They have a *Class 1 surface spread of flame* (BS 476: Part 7: 1971) and can be washed with a solution of mild detergent or with soapy water.

Perforated and slotted plasterboards These boards are usually fixed with a glass-fibre or mineral wool backing to increase sound absorption.

Fixing plasterboards The thickness of boards must relate to the span between fixings, thus:

Plasterboards should be fixed with their longitudinal edges at right angles to joists or other supports. All four edges of wallboards and baseboards should have a minimum bearing of 25 mm, 51 mm wide noggings for edge support being inserted between the main framing where required. Plaster laths should be fixed with longitudinal edges at right angles to the main supports, 'breaking joint' on each course and with 3 mm gaps between their edges.

Thickness of board mm	Maximum centres of joists, studs and battens (spans for plaster 'ribbons' for dry linings are given in **bold** type)	
	Walls mm	Ceilings mm
9·5 12·7	381 **457** 457 **610**	457 610

Fixing by nails Nails should be 14 swg (2 mm) galvanized, and with small flat heads and smooth shanks, 32 mm long for 9.5 mm thick boards and 38 mm long for 12.7 mm thick boards. Nails should be driven slightly below the surface without breaking the paper, starting from the centre of the boards, at 152 mm centres for ceiling, 203 mm centres for walls and partitions, and ar 102 mm centres 13 mm from all edges.

Fixing as 'dry linings' The expression *dry lining* is applied to the fixing of *gypsum tapered edge wallboards* to walls by plaster dabs or on battens so that a true and jointless surface is obtained as described in *BRE Digest 9* and *D of E Advisory Leaflet 64*. On walls which are reasonably true in line an allowance of 19 mm should suffice for the thickness of the finish. The method has the advantages of being 'dry' and rapid, particularly if cutting of boards is minimized. Efflorescence problems are eliminated and the cavity improves thermal insulation particularly where foil-backed boards are used.

PLASTERING

(On the other hand, on walls of brick or blocks, sound insulation is lower than that provided by wet applied plaster.) Heavy objects can be fixed by drilling a hole in the plasterboard and injecting plaster to form a solid mass in the cavity behind, into which, when the plaster has hardened, a hole can be drilled for a plug and screw.

In the method of fixing advocated by British Gypsum Ltd, 76 x 51 mm *dots* of thin bitumen-impregnated fibreboard are bedded in *Board finish* plaster at 457 mm centres horizontally (to suit 914 mm boards) and about 1067 mm centres vertically — their purpose being to *straighten* the wall and to provide a temporary means of fixing the boards. When the dots are firm, neat *Board finish plaster* dabs, slightly thicker than the dots, of trowel length and 51-76 mm wide are applied with gaps of 51-76 mm between them. One vertical line of dabs is required at the centre of each 914 mm wide board with others set in about 25 mm from each vertical edge. Dabs are also applied horizontally between the top and bottom dots. Each wallboard which should be at least 26 mm shorter than the floor—ceiling height is pressed with a foot-operated wedge until it is tight to the ceiling. The board is then secured to the outer dots by doubleheaded galvanized nails which can be removed and re-used when the plaster dabs have set.

The depressions formed by the tapered edges of adjacent boards are filled with proprietary *joint filler* and a special 44 mm wide *paper tape* is pressed into it. A further application of filler is used to bring the surface flush with the face of the boards and when this is hard a *joint finish* is laid in two applications in a band 203 to 254 mm wide and the edges are feathered out with a sponge. Finally, a very thin slurry of joint is spread over the entire board surface to remove differences in texture between the jointed areas and the plasterboards. Cut edges are less easily concealed and should be chamfered with a *Surform* type tool and be placed at internal angles. Metal reinforced tape is available for external angles which require special protection.

Preparation for plaster All joints of square-edged plasterboards. and wall to ceiling and wall to wall junctions (including external angles) between *gypsum laths*, are reinforced with 90 mm jute scrim bedded in neat *board plaster*. Boards should not be wetted before they are plastered.

3b *Asbestos boards*
(See *MBS: Materials*, chapters 3 and 10.)
Asbestos *insulating boards and wallboards* (BS 3536: 1962), unlike *semi-* and *fully-compressed asbestos cement boards* are suitable for plastering if porosity is reduced with suitable primers.

3c *Expanded plastics boards*
(See *MBS: Materials*, chapter 3).
Boards such as expanded polystyrene and foamed polyurethane, have low suction and provide adequate key for appropriate types of plaster. They have low resistance to impact and should be fully bonded to a firm background.

3d *Insulating fibre building boards*
(See *MBS: Materials*, chapter 3.)
These boards, described in BS 1142: 1972 provide better thermal insulation than plasterboards but are combustible, have high moisture movement and are liable to fungal attack in damp conditions. They can be nailed to joist, battens or studs as follows:

Thickness of board, mm	Maximum centres of supports, mm
12·7 (1220 mm wide)	405
12·7 (915 mm wide)	455
19·0 and thicker	610

Alternatively, boards can be used as permanent formwork to concrete structures.

Insulating fibre building boards should be wetted before fixing to give a 'shrink fit' but they must dry before plastering or the bond between plaster and board may fail. The 'rough' side provides the better key for suitable gypsum plasters.

All joints must be scrimmed. (FIDOR recommend wire mesh.)

4 *Wood-wool slabs*
(See *MBS: Materials*, chapter 3.)
As described in BS 1105: 1972 have low suction and provide a good key. Although they have high moisture movement, if they are dry when they are fixed the likelihood of shrinkage damaging the plaster is small. They may be fixed as *permanent formwork* for concrete, or nailed with sufficiently

74

long nails. Joints between slabs should be reinforced in accordance with the manufacturers' instructions.

5   *Compressed straw building slabs (Stramit)* BS 4046: 1971 (See *MBS: Materials,* chapter 3.)

Slabs must be kept dry. *Plaslin* slabs have plaster liners on both sides and plain paper liners treated with a PVA bonding agent provide a good mechanical key. Joints between slabs should be scrimmed.

6   *Cork slabs*

Cork has low suction and a variable key but premixed gypsum lightweight bonding coats adhere well. With certain methods of fixing slabs, joints may require to be reinforced.

7   *Metal lathing*

This provides a mechanical key for general surfaces, or locally where changes in background materials occur. Metal lathing being a good conductor of heat, ordinary plaster is liable to show *pattern staining*[1] but plaster on metal lathing can provide a good standard of *fire resistance* (see *MBS: S and F Part 2*). The lathing should be protected from corrosion by galvanizing[2] or by bituminous paint (see chapter 17, page 97). BS 1369: 1947 *Metal lathing (steel) for plastering* describes the following types:

   Plain expanded metal
   Expanded metal with internal ribs
   Expanded metal with attached ribs
   Perforated expanded metal
   Dovetailed expanded metal

Plain expanded metal with diamond shaped mesh having at least two strands per 29 mm and an aperture not less than 5 mm wide is the commonest type. It should weigh not less than 1.62 kg/m² for sanded plasters and 1.22 kg/m² for premixed lightweight gypsum plasters and be fixed to supports at 356 mm centres with the long way of the mesh across the supports. The strands of the mesh should slope inwards and downwards from the face on vertical surfaces, and on soffits the strands in adjacent sheets should all face in one direction.

It should be tensioned as tightly as possible and fixed with galvanized nails at 102 mm centres driven at an angle across the grain of timber, or

with wire or suitable clips to steelwork. Edges of adjacent sheets should be lapped 26 mm over supports and wired together at 102 mm centres with 18 swg (1.2 mm) galvanized wire. To avoid rust stains appearing through the plaster, the ends of sheets and wire should be bent back from the face of the work. To ensure continuity of the key for plaster over wide supports rods or strips should be fixed between the supports and the lathing. A spiral of 3.2 mm wire at 305 mm pitch is commonly used as a spacer around steelwork and to increase the rigidity of the lathing. A lighter gauge is suitable where the lathing is fixed at frequent centres and is required only to give a key.

Plastering on expanded metal As normally fixed, metal lathing lacks rigidity and is less able than 'solid' backgrounds to restrain the drying shrinkage of cement undercoats which tend to crack and expose the lathing to corrosion. Cement undercoats are necessary in damp conditions or where cement or *Keene's Class D* (BS 1191) finishes are to be applied, but for other gypsum finishes a *Class B metal lathing grade*[3] undercoat and float coat is to be preferred and for *lightweight gypsum finishes* a *gypsum lightweight metal lathing* undercoat and float coat is usually required. Three coats are essential to obtain a smooth and true finish.

8   *Dovetailed bitumen-impregnated fibre sheet (Newtonite lathing)*

This is particularly suitable for fixing to existing walls where a barrier to damp is required. The manufacturers' advice should be obtained as to its suitability and methods of use.

9   *Wood laths*

These are unlikely to be used today except possibly for repairing old plasterwork. They should comply with BS 4471: Part 2: 1971 *Small resawn sections.*

4   MIXES AND APPLICATION OF PLASTERS

Adhesion requires intimate contact between surfaces, air must be expelled by force during or after applications, and for finishes subject to high drying shrinkage or to constant temperature changes a

---

[1] See *MBS: Materials*, chapter 1.
[2] See *MBS: Materials*, chpater 9.

[3] The *metal lathing grade* contains a rust inhibitor which dispenses with the need to add lime for this purpose.

mechanical key is essential. *Bonding agents* (see page 67) are useful in less exacting stress conditions. Generally no coat should be stronger than the background or the undercoat on which it is applied. Table on page 77 gives approximate thicknesses of plaster coats on common backgrounds Table on page 78 give typical plastering systems for premixed-lightweight and site mixed *Class B, BS 1191* gypsum based plasters, and table on page 79 gives systems for use with Portland cement based undercoats.

The number of coats required depends upon the rigidity of a background, the 'truth' of the background and that required of the finish, and to some extent upon the type of plaster which is used. In the past, on most backgrounds after *dubbing out* any depressions, three coats of plaster were required. Today backgrounds tend to be more accurate, and while three coats are still needed to obtain a level surface on metal lathing, two coats not less than 13 mm thick can give a surface with not more than about 3 mm deviation in a length of 1830 mm (about 1 in 600) on backgrounds which reach a good standard in line and plumb. Thinner plaster is bound to closely follow the contours of backgrounds, but on very accurate backgrounds a single coat is often considered to be sufficient.

We now consider single coat and multi-coat finishes:

Single coat finishes

Single coat finishes comprise:

(a) *Class B Retarded hemi-hydrate low setting-expansion board plasters* (see page 64) can be applied as skim coats at least 5 mm thick. Salts which may take as long as six weeks to emerge, should be brushed off.

Projection plaster (British Gypsum Ltd) is applied in one coat 13 mm thick. It cannot contain lime so that expanded metal must be galvanized to prevent corrosion.

(b) *'Thin-wall' plasters*

These have gypsum and/or organic binders. Less labour is involved in handling and application, it is possible to spray a surface and level it later and there is less water to dry out, although to secure these advantages backgrounds must be very true.

Well fixed plasterboards, compressed straw slabs, some cellular plastics boards, good quality concrete slabs and in-situ concrete are sufficiently true.

(i) *Gypsum based thin-wall plasters* These can be applied in an economical thickness of 2 to 3 mm.

(ii) *'Scandinavian', 'Swedish sand putty' or veneer type' thin-wall plaster.* On exceptionally accurate backgrounds a thickness of 1 to 2 mm is sufficient. Bond is good. The semi-liquid is normally sprayed on (although small areas can be applied by hand), and levelled with a broad spatula which can have a long handle to obviate the need for scaffolding.

Trade name is *Breplasta*.

Multi-coat finishes

We now consider:
1 the first undercoat
2 the second undercoat (where applicable)
3 the final coat

1 *The first undercoat*

Before applying the first undercoat it is necessary to *dub out* any depressions. Cement and gypsum plaster undercoat must be pressed well into the background which should provide a good key. Lime reduces adhesion and should never be added to first coats on plasterboards or other boards.

Undercoats must be scratched with a crossed undercut key for a cement of gypsum second undercoat and scratched for a final coat of those plasters.

Undercoats are of the following types:

Cement based undercoats – (see table 22), are necessary in damp conditions and to hold back water and less effectively, water vapour. Water repellent admixtures can help. 1 Portland cement:3 sand (by volume) is usual on rigid and well keyed backgrounds for cement, *Keene's* and *Class C* gypsum plasters which require a strong undercoat. Cement based undercoats are suitable for *Class B* gypsum and for Scandinavian thin-wall plasters.

Gypsum based undercoats – (see table 21) adhere better than Portland cement mixes, particularly *Premixed bonding grade lightweight gypsum plaster;* also they do not shrink in drying.

Organic based undercoats On accurate backgrounds a *backing grade* plaster may be necessary to 'true up' surfaces and normally two coats of *finish grade* applied with an interval of twenty-four hours. A *rendering grade* is available for use on less accurate backgrounds with the advantage of greater speed over cement and gypsum based first coats.

2 *The second undercoat*

Before this coat is applied Portland cement based first coats should be allowed to develop sufficient strength before being allowed to dry and shrink. Gypsum based first coats should have set but not dried out when the second undercoat is applied. The second undercoat must be ruled to a plane surface, if necessary consolidated with a wood float, and keyed to receive the final coat.

3 *The final coat*

Finishing coats must set at a rate which enables the plaster to be applied and finished level and smooth as a base for decoration. It must then provide the required degree of hardness. Finishes must not be stronger than undercoats and otherwise be compatible with them — see tables 21 and 22.

Types of finishes are now decribed in order of increasing hardness from (a) – (g):

(a)   *Lime putty* which is a paste of water and hydrated lime could be applied on any normal undercoat but strength develops extremely slowly and is insufficient for modern buildings. The addition of sand decreases shrinkage. If lime is slaked from quicklime the process must be thorough to avoid

Backgrounds	*First undercoat mm*	*Second undercoat mm*	*Final coat mm*	*Total* *mm*
Plasterboards and insulating fibre building boards	— 8	— —	5 2	5 minimum 10 minimum
Concrete	— 8	— —	2–3 2	2–3[1] – *Class B* *Board finish*[2] or *'Thin-wall' plaster on* very true close texture surfaces only 10 maximum*
Most brickwork and block-work No-fines concrete	11 11	— 6	2 2	13 maximum* 19 maximum*
Metal lathing	0[3] 0[3]	8[3] 11[3]	2 2	10[3] approx. – *Lightweight gypsum plasters* 13[3] approx. – *Other plasters*
Wood-wool slabs	11	—	2	13
Expanded polystyrene	8 11	— —	2 2	10 approx. – on ceilings 13 minimum – on walls
Backgrounds treated with bonding agents	— 8	— —	2–3 2	2–3 } *Class B Board finish plaster* 10 }

[1] Thickness should be obtained from the manufacturer
[2] A bonding treatment may be needed on some concretes
[3] Thickness measured from face of lathing
* The greater the thickness the smaller the strain to cause failure

Table 20   *Approximate thicknesses of gypsum based plaster coats on common backgrounds*
Greater thicknesses may be necessary on inaccurate backgrounds, or for increased sound insulation or fire resistance.

Premixed lightweight aggregate plaster (BS 1191 Part 2)		Background[1]	Site-mixed plasters		
			Undercoats(s)		Finish coat
Finish coat	Under-coat(s)		Class B (BS 1191 Part 1) plaster	Type 1[2] (BS 1191) sand	Class B (BS 1191 Part 1) plaster
Finish grade (b1)	—	Boards True concrete surfaces Expanded plastics boards	—		Board finish plaster – neat (or 'Thin-wall' plaster)
	—	Aerated concrete slabs and block-work	not recommended		—
	Bonding grade (a3)	Compressed straw slabs[3] Glazed surfaces treated with bonding agent Close texture lightweight aggregate concrete[3,7] Dense concrete[3] Clay engineering brickwork[3]	1 Browning grade (a1)	1½ (1)	Finish grade – neat or with up to 25 per cent lime putty
	Metal lathing grade (a2)	Plasterboards (grey side) Insulating fibre building boards	1 Haired browning grade (a1)	1½ (1)	
		Expanded plastics boards		1[4] (2–3)[4]	
		Metal lathing[5]	1 Metal lathing grade (a2)	1½ (1) render	
				2 (1½) float	
	Browning grade (a1)	Wood wool slabs[6]	1 Browning grade (a1)	2 (1½)	
		Dense clay brickwork with joints raked[3] – other than engineering brickwork Dense clay blockwork Calcium silicate and concrete brickwork No-fines concrete[7] Open-textured lightweight aggregate concrete[7]			
		Normal clay brickwork and block-work		2–3[4] (1½–2)[4]	

[1] For description and preparation of backgrounds, see page 68
[2] If BS 1198 type 2 sand is used the proportions of sand should be reduced as indicated in parentheses
[3] May require bonding agent
[4] According to plaster manufacturers' instructions
[5] Two undercoats are required
[6] Two undercoats may be necessary
[7] Manufacturers of lightweight aggregates should be consulted

Table 21   Premixed plasters and site-mixed plasters based on Class B (BS 1191) gypsum plasters (mixes by volume)

The mixes shown are intended as a guide only and should be confirmed with the plaster manufacturer in each case.

Background	Undercoat[1]	Finish coat	
		Portland cement based	Gypsum based (BS 1191)
Strong brickwork with raked joints Strong no-fines concrete	1 PC : 3 S	Any Portland cement based finish not stronger than the undercoat	Keene's – Class D – neat
Clay, calcium silicate and concrete brickwork Clay and concrete blockwork Strong no-fines concrete	1 PC : ¼ L : 3 S		Classes B or C – neat or with up to 25 per cent lime
Backgrounds as above No-fines concrete – moderate strength Aerated concrete	1 PC : 1 L : 5–6 S 1 PC : 5–6 S with plasticizer 1 Masonry cement : 4½ S		
Backgrounds as above Metal lathing	1 PC : 2 L : 8–9 S 1 PC : 7–8 S with plasticizer 1 Masonry cement : 6 S		

[1] Undercoats containing cement or lime are not normally suitable on engineering brickwork, dense concrete, close textured lightweight aggregate concrete, and they are not suitable on boards
PC – Portland cement   L – Non-hydraulic lime putty   S – Sand – BS 1199

Table 22   *Plaster mixes with Portland cement based undercoats (by volume)*

popping and *pitting* of reactive particles. *Soaking overnight* improves workability.

(b)   *1 lime putty: ¼-1 Class B plaster* (BS 1191): *0-1 sand (by volume)*. With the higher gypsum plaster content mixes are moderately strong and provided the surface is not over-trowelled the gypsum restrains the shrinkage of the lime. The mix could be applied on most normal undercoats but not on Portland cement : fat lime : sand mixes.

(c)   *Premixed gypsum lightweight plasters*. These finishes (see page 67) are intended for use on gypsum lightweight plaster undercoats.

(d)   *Class B* (BS 1191) *gypsum plaster*. The addition of up to 25 per cent lime putty (by volume) slightly reduces hardness and improves workability but accelerates setting.

(e)   *Class C – Anhydrous* (BS 1191) *gypsum plaster* is very slightly harder than *Class B* plasters. They set slowly and can be retempered allowing ample time for finishing. The addition of up to 25 per cent lime makes for easy application.

(f)   *Class D – Keene's* (BS 1191) *gypsum plaster* has a more gradual set and can be brought to an even smoother finish than *Class C.*

(g)   *Cement: lime sand mixes*. These finishes would normally be used internally only for extremely heavy duty where dampness cannot be avoided and where a non-alkaline and craze-free surface is not essential. A rich mix such as 1 Portland cement : 0-¼ lime putty : 3 sand (by volume) gives maximum hardness on an undercoat of the same mix and strength. Increases in the lime:sand ratio reduce hardness and the associated tendency to crack and craze.

Precast plasterwork

On the continent, partition blocks made from gypsum plaster and straw are common. In Australia sisal fibre reinforced slabs 11 mm thick of storey height and 12 m long are used extensively as an inner leaf in framed construction requiring support only at 450-600 mm centres. In this country precast plaster takes the form of: *Bellrock* partition slabs with outer 'walls' of plaster and honeycomb cores; fibrous plaster and glass fibre reinforced gypsum (GRP).

FIBROUS PLASTER

Fibrous plaster (or *'stick and rag work'*) (not to be confused with plaster which contains fibres), is pre-cast *Plaster of Paris* reinforced with jute scrim, wood laths and occasionally with wire netting. Plane surfaces are superior to those which can normally be obtained in trowelled work although distortion can present some difficulty in accurate matching of adjoining units. Flexible moulds enable intricate details to be cast, and at low cost for quantity production. For internal use standard louvres for air bricks and encasures for columns and beams are made in fibrous plaster.

Units of fibrous plaster can be made in any size which is convenient for conveyance to the site and for fixing. Fixing is rapid and simple, usually by nails to timber grounds, or by galvanized wire fixed to metal grids. Wads of scrim soaked in plaster are used to reinforce fixing where additional strength is required. Only nail holes and joints require to be made good with plaster, so that the process on the site is almost completely dry.

GLASS–FIBRE REINFORCED GYPSUM
See also *MBS: Materials,* chapter 10

The BRE has developed spraying and pressing techniques for the manufacture of *glass-fibre reinforced gypsum (grg)* products such as partition units, slabs for use instead of floor boards, and diamond shaped pyramidal panels which can be bolted together to form a dome. Although unsuitable in damp conditions, glass-fibre reinforced gypsum products have good strength properties, fracture is quasi-plastic rather than brittle and there is no loss of strength after 6 months at 40 per cent RH and 18°C. Fire resistance is excellent and moisture expansion is low. Table 23 compares the properties of an asbestos cement sheet with those of a glass-fibre reinforced gypsum plaster board.

	Flexural strength N/mm^2	Tensile strength N/mm^2	Impact strength N/mm^2	Moisture expansion per cent	Fire resistance
Asbestos cement[1] sheet	28	14	1·75–2·50	0·2	Poor
Glass-fibre reinforced gypsum plaster board[2]	24–35	12–18	44–53	0·02	Excellent

[1] 10–15% asbestos: ordinary Portland cement by weight. See *MBS: Materials*, chapter 10.
[2] 6–10% glass fibre: gypsum plaster by weight

Table 23   Comparison of the properties of an asbestos cement sheet and a glass-fibre reinforced gypsum plasterboard

3 Renderings

Renderings[1] modify the weather resistance, colour and texture of external wall surfaces. The recommendations in CP 221 : 1960 *External rendered finishes* should be followed.

We consider, in turn: 1 Durability and weather resistance; 2 Backgrounds; 3 Mixes; 4 The coats; 5 Application; 6 Detailing.

1 DURABILITY AND WEATHER-RESISTANCE

Differential drying and moisture movements, and thermal movements greater than occur internally, give rise to shear and/or tensile stresses between the background and rendering, or between coats. Ice prevents adhesion to backgrounds, and in persistently wet conditions sulphates derived from clay bricks or other sources attack Portland cement in mortar joints and in the rendering. Expansion of jointing material cracks renderings, further water enters and the deterioration becomes progressive.

In ordinary exposures moderately strong and dense cement:lime:sand rendering mixes provide satisfactory weather resistance. They absorb some rain, but when it stops it can evaporate freely if the outer surface is left unpainted. Incidentally, mixes containing lime are better able to retain water, which makes for thorough hydration of cement on absorptive backgrounds. However, dense renderings are necessary in severe exposures although they are particularly prone to *crazing*[2] and because they are strong their shrinkage is less easily restrained by the background and cracks result. Water which flows down the non-absorptive surface enters the cracks and is unable to evaporate outwards so that a dense rendering can, in fact, reduce the weather resistance of a wall. In practice in severe exposures if often

[1] The term *rendering* is confusingly also applied to first coats on brickwork, blockwork and masonry internally.

[2] Crazing is a surface network of fine cracks produced by the carbonation of cement laitance caused by overworking a surface or by evaporation of excess water. Disfigurement is less with mixes of lower cement content and with textured and scraped finishes.

befomes necessary to fill cracks as they occur and to paint renderings.

2 BACKGROUNDS

Table 24 summarizes the main properties of common backgrounds. For good adhesion they must be rigid, free from dust, dirt, oil, grease, paint and efflorescence. Some suction is necessary to prevent the material sagging or sliding after application, and a spatterdash treatment is recommended where suction is high or irregular.

Physical adhesion is insufficient and an effective mechanical key must be provided. Mortar joints in brickwork and blockwork should be raked out to a depth of at least 13 mm and brushed clean. Smooth concrete should provide a dovetailed key from rubber formwork liners or by the use of surface retarders (see chapter 5, page 95). Hacking hardened concrete is a costly alternative while superficial treatments such as light *sparrow picking* are of little value.

No-fines concrete provides a good mechanical key and so do wood-wool slabs, although here little restraint is afforded to thermal and moisture movements, and bitumen coated metal lathing should be fixed over them.

Renderings cannot 'bridge' structural movement joints and at junctions between dissimilar backgrounds, eg reinforced concrete columns and adjacent lightweight concrete infill panels, joints should be provided. Alernatively, expanded metal can be used to prevent concentration of movement as described for plastering in chapter 2.

Renderings must not be stronger than the background, so that it may be necessary to apply strong renderings on expanded metal lathing fixed to battens which have been impregnated with preservative.

3 MIXES

Table 25 recommends mutually compatible undercoat and final coat mixes for various backgrounds

Type	Properties			Remarks
	Suction	Key or bond	Movement	
Dense, strong and smooth, eg — high density bricksand blocks — dense concrete	Low to moderate	Poor. Mechanical key needed. Hacking may be needed even if brick joints are raked	Low to high. Clay materials may expand Concrete materials may shrink	The risk of efflorescence is lower than with more porous backgrounds
Moderately strong and porous, eg — most bricks and blocks	Moderate to high	Good if joints well raked out, keyed bricks are used, or if spatterdash or other bonding treatment is applied	Shrinkage moderate to high for materials other than clay brickwork or blockwork which may expand	If suction is high or irregular, a spatterdash treatment is recommended Risk of efflorescence with some products
Moderately weak and porous, eg — lightweight aggregate and aerated concretes — low strength bricks	Moderate to very high	Moderate to good	Shrinkage, low to high	Background should be dry, (and therefore 'preshrunk') Risk of efflorescence with some products Strong renderings may shear the background surface
No-fines concrete	Low to moderate according to aggregate type	Good mechanical key	Low to moderate	Sufficient strength to resist shrinkage stresses
Metal lathing (BS 1369)	—	Good	None if lathing is tightly stretched	Use a dense and relatively impervious mix for the first undercoat, and 'back plaster', if possible, to prevent rain penetration and to protect the lathing

Table 24 Backgrounds for renderings (Based on CP 221 : 1960)

and exposures, and for four types of finish. It will be seen that 1 Portland cement:1 lime:5–6 sand is suitable for most purposes and is preferred for many purposes, the stronger mixes being recommended only for strong backgrounds or where they are needed to resist knocks and abrasion or to retain dry-dash.

Background (see table 24)	Type of finish	Type of mix* for given exposure conditions†			
		'Severe'		'Moderate' or 'Sheltered'	
		Undercoat(s)	Final coat	Undercoat(s)	Final coat
Dense, strong and smooth Moderately strong and porous	Wood float	1, 2 or 3	1 or 3	1, 3 or 4	1, 3 or 4
	TEXTURED (Including SCRAPED)	3	3	3 or 4	3 or 4
	ROUGHCAST	1, 2 or 3	as undercoats	1, 2 or 3	as undercoats
	DRY-DASH	1 or 2	2	1 or 2	2
Moderately weak and porous	Wood float	} 3	} as undercoats	{ 3 or 4	} as undercoats
	TEXTURED (Including SCRAPED)				
	ROUGHCAST	3		3	
	DRY-DASH	2 or 3		2 or 3	
No-fines concrete	Wood float	1, 2 or 3	1, 2 or 3	1, 2, 3 or 4	1, 3 or 4
	TEXTURED (Including SCRAPED)	1, 2 or 3	3	2, 3 or 4	3 or 4
	ROUGHCAST	1, 2 or 3	1, 2 or 3	1, 2 or 3	1, 2 or 3
	DRY-DASH	1 or 2	2	1 or 2	2
Metal lathing	Wood float	1, 2 or 3	1 or 3	1, 2 or 3	1 or 3
	TEXTURED (Including SCRAPED) ROUGHCAST	1, 2 or 3	3	1, 2 or 3	3
	DRY-DASH	1 or 2	2	1 or 2	2

*MIXES:

Type 1 1 Portland cement:0-¼ fat lime:3 sand (by volume)
Type 2 1 Portland cement: ½ fat lime:4–4½ sand (by volume)
Type 3 1 Portland cement:1 fat lime: 5–6 sand (by volume)
Type 4 1 Portland cement:2 fat lime:8–9 sand (by volume)
Spatterdash – to provide a key – 1 Portland cement:1½–2 sand (by volume); to overcome irregular suction on porous backgrounds – 1 Portland cement: 2–3 sand (by volume)

†*Exposure gradings*

Severe Exposure to the full force of wind and rain, as with buildings on hills or near the coast, and tall buildings in towns.

Moderate Walls protected by eaves or other projections, and by neighbouring buildings, such as buildings in towns and suburbs.

Sheltered Walls in districts of low rainfall, and those in close proximity to other buildings, such as ground and first floor walling in towns.

Proprietary *masonry cement*:sand mixes may be used as alternatives to Types 3 and 4 but mix proportions should be in accordance with manufacturers' instructions.
Where renderings are required to resist moderate sulphate action, *sulphate-resisting Portland cement* may be used instead of the Portland cement given in the mixes above.
Sand to BS 119:1955 – preferably Table 1 of the BS.
Where alternative sand contents are shown, (eg 4–4½, 5–6, and 8–9) the higher proportion should be used if the sand is well granded, and the lower content if the sand is coarse or uniformly fine.

Table 25 Recommended mixes for external renderings (Based on CP 221:1960)

The types of finish shown in captals and the mixes shown in bold type in the table are those to be preferred in most circumstances.

Materials used in rendering include:

Ordinary and rapid hardening Portland cements	BS 12
Sulphate-resisting Portland cement[1]	BS 4027
Masonry cement	
High alumina cement[2]	BS 915
Limes	BS 890

Plasticizers BRS tests have indicated that cement/sand mixes plasticized by air-entraining agents or mortar plasticizers sometimes have less satisfactory resistance to rain penetration than cement/lime/sand mixes of similar strength. Proprietary mixes based on masonry cement which contain a fine mineral filler in addition to an air-entraining agent were nearly as effective as cement/lime/sand mixes.

For the above materials see *MBS: Materials* chapter 7.

Sand should be clean, sharp and preferably comply with table 1 of BS 119:1955 *Building sands from natural sources, Sands for external renderings, internal plastering with lime and Portland cement and floor screeds* which is quoted below:

BS sieve	*Percentage by weight passing BS sieves*
5 mm	100
no. 7	90 – 100
14	70 – 100
25	40 – 80
52	5 – 40
100	0 – 10[3]

Impurities – see Sand for plaster, page 67.

Natural aggregates other than sand BS 882:1965.

Pigments White or coloured Portland cements can be used in the finish coat or pigments can be added to ordinary Portland cement on the site. Unfortunately the white film of calcium carbonate (*lime bloom*) which forms on drying, tends to give

[1] Sulphate-resisting cement is advisable for renderings, and mortarts in chimneys, parapets and fre-standing walls which are constructed with clay bricks of *ordinary quality* (BS 3921:1969).
[2] High alumina cement is used only where special conditions justify its high cost.
[3] In the case of certain crushed stones, higher proportions may be satisfactory.

coloured renderings a faded look, more so on the darker colours.

Water should be free from salts and other deleterious substances.

Metal lathing (steel) for plastering BS 1369:1947.

4 THE COATS

One coat is rarely able to accommodate the irregularities of suction which occurs between small units or to prevent mortar joints 'grinning through'. One undercoat and a final coat are usually sufficient in moderate exposures but in severe exposures three coats are recommended. A *spatterdash* (thrown-on) coat bonds well and evens out the suction on backgrounds, and applied as a continuous covering on relatively even surfaces it may be considered as being the first coat in a three-coat (but not in a two-coat) system.

Undercoats should be 10 to 16 mm thick. Final coats are normally 6 to 10 mm thick, but where they are machine applied, as little as 3 mm.

Undercoats

Undercoats can prevent rain penetrating, align or straighten uneven surfaces and prevent back-grounds 'grinning through', and they must provide uniformly moderate suction and good adhesion for the finishing coat. Mixes must be sufficiently strong to obtain a good key but if they are stronger than the background or a previously applied undercoat, cracking and loss of adhesion often occur.

Undercoats, if not left rough, should be scratched to provide a key. Each coat should be left to dry and shrink for at least two days in summer and a week in cold or wet weather, before the next coat is applied.

Undercoats (and spatterdash coats) which will be subject to moderate or severe exposures may benefit by the inclusion of water-repellent cement or a water-proofing admixture.

Finishing coats

Finishes, especially those rich in cement, containing fine sands or finished with a steel trowel are liable to surface crazing and unavoidable variations in surface texture give a patchy appearance. Rain streaks are more obvious on smooth than on textured surfaces. Finishes considered in order of increasing durability, resistance to rain penetration and to irregular discolouration are:

Wood floated finishes

Renderings lightly patted with a wood or felt-faced float provide a uniform, flat surface free of scouring marks. Crazing, cracking and uneven weathering may result if too much cement and/or fine sand are used or if surfaces are overworked.

Scraped surfaces

A truly aligned, recently set finish is usually scraped with a steel straight-edge or old saw blade thereby removing 2 to 3 mm from the surface which includes the laitance which would tend to crack or craze. Scoring marks result where granular material is dragged across surfaces and coarse particles produce a 'travertine' effect.

Ornamental textures

During application and while a surface remains plastic (suction of undercoats must be low), combed, ribbed, stippled and the bold *English cottage texture* effects can be obtained.

Thrown finishes

These comprise *wet dash* and *dry dash*. A typical hand-thrown wet dash (or *roughcast*) is 6 to 13 mm cement coated aggregate thrown on a suitably matured undercoat.

Dry-dash finishes result where 'dry' 6 to 13 mm pebbles (hence *pebbledash*), shingle or spar, are thrown on and lightly pressed into a freshly applied final coat of mortar so the aggregate is left substantially exposed. The final coat must be strong enough to hold the aggregate, ie not weaker than 1 cement:1 lime:6 sand.

Dry proprietary compositions, obtainable in a wide variety of colours, give a range of textures (including *Tyrolean*), when they are machine applied. Some manufacturers provide pre-mixed undercoats.

5 APPLICATION

After 'slaking the thirst' of absorptive backgrounds but without saturating them, a high standard of workmanship is needed to produce functionally and visually satisfactory renderings. Force is necessary to expel air and bring the rendering into intimate contact with the background. Throwing on, manually or by machine, gives better adhesion than 'laying-on' with a trowel and is particularly advisable for first coats on smooth backgrounds.

Apart from *English cottage textures*, renderings should be applied from the top downwards. If work cannot be completed in one operation, straight *day joints* should be located at window heads, sills or other architectural features.

Work should not continue at freezing temperatures or when night frosts are likely. On the other hand, work should be done out of bright sunlight or drying winds, and in hot weather damp curing is recommended.

6 DETAILING

The following principles should be observed in detailing renderings:

1 Large areas should be avoided by providing movement joints at intervals.
2 Horizontal surfaces must be protected by flashings, copings and sills, with drips to throw water well clear of walls. Damp-proof courses should be provided below mortar jointed copings and sills. See figure below and figures 110 and 116 in *MBS: Components*

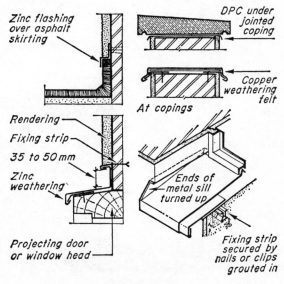

Zinc flashing over asphalt skirting

DPC under jointed coping

Copper weathering felt

At copings

Rendering

Fixing strip

35 to 50 mm

Zinc weathering

Ends of metal sill turned up

Projecting door or window head

Fixing strip secured by nails or clips grouted in

3   Protection of renderings

3 Where there is any possibility of water penetrating behind renderings, flashings and weep holes must be provided to conduct it outwards.

4 Parapets and free-standing walls should not be rendered on both sides and it is better not to render chimney stacks.

5 Renderings carried across damp-proof courses are a common cause of dampness in the lower parts of walls. Renderings on walls below dpcs are pushed off by salts from soils, and water rises by capillary movement between the rendering and wall and by-passes the dpc.

4 Wall tiling and mosaics

Wall tiling and mosaic wall coverings consist of relatively thin and small units which are usually fixed by adhesion. They may be required to improve appearance or to improve resistance to abrasion or staining. Glazed tiles are particularly easy to clean and special epoxide based jointing grouts can be used where sterile conditions are essential. Materials include ceramics, concrete — including terrazzo, glass, stainless steel and plastics. In addition, quarries and tiles such as linoleum, cork and rubber which are intended primarily for flooring are often used for walls, particularly at dado level. Tiles which absorb sound include perforated and slotted insulating fibre building boards. The choice of materials which are durable externally is limited to high grade ceramics, concrete, glass and stainless steel.

Ceramic wall tiling

Ceramic, ie clay, wall tiles are resistant to staining and attack by chemicals and if properly fixed good clay tiles retain their natural colour and gloss indefinitely. They are hard and robust but should not be used, particularly on arrises, where collisions are likely to occur. Externally a frost resistant product is essential and where severe chemical attack may occur clay tiles should comply with BS 3679:1963 *Acid-resisting bricks and tiles* and the jointing material and possibly the bedding must be chemically resistant. See BRE Digest 120.

CERAMIC TILES FOR INTERIOR USE

Most ceramic tiles for interior use have an earthenware body made from a mixture of ball-clay, china clay, calcined flint and cobalt oxide which help to produce whiteness, and limestone to limit shrinkage in firing. Each ingredient is ground and mixed with water, the separate slurries being mixed together to form a *slip*. Water is extracted and the clay is pressed into packs which are dried and crushed. The resulting dust is moistened slightly and tiles formed by die-pressing have finer surfaces than can be obtained by other means. Firing in kilns at about 1100°C takes up to ten days.

A glaze ground to a fine powder and suspended in water is put on the *biscuit* which is fired again in a tunnel kiln. Usually there are two qualities, *normal* and *seconds*, the later being adequate for some purposes.

Surfaces are: *high glaze* (glossy), *eggshell, satin* and *matt*.

Tiles are made in white and a very wide range of colours (*enamel glazes*). One manufacturer produces two hundred colours, thirty-five of which are available from stock. Mottled effects and patterns are also available.

It may not be easy to match old colours, even if the manufacturer's colour number or description is known but modern colour ranges are very consistent and a reasonable match should be obtainable. In the past, colour designs other than mottled effects had to be done by hand and their high cost, particularly where many colours are used, may still be justified for important work. Today, however, patterns are silk-screen or transfer printed, and some ripple-textured tiles are available at the same price as plain tiles. Some patterned tiles can be arranged in various ways and combinations to form larger patterns.

Tiles with a moulded face, termed *profiled* or *sculptured* tiles, are available in a range of standard designs.

Sizes

BS 1281:1974 *Glazed ceramic tiles and tile fittings for internal walls* specifies properties and gives details of tests for warpage and curvature, water absorption and resistance to chemicals, impact and crazing. It gives the following *preferred nominal sizes for non-modular tiles:*

152 × 152 × 5.0, 5.5, 6.5 and 8.0 mm
108 × 108 × 4.0 and 6.5 mm
⎫ tiles with cushion edges and spacer lugs ⎬

152 × 152 × 9.5 mm
⎫ tiles without cushion edges and spacer lugs ⎬

Modular Tiles

BS 1281 recommends *basic sizes* (which include the tile and its share of the joint) for tiles with cushion edges and spacer lugs of:

100 × 100 × 5.0 and 200 × 100 × 6.5 mm.

Great advances have been made in the control of sizes. For non-modular tiles the maximum permitted deviations in facial sizes are +0.6 and −0.3 mm and for modular tiles +0.8 and −0.6 mm on the greater dimension and +0.5 and −0.3 mm on the lesser dimension. The maximum range of deviation of average dimensions is 0.5 per cent on a batch of at least 35 tiles samples from any one consignment as laid down in the Standard and measured to the nearest 0.02 mm.

Internal tiles are at present also made in the following sizes:

Square tiles

25.4 ×	9.5 mm
50.8 × 6.35, 9.5 mm	
76.2 × 6.35, 9.5 mm	
101.6 × 6.35	mm
101.6 ×	*9.5 mm (12.7mm three dimensional tiles)*
107.95 × 3.97, 6.35 mm	
152.4 × 4.76, 6.35, 9.5 mm (15.9 mm three dimensional tiles)	

Rectangles

101.6 × 12.7, 25.4, 50.8,   × 6.35, 9.5 mm
107.95 × 6.35   × 6.35 mm
152.4 × 6.35, 12.7, 25.4, 50.8. 76.2 × 6.35, 9.5 mm
152.4 × 101.6 × 9.5   mm
203.2 × *101.6 × 6.35, 9.5 mm*
215.9 × 107.95 × 6.35   mm
217.5 × 107.95 × 6.35, 9.5 mm

Hexagons

50.8, 57.15, 76.2, 101.6 measured from side to side × 9.5 mm thick.

Fittings

Fittings are tiles which provide curved junctions at internal and external right angles and a finish to exposed edges of tiled areas. They include *round edge, cushion edge* and *attached angle* tiles, *beads* and *cappings.*

Round edge tiles are flat tiles with one edge, or two opposite or adjacent edges rounded, the latter being termed an *external angle tile.*

Cushion edge tiles have a very slight radius at the glazed edges, and must not be confused with round edge tiles.

Attached angle (or *combination*) *tiles* are flat tiles with a short return on one or two edges. They are glazed outside for external angles and inside for coves.

External angle (or *quadrant*) *beads and internal angle* (*or cove*) *beads* are made with maximum overall widths of 31.75 and 50.8 mm.

Cappings are 50.8 and 76.2 mm wide with one or two attached external angles to the long edges.

Angle beads, attached angles and cappings are made with external radii of 22 and 35 mm. Coves and attached angles are made with internal radii of 12.7 and 25.4 mm.

Accessories

Soap dishes, tumbler and tooth brush holders, coat hooks, toilet paper holders and other accessories are made to suit standard tile sizes.

EXTERNAL AND HEAVY-DUTY CERAMIC TILES

Externally in this country frost resistant tiles are essential. These may be internal tiles the surfaces of which have been treated with a water repellent or the pores of which are filled with wax. Alternatively, highly vitrified tiles (fired at about 1250°C), usually extruded and necessarily thicker than internal tiles, can be used. Some of the latter type are unglazed.

Heavy-duty tiles (not all of which are frost resistant), are often used internally for their decorative appearance and/or for hard wear. Applications include floorings, swimming pools and industrial uses such as vessel linings, eg stock chests in paper mills.

Available sizes include most of those given for internal wall tiles and in addition:

73 × 73	
98 × 98	
149 × 73	× 10 mm
152 × 152	
102 × 102	
152 × 51 and 76	
241 × 114	× 13 mm
250 × 60	
152 × 152	
196 × 96	
200 × 48	
203 × 102*	× 16 mm
242 × 51 and 114	
250 × 51	
254 × 63 and 127	
220 × 40	
228 × 73, 79, and 152	× 20 mm
242 × 57	
203 × 203	
228 × 228	× 25 mm
305 × 203 and 228	

*This modular size includes one joint. Some tiles of this size are extruded in pairs back to back and must be separated before use.

Larger sizes up to 610 × 304 × 32 mm are usually called *Ceramic wall facing tiles.*

Blocks can be purpose-made in glazed faience or unglazed terra-cotta – see *MBS: Materials,* chapter 5.

Fittings such as angle returns are made to suit some external tiles.

FIXING TILES

The relevant Codes of Practice are: CP 212:Part 2: 1978 *External ceramic wall tiling and mosaics* and BS5385:Part 1:1976 *Code of Practice for internal ceramic wall tiling and mosaics in normal conditions.*

Expert advice is available from the *British Ceramic Tile Council*, Federation House, Stoke-on-Trent, Staffordshire.

Almost all surfaces can be satisfactorily tiled but the method of fixing must be appropriate to the properties of the tiles and background, and to the climatic exposure and other service conditions. Bedding materials and joints have a very important bearing on success. Each of these factors is considered in turn:

Properties of tiles

Ceramic tiles are rigid and thermal movement can normally be ignored. New tiles, however, like bricks (see *MBS: Materials*, chapter 6), absorb moisture and expand when they are removed from the kiln, although this movement is likely to be partially complete when tiles are fixed. Reversible moisture movement is negligible.

Properties of backgrounds

Some backgrounds are too weak, in themselves or in their adhesion to a wall, to support tiling. Tiles, as distinct from slabs, are fixed by adhesion and movement of backgrounds is the most common cause of loss of bond and cracking of tiles. Such movements arise from structural deformations, including creep, and from changes in temperature and moisture content. Fixing should not be undertaken on certain calcium-silicate bricks, on dense concrete and in particular on lightweight aggregate and aerated concretes, until they have thoroughly dried and shrunk. Serious reversible movements may occur in fibreboards, chipboards and plywood. To avoid tiles being cracked by disparate movements of adjacent backgrounds, metal lathing or wire netting is sometimes fixed across the junction, but a movement joint in the tiling is recommended. Other properties of backgrounds which affect adhesion are mechanical key, porosity, suction and chemical characteristics. Soluble salts may be harmful, particularly sulphates if the background is constantly wet.

On some true backgrounds tiles can be fixed directly with a thin-bed adhesive. On backgrounds which are not plumb and level, however, and on expanded metal a *floated* or *rendering coat* of cement and sand (rather than plaster) should be provided.

Floated coat

Backgrounds must provide an effective key. Smooth surfaces must either be hacked to a depth of 3 mm over at least half the area, or a *bonding agent* may be used as advised by the manufacturers. Surfaces must be wetted to adjust suction before applying the floated coat.

The floated coats must be firmly applied but not overworked. They must be sufficiently strong, but not stronger than the background or the undercoat on which they are applied. The high drying shrinkage of unduly rich cement mixes may cause failure. Where appropriate, sulphate resisting Portland cement should be used.

It a greater thickness than 13 mm is needed to provide a level surface it should be built up in coats each not more than 10 mm thick, the undercoat being allowed to dry out and shrink before the following coat, which should not be stronger than the undercoat, is applied. Additions such as lime, and air entraining agents should only be used under strict control.

CP 212 Part 1:1963 and Part 2:1966 recommend mixes for floated coats on various backgrounds as shown in table 26.

Background		Floated coat§ **
Glazed bricks and tiles Sheets, boards and compressed straw slabs‡ Plasterwork (dry, strong and adherent)‡		None
Dense, strong and smooth	High density clay brickwork and blocks*† Dense concrete (pre-cast or in-situ)* Natural stone*†	1 Portland cement : 3 sand[1] to
Moderately strong and porous	Clay and concrete bricks – raked joints Hard sand lime bricks – raked joints† Medium density concrete – hacked	1 Portland cement : 4 sand[2]
Metal lathing No-fines concrete – dense or lightweight aggregate		
Moderately weak and porous	Lightweight aggregate concrete Aerated concrete Soft sandlime bricks – raked joints	1 Portland cement : 4 sand[1] to
Metal lathing on wood wool‡ or compressed straw slabs‡		1 Portland cement : 5 sand[2]

* May require hacking
† May require metal lathing or wire netting
‡ Not recommended externally
§ Alternatively, masonry cement and sand or air-entrained cement and sand mixes of equivalent strengths, can be used as recommended by manufacturers.
** Floated coat mixes must also suit the method of fixing to be adopted.

[1] and [2] To improve workability fat lime is sometimes added to cement : sand mixes as follows:
  [1] up to ¼ part; [2] up to ½ part. Thorough mixing is, however, essential.

Table 26   Floated coats for tiling on various backgrounds – mixes by volume

Methods of fixing

Tiles can be fixed in four ways depending upon the flatness and other characteristics of backgrounds. The advice of manufacturers of proprietary products should always be followed, particularly as to the time which should elapse between applying a float coat and fixing tiles. After fixing, external tiling should be protected from frost and rain.

1 The sand-cement (traditional) method

1 Portland cement:3 to 4 sand (by volume) is usually suitable on Portland cement-based floated coats which have been scratched to provide a key (see table 26). Mixes stronger than 1:3 should not be used and although plasticizers, waterproofers, fungicides and other admixtures are sometimes useful it is most important to ascertain that they will not adversely affect adhesion. Tiles should preferably not be fixed until the floated coat is at least two weeks old and thoroughly dry. Immediately before tiling it must be wetted sufficiently to prevent loss of water from the bedding material. The more porous tiles should be soaked in clean water for at least half an hour, drained and stacked before use in the manner described in CP 212. Each tile should be 'buttered' with mortar over the whole of the back. Solid bedding is particularly important where mechanical damage is likely or where entrapped water might freeze. After tapping tiles firmly into position the bed thickness should not be less than 6.5 mm for tiles up to 152 x 152 mm and up to 9.5 mm for larger tiles. The surface should be cleaned off after 1 to 2 hours.

2 The cement-based mortar (thin-bed) method

CP 212:Part 1:163:Appendix B gives performance standards for these adhesives. They are satisfactory for fixing tiles which are not deeply keyed on many backgrounds which are true and plumb to within ± 1.6 mm in any distance of 3 m. Cement-based thin-bed adhesives are suitable both internally and externally, but not on wood-wool slabs, plasterwork, compressed straw slabs, plasterboards, glazed bricks or tiles.

Cement-based mortar can either be applied to walls with a notched trowel as a thin screed, or be 'buttered' over the backs of tiles so its thickness does not exceed 3 mm. Tiles must be dry when they are fixed.

3 The mastic adhesive (thin-bed) method

These proprietary mastics permit a bed thickness of about 2 mm. Some are flexible, and bond dry tiles even to surfaces such as chipboards, plaster work and glazed tiles. Some are suitable for service in hot or damp conditions. In all cases they should comply with CP 212:1963:Appendix A *Performance requirements for mastic adhesives (organic)* and be used in strict accordance with the manufacturers' instructions. Grouting or pointing should not be done for twenty-four hours after fixing, and preferably longer where tiles are fixed on low porosity backgrounds.

4 The thick-bed adhesive method

Adhesives are available which can accommodate surface irregularities up to about 13 mm in the length of a wall.

Joints

Joints must allow a degree of micro-movement. The jointing material must, therefore, not be too strong and the joint must not be too narrow. Crushable spacer lugs are provided on most tiles and these assure joints of sufficient and uniform width.

For small tiles on a stable background a minimum joint of 2 mm is recommended but wider joints are necessary for larger tiles and less stable backgrounds, eg 10 mm is recommended for some external tiles. Additionally, movement joints at least 6 mm wide should be provided in the bedding and tiling. Inside buildings they should occur at internal angles and at distances not exceeding 4.5 m vertically and horizontally. Externally, they should occur at storey heights, preferably where changes in structural materials take place, and vertically at about 3 m intervals. Movement joints in the structure must of course be carried through the floated coat, bedding and tiling.

Joints must be grouted or pointed, preferably with proprietary products, to prevent ingress of dirt, moisture and corrosive substances. The mix should be crushable; neat cement should never be used. For joints up to 5 mm wide the mix is brushed on as a grout, worked into the joints with a squeegee and 'pencilled in'. Wider joints are filled with a pointing tool. In both cases surplus material is removed as the work proceeds and when the mix is hard the tiling should be polished with a dry cloth. Movement joints should be filled with a suitable elasto-meric mastic, see *MBS: Materials,* chapter 16.

Mosaics

Mosaic tesserae, typically 19 X 19 X 5 mm, of glazed or unglazed ceramics, glass and marble are usually supplied glued face down on paper which is later removed, or with nylon strips, nylon net or similar material glued to their backs which will be embedded in the bedding mortar.

Floated coats should be provided as for tiles, to which a bedding mortar of 1 Portland cement:3 to 4 clean sharp sand (by volume) is applied not more than 10 mm thick. Up to ½ volume of hydrated lime can be added to the richer cement mix provided it is thoroughly mixed in. The backs of paper faced mosaic should be pre-grouted to fill the joints between the tesserae, and differences in level of the backs of marble mosaic should be made out with 1 cement:2 fine silver sand. The mosaic is then beaten into the bedding without delay. Nylon-backed and similar mosaics are grouted after fixing is completed.

Alternatively, mosaics can be fixed to floated backgrounds with cement-based *thin-bed* mortar not more than 3 mm thick or to backgrounds such as plaster with a mastic adhesive. *Thick-bed* adhesives are sometimes used.

After removing any paper facing and glue, and rubbing a grout over the mosaic it should be cleaned down.

Movement joints should be provided as for tiling.

5 Integral finishes on concrete

Structurally sound concrete[1] is essential, but many other criteria must be satisfied in order to achieve concrete surfaces which are aesthetically satisfactory. References include: *Recommendations for the production of high quality concrete surfaces*, Cement and Concrete Association Limited and *Guide to Exposed Concrete Finishes*, M. Gage, The Architectural Press Limited.

Colour can be provided by cements and aggregates, and some of the latter sparkle. Formwork imparts shapes and textures which can be modified mechanically and to a small degree chemically. Nevertheless, unless special precautions are taken, concrete may be patchy in colour and texture and defects such as the following may occur:

Efflorescence (or *lime bloom*) — is a persistent chalk film which may form rapidly on surfaces where lime liberated by cement and carried through concrete as it dries is carbonated by carbon dioxide from the air.

Crazing — is a pattern of fine, shallow cracks which often divide very smooth surfaces into areas about 5 to 25 mm across. It is associated with carbonation of 'wet' mixes which have not been adequately cured.

Honeycombing results from undersanded mixes, segregation if concrete is allowed to flow in the formwork, inadequate compaction or leakage of mortar from formwork.

Blow holes Small blow holes in surfaces are almost unavoidable but their number and size can be reduced by the use of absorptive linings (the use of vacuum forms prevents them).

Surfaces of uniform colour and texture are the most difficult to obtain, crazing and other defects are more apparent and runnels of water show as dirt stains in polluted atmospheres and of algae in clean air.

In so far as visual requirements affect the type of cement, type, size and grading of aggregate and the

[1] See *MBS: Materials*, chapter 8.

depth of cover required on reinforcement, the structural engineer must be consulted at an early stage, and special care must be taken to ensure:

(i) *Uniformity of batching and mixing* The colours of cements and aggregates vary and they should be obtained in large batches from the same sources. Variations in grading of aggregate, and water migration between parts having different mix proportions cause variations in colour. Because cement and sand adhere to the mixer drum and blades, the first batch of concrete should not be used for work which is to be exposed to view.

(ii) *Low water/cement ratio*—crazing is more likely to show where a high water/cement ratio both facilitates the migration of lime and reduces the density and strength of concrete. Absorbent formwork is not recommended as a means of reducing the water/cement ratio of surfaces — see (vii).

(iii) *Avoidance of segregation during handling, placing and compaction.* Placing should be in shallow layers, commence as soon as possible and proceed continuously until in-situ concrete has been placed between construction joints, or moulds for precast work have been filled.

(iv) *Complete compaction* especially at vertical surfaces, where a slicing tool may be usefully employed to avoid honeycombing.

(v) *Correct positioning and design of construction joints in in-situ work* because they are always apparent, even after a surface has been bush hammered.

(vi) *Freedom from rust stains* Ends of binding wires should be turned inwards, and wire, nails and other ferrous debris must be removed from the formwork before concrete is placed.

(vii) *Limited and uniform suction of formwork surfaces* Absorbent formwork is generally more likely to ·cause variations in the colour of finished concrete surfaces than non-absorbent formwork (although it is less likely to cause *blow holes*). Uniform suction can be obtained by applying a thin but complete coat of a *parting agent* to formwork, which can be done more evenly by spraying rather than by brushing. Straight oil often gives good results, particularly on impermeable formwork, but water in oil (not oil in water), or chemical release agents have the advantage of remaining effective for a number of uses. Good results have also been obtained by soaking formwork before concrete is placed in it and keeping it wet until the concrete has hardened.

(viii) *Leak-proof joints to formwork* Migration of water and entry of air through joints causes variations in colour and honeycombing. Butt joints, and even tongued and grooved joints, in timber should be sealed with foamed plastics strips. Joints in formwork constructed of materials which have less movement, such as plywood, plastics and steel, should be sealed with masking tape.

(ix) *Rigid formwork* Lack of rigidity causes distortion, and air which enters open joints discolours concrete.

We now consider integral surface finishes, first on in-situ concrete and then on precast concrete.

INTEGRAL FINISHES ON IN-SITU CONCRETE

1 Effects obtained from formwork or liners

Shapes, including complex shapes in high relief, can be formed by timber, steel or glass-fibre reinforced plastics (GRP). Almost any texture can be obtained, either from the formwork itself or from liners such as: hardboard, plywood, vacuum-formed plastics sheets, moulded rubber sheets, rigid cellular plastics or foamed polystyrene which is easily worked and removed when it has served its purposes; it can be used once only. Surface retarders can be applied to formwork to delay the setting of cement — see 3(v). The tendency of glass-like surfaces to craze can be reduced by adding a water repellent to concrete mixes. Where a smooth finish is required formwork should be struck as soon as possible so that minor projections can be removed by rubbing down the whole surface with a planed end-grain wood block, or a rubber-faced float lubricated with water. Surface voids can then be stopped with fine mortar.

Board-marked surfaces In recent years sawn timber boards — sometimes sand-blasted to em-

phasize the grain — have been used as formwork. For a satisfactory impression on the concrete, absorbency should be reasonably uniform and edges and ends should be jointed with tongues. By chamfering the edges of the baords projecting fins can be formed on the concrete.

The aggregate transfer method conceals any variations there may be in the colour of the structural concrete. Selected aggregate is stuck to the rough side of peg-board type hardboard formwork liners which have been coated with water soluble cellulose-bound mortar. After the concrete has been placed and hardened, the peg-board is stripped, leaving the aggregate adhering to the concrete. The surface is then scrubbed to remove adhesive and sand.

2 Effects obtained in placing concrete

(i) *Hand-placed aggregate* Aggregate can be positioned by hand, or distributed over and then pressed into, horizontal slabs of 'green' concrete.

(ii) *'Sand-bed' method* On the site, this method is suitable only for soffits. Larger aggregate is embedded by hand in a layer of dry sand which has been spread evenly on the formwork. The backs of the stones are covered with 1 cement:3 sand (parts by volume), followed by ordinary concrete. When the formwork is removed the sand falls away leaving the aggregate exposed in one plane on the surface. Vibration would displace stones and cause mortar to run through to the face.

(iii) *'Naturbetong'* This system, developed in Norway, exposes coarse aggregate so that it lies in one plane. Either dry coarse aggregate, which excludes materials smaller than 15 mm, is placed in the formwork and mortar is injected into it, or alternatively the aggregate is vibrated into mortar which has been placed in the formwork. The first method is generally more suitable for slender vertical elements and the second method for horizontal elements. After 12 to 20 hours the cement and fine aggregate is removed from the face by sand blasting.

3 Effects obtained after placing but before concrete has hardened

(i) *Floated and trowelled surfaces* The hand operations for finishing horizontal surfaces are dealt with under *Floorings*, chapter 1.

(ii) *Rotary surfacers* can be used to give a smooth and reasonably level finish to flooring and other large horizontal surfaces.

(iii) *Screedboard tamped and rolled surfaces* Upper surfaces of slabs can be patterned in relief by dropping a screed board, or for a bolder texture a scaffold pole, on them at regular spacings. Notched screed boards can be drawn over a surface, or rollers or tampers with patterned surfaces can be used.

(iv) *Spraying* Where new concrete surfaces are not enclosed by formwork, cement and fine material can be removed with a water spray.

(v) *Brushing* 16 to 18 hours after casting ordinary Portland cement concrete and curing it at an air temperature of about 15°C, aggregate can be exposed by brushing vigorously while hosing with clean water. The damp surface is then brushed with a 10 per cent solution of hydrochloric acid and finally hosed with water. Where it will not be possible to obtain access to surfaces at such an early stage the setting of cement near surfaces can be safely delayed by spreading a *retarder* uniformly on the contact surfaces of formwork at the rate of coverage recommended by the manufacturer. If this is done, immediately after carefully removing the formwork, the aggregate can be exposed by brushing, followed by hosing down, and light brushing to remove remaining loose material.

(vi) *Scraping* Surfaces which are accessible soon after casting can be scraped, eg with an old saw blade.

4 Effects obtained on hardened concrete

(i) *Tooling* Hardened concrete surfaces can be worked with a point or other mason's tool. After at least three weeks the larger aggregate can be exposed by *bush hammering* which should be done uniformly and without chipping the aggregate. Tooled surfaces usually look best when they are either contained within smooth faced margins or carried round chamfered corners.

(ii) *Abrasive blasting* Interesting textures and modelling can be obtained by this method although like other mechanical treatments it emphasizes rather than conceals imperfections in concrete surfaces. It can be carried out at any time but more rapidly on green concrete. Precautions must, of course, be taken to avoid inhaling dust. Varying degrees of texture are given by sand, grit and shot. *Blast carving* of cellular concrete has been skilfully exploited by William Mitchell. Coarse aggregate which is harder than the matrix can be exposed to up to one-third of its mean size. It is worth noting that shot which lodges in cavities can cause stains.

(iii) *Grinding and polishing* Grinding is usually done 'wet' with a carborundum wheel, often to remove unintended projections, preferably 24 to 36 hours after striking formwork. Surface voids are stopped with fine mortar. Grinding and polishing after a further seven days or so, are costly and are usually confined to small areas. Terrazzo is always ground. See chapter 1.

INTEGRAL FINISHES ON PRE-CAST CONCRETE

The control which can be exercised over materials and processes, and the availability of techniques such as hydraulic pressing make for the production of superior products in the factory which can, and should, be thoroughly matured and thereby 'preshrunk' before use.

Most of the processes which have been described for finishes on in-situ concrete are applicable also to pre-cast concrete but techniques which are not practicable on the building site include the use of:

(i) *Special moulds*, eg stainless steel, vacuumformed thermoplastics, plastics-glass-fibre, and for 'pre-cast' stone, rubber bearing the imprint of natural stones.

(ii) *Special mixes* (a) *non-homogeneous* By casting special mixes as a facing on ordinary concrete, the use of relatively costly aggregates and cements may become economic.
(b) *Homogeneous 'Faircrete'* (John Laing Concrete Ltd) is a patented air-entrained concrete incorporating fibres with either dense or lightweight aggregate. It is extremely workable so that it gives a very faithful impression from formwork and can readily be formed while it remains plastic, into complex and deeply profiled shapes. However, slump is negligible and such shapes are accurately retained.

(iii) *Casting, either face up or face down – as convenient.*

(iv) *Acid etching*   The surface should be wetted thoroughly before applying dilute hydrochloric acid which after five minutes should be well hosed off to prevent yellow stains.

(v) *Splitting* Exposes irregular surfaces which are free from efflorescence, the cause of pronounced crazing. In a process developed at the BRE, tubes which are incorporated in concrete slabs are inflated while the mix is still green to split them into two units with a contrast between the appearance of smooth grooves and irregular projecting ridges.

(vi) *Mosaic*   Used as permanent shuttering, the tesserae are placed individually or mounted on paper in the base of the mould, the joints are grouted with 1 white or coloured cement:5 sand (parts by volume) and the normal backing concrete is placed.

Finishes may be required to protect surfaces from rain, sunlight, abrasion, chemical liquids and fumes, micro-organisms, fungi, insects and fire. They may be required for hygiene, to reflect or diffuse light, to provide colour and/or pattern, to define areas visually or to absorb sound.

This chapter deals with thin surface-finishes under the following headings:

Painting

Painting is the application to surfaces of pigmented liquids or semi-liquids, which subsequently harden. We are concerned here mainly with site-applied finishes.

Useful references are:
BRE Digest 21 *New types of paints*, HMSO
BS 2015:1965 *A glossary of paint terms,* BSI
CP 231:1966 *Painting of buildings*, BSI
Introduction to paint technology, The Oil and Colour Chemists' Association.
Painting from A to Z, J. Lawrence, The Sutherland Publishing Co. Ltd.

COSTS OF PAINTING

Surface finishes represent up to five per cent of the initial cost of a typical building, but the recurring costs of materials, plant, labour and inconvenience occasioned by their maintenance may represent as much as twenty-five per cent of the cost of a building during its life. It follows that more costly but more durable finishes, in particular many factory-applied finishes, are often cheaper in the long run.

Because the cost of labour, plant, etc, greatly exceeds the cost of paint, using cheap and inferior paint or skimping the preparation of surfaces is false economy, and generally for external work an extra coat is a good investment. It is also sound economy to reinstate the surface of a paint film before it has deteriorated to the extent that it becomes necessary to remove the whole film, to repair any rotted timber and corroded metal, and to prepare, prime and paint the background.

LIVES OF PAINT SYSTEMS

Inside buildings the life of a paint film is usually thought to have ended when it is faded, dirty, chipped or scratched. Externally, protection is usually the main need. Table 27 gives life expectations for various protective systems applied to vertical surfaces, but lives may be much shorter:

on horizontal and inclined surfaces,
in abnormally corrosive atmospheres,
where the wrong system is adopted,
where preparation is inadequate,
where application techniques, or conditions during application were poor.

NUMBER OF COATS

The minimum number of coats for ordinary work are given below. The durability of an external paint film is usually directly related to its thickness.

Surface	Externally	Internally
New	4*	3*
Old paint in good condition	2	1

* Including primer.

Externally this should be at least 0.125 mm. A normal coat of paint rarely exceeds 0.05 mm thick,[1]

[1] There is a temptation to apply paint in thick coats but they are more liable to form wrinkles. Also, in evaporating, solvents in paints tend to form pin-holes or to soften the outer layer. Paints which combine with oxygen from the atmosphere are therefore generally mechanically sounder where they are applied in thin coats.

and at least four coats are usually required. A greater number of coats is justified on surfaces which are difficult to reach, which are not vertical, face south, or are in severe exposures.

Internally, a greater number of coats may be needed to provided acceptable opacity and a superior finish.

THE PAINT SYSTEM

Ordinary paint systems comprise: a primer, undercoat(s) and finishing coat(s), each of which performs a specific function, although in finishes such as emulsion paint two or more functions are performed by one material. All coats must be compatible with each other and with the background.

Primer

The primer must adhere to surfaces, including those which are shiny, chemically aggressive and those which move or are very hot. Suitable primers are used to seal porous surfaces which would cause loss of gloss in the finish, and to equalize suction on surfaces such as old plaster which has been repaired and would lead to a very uneven sheen or gloss. Various primers minimize *bleeding*, eg of bitumen, staining by resin or sapstained timber and attack by alkalis in the background.

On metals, etching and corrosion-inhibiting primers are important.

Undercoats

The first undercoat should follow as soon as the primer is hard.

Type of coating (normal number of coats)	Background	Average life – years
Long-oil alkyd-based paint finishing systems with suitable primers and undercoats	timber ferrous metals	3 – 5 3 – 7
	aluminium concrete masonry renderings	3 – 8
Cement paint	brickwork, concrete, renderings	5
Special protective paints, eg micaceous, iron oxide, aluminium, coal-tar epoxy	steel – with thorough surface preparation	5 – 10
Thick PVC coatings Thin PVF films	galvanized sheet wood, asbestos cement, metals etc.	10 – 20
Thick coatings containing mineral aggregate	concrete renderings masonry	
Vitreous enamel	steel, cast iron, aluminium	at least 20

Table 27 Lives of protective systems on vertical surfaces

The shorter lives in the ranges given can be expected facing south and in severely polluted or marine atmospheres. Lives are even shorter on sloping surfaces and where materials and workmanship are poor. Longer lives of certain paints can be obtained by stoving in factory conditions.

Undercoats must provide obliteration, and adhere well to the primer and to each other. They should fill minute surface depressions and provide a good base so that the finishing coat will not 'sink' and lose its gloss. With paints containing synthetic ingredients it is no longer necessary to rub down newly applied coats to obtain a key, but 'flatting' of undercoats — preferably 'wet' — is necessary to obtain a first-class finish.

In applying coloured paint each succeeding coat should be readily distinguished, although the colour of the last undercoat should be near to, but lighter than the finishing coat, the latter often being less opaque than the undercoats.

Finishing coat

The finishing coat forms the final protection against the weather, chemical and mechanical damage, and finally determines texture and colour.

In diminishing order of smoothness surfaces can be described as: *full gloss; semi-gloss; eggshell* (*lustre, satin, velvet* or *suede*) — these have 'sheen'; *flat* or *matt*.

Gloss reflects light directly, so that its effect on surfaces illuminated with a point source of light is to accentuate the slightest irregularities.

Gloss and eggshell paints do not collect grime as readily as matt and textured paints, and give good protection. Resistance to moisture is good and some of them are suitable externally. Flat paints are usually permeable and partly 'hide' condensation.

Colour

British Standard Specifications for paints used in building employ the terminology of the *Munsell system*, ie *hue, value* and *chroma* (*HV/C*) defined in BS 4727:Part 4 *Terms particular to lighting and colour*, as follows:

Hue — commonly referred to as 'colour', eg red, yellow, blue green, etc.

Value (*reflectance value* or *lightness*) is a measure of the light reflected, irrespective of hue and chroma.

Chroma (*saturation* or *intensity*) is the intensity of a particular hue compared with a neutral grey of similar lightness.

A very wide range of paints of varying hues, values and chroma, including the 86 colours, black and white of BS 4800:1972 *Paint colours for building purposes*, is held in stock by paint manufacturers, and special paints can be made to order.

BS 5378:1976 *Specification for safety colours and safety signs.* (A system for prevention of accidents and health hazards and for meeting certain emergencies.)

It is important to note that all colours 'fade' when exposed to short wave radiation and that many paints which are suitable for use inside buildings would not achieve a satisfactory *Paint Research Station 'colour premanency rating'* if they were used externally.

Because the finishing type of many modern paints, such as modified alkyds, is more durable than the undercoat type, externally two finish coats are sometimes applied *gloss on gloss*, one of them taking the place of the last (or only) undercoat. Internally, however, since the finish type paint tends to flow away from high spots the undercoat is required to give obliteration on rough surfaces.

COMPOSITION OF PAINTS

All paints contain a *binder* (or *medium*) which hardens. Other ingredients found in various paints include:

pigments, stainers, extenders, driers, catalysts (or *hardeners*), *thinners* or *solvents* and *gelling agents.* Some water-thinned paints (see page 104) include *emulsifiers.*

The preparation, proportioning and mixing of paint ingredients was formerly done by the craftsman, but today most paint is provided ready for a stated use. Paints of the same brand and type can be intermixed to vary their colour and a suitable thinner may be added if it is required but otherwise no addition should be made to the factory product, and different brands should not be intermixed.

Binders (*media* or *vehicles*)

The binder must bind the other ingredients together, adhere to and sometimes penetrate or seal the surface. When the paint has been applied, the medium must harden at a rate suited to the method of application, whether by brush, roller, spray or by dipping.

Various hardening mechanisms of paints are set

Binder	Durability	Cost	Hardening mechanism
Cements	High	Low	Chemical moisture reaction
Glue and casein-bound non-washable distemper	Low	Low	Evaporation of water and gelling
Polymer emulsions	Medium/high	Medium	Evaporation of water and coalescence
Drying oils eg linseed, tung and soya – in washable distempers	Low	Low/medium	Evaporation of water and some oxidation
– in paints – straight oil and oleo-resinous	Low/medium	Low/medium	Evaporation of thinner, absorption of oxygen from air and polymerization
– oil modified resins, eg air-drying alkyds	Medium/high	Medium/high	
Natural resins uncombined with oils, eg shellac	Low	Medium	Evaporation of thinner and deposition of resin
Thermoplastics in solution, eg celluloses, vinyls, acrylics	Medium/high	Medium	Evaporation of solvents
Bitumen	Medium/high	Low/medium	
Chlorinated rubber	Medium/high	Medium	
Two-pack epoxides and polyurethanes Coal-tar epoxides	Medium/high	High	Evaporation of solvents and complex chemical change
Thermosetting polymers – some urea and melamine formaldehydes	Medium/high	Medium	Evaporation of any solvent present, crosslinking and oxidization
– alkyds	Medium	Medium	
– polyesters	High	High	Polymerization by catalyst
Plastisols[1]	High	High	Coalescence on heating
Organosols[1]	High	Medium	

[1] See plastics coatings, page 120

Table 28   Types of binders and their hardening mechanisms

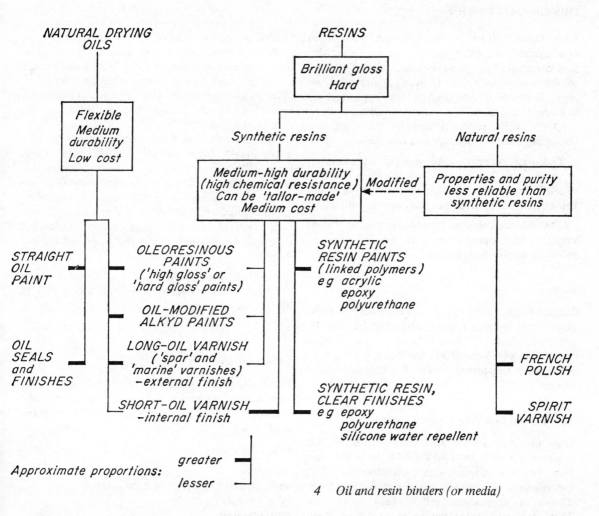

NATURAL DRYING OILS

Flexible
Medium durability
Low cost

RESINS

Brilliant gloss
Hard

Synthetic resins

Medium-high durability
(high chemical resistance)
Can be 'tailor-made'
Medium cost

Modified

Natural resins

Properties and purity
less reliable than
synthetic resins

STRAIGHT OIL PAINT

OLEORESINOUS PAINTS
('high gloss' or
'hard gloss' paints)

OIL-MODIFIED ALKYD PAINTS

OIL SEALS and FINISHES

LONG-OIL VARNISH
('spar' and
'marine' varnishes)
–external finish

SHORT-OIL VARNISH
–internal finish

SYNTHETIC RESIN PAINTS
(linked polymers)
e g acrylic
epoxy
polyurethane

SYNTHETIC RESIN, CLEAR FINISHES
e g epoxy
polyurethane
silicone water repellent

FRENCH POLISH

SPIRIT VARNISH

Approximate proportions: greater

lesser

4   Oil and resin binders (or media)

out in table 28. Common binders are glue, casein, natural drying-oils – now usually *modified*, natural or synthetic thermoplastic and thermosetting resins, bitumen and cement. The distinction between paints and plastics coatings is not clearly defined; most paints are now based on synthetic polymers, but some 'plastics coatings' are deposited from solution in the same way as cellulose paints.

Driers and catalysts

Paints which contain drying oils dry in two stages, first by evaporation of thinners and solvents, then by oxidization and polymerization of the oil. Driers catalyse and speed up the process of early drying.

Catalysts – or *hardeners* – either as a separate component, or incorporated in *single part* (or *single pack*) paints, induce an irreversible chemical change leading to hardening of non-oxidizing systems.

Pigments

Pigments are fine powders or flakes derived from organic and inorganic sources which impart colour to paints, together with opacity, 'body' and sometimes chemical resistance, rust inhibition and increased durability.

White pigments – *Titanium dioxide* the most common white pigment has excellent opacity and is available in *chalking* and *non-chalking* forms.

White lead (basic lead carbonate) combines well with oil and is easy to apply. The film is very elastic and highly resistant to penetration of moisture and weathers by *chalking*, providing a good surface for

101

redecoration. However, sulphur gases in urban atmospheres turn white lead to black sulphide. Also lead compounds are poisonous and paint containing soluble lead must not be sprayed, or rubbed down 'dry'. It should not be used indoors — particularly in kitchens and nurseries — and never on toys!

Other white pigments include: *zinc sulphide* (lithopone), *antimony oxide* and *zinc oxide.*

Coloured pigments   All colours are available, although they are not all equally light-fast. For example iron oxides provide reds and browns and zinc and lead chromates give the brighter yellows.

Stainers   are coloured pigments ground in a paint vehicle which can be added to already prepared paints to modify their colour.

Extenders

Extenders are finely ground minerals such as china clay, mica, whiting (chalk), silica and barium sulphate (barytes). They have little or no opacity when they are mixed with oil but give body, help to keep pigments in suspension, harden the film and reduce its cost.

Solvents and thinners

Generally, solvents are added in manufacture and thinners are sometimes added later to render oils, resin and wax miscible with each other, to adjust the viscosity of paint, to suit the method and conditions of application, and to help penetration. They evaporate during the drying of the paint and should leave no deleterious residue. Excessive thinning reduces gloss and density of the paint film.

Oil and oleo-resinous paints were traditionally thinned with turpentine, but now *white spirit* (*turpentine substitute*) (BS 245:1956 amended to 1963) is used. Bitumen is thinned with naphtha. Thinners such as those used in cellulose lacquers have low flash points and require special care in use. Cement paint, emulsion paint, washable and non-washable distempers are thinned with water and this non-combustible and cheap thinner is being used increasingly for factory-applied primers.

Other constituents

Flatting agents are sometimes added to reduce the gloss of the dried film.

Gelling agents   Gelled or thixotropic paints include ingredients which give 'false body' to gloss, semi-gloss and emulsion paints. They do not settle in the can and do not require stirring before use. More paint can be carried by the roller or brush and larger brushes can be used because they drip less than 'liquid' paints.

The movement of a roller or of the bristles of a brush breaks down the gel and the paint flows freely, although in so doing it tends to follow surface irregularities. The paint resumes its gelled condition after application so that heavier coats can be applied which provide better obliteration, although thick coats of ordinary paints dry and harden less thoroughly throughout their thickness and are less durable.

Emulsifiers are included in washable distempers (oil-bound water paints), emulsion paints and in bituminous emulsions.

TYPES OF PAINTS

The main types of paints are now described. (It should be noted at this point that some terms such as *enamel, lacquer, synthetic* and *plastics* are often used loosely.)

Paints for general uses:

straight oil
oleo-resinous (*high-gloss* or *hard-gloss*)
oil-modified alkyd
synthetic resin
    acrylic resin
    polyurethane
    epoxy (epoxide) resin
cellulose nitrate
chlorinated rubber
bituminous

water-thinned paints
    limewash
    non-washable distemper
    washable distemper
    emulsion paints
    cement paints
    synthetic resin/aggregate finishes

Paints with special properties: pages 105 and 106
    special properties in application
    special properties in service

Paints for general uses

Straight oil paints

These paints are uncommon today except as primers. BSs 2528–2532:1954 described *Ready-mixed oil-based undercoating and finishing paints (exterior quality)*. Based on natural drying oils, usually thinned with white spirit, straight oil paints have relatively low flow properties, and gloss. The oil, which dries by the absorption of oxygen causing polymerization, is liable to *saponification* by alkalis of which Portland cement is a common source in building.

Drying oils include the following:

Linseed oil occurs in various forms:

Raw linseed oil (BS 243:1969), produced by crushing flax seed pods, is yellow in colour. It is available as:

Boiled linseed oil (BS 242:1969), produced by heating raw oil in air for several days and adding driers, is much darker in colour, quicker drying and gives a film which is more resistant to moisture, harder and glossier than that provided by raw oil.

Pale boiled oil (BS 242:1969) bleached with Fuller's earth is suitable for delicate tints.

Stand oil produced by prolonged heating of a refined oil to a high viscosity is pale and flows well, giving a full gloss.

Blown oil is produced by blowing air through a heated oil so that it thickens, becomes much darker and dries faster.

Other natural drying oils – For light tints linseed oil has been largely superseded by tobacco oil, soya bean oil, dehydrated castor oil and others, which all show less yellowing on ageing.

Oleo-resinous paints (high-gloss or hard-gloss paints)

Oleo-resinous paints (cometimes misleadingly referred to as 'synthetic paints'), comprising drying oils reinforced with natural or synthetic resins, show a marked improvement in gloss, durability and other properties over straight oil paints, but like them oleo-resinous paints have been largely supplanted by oil-modified alkyd paints.

Oil-modified alkyd paints

These paints which are flexible and very durable are the most common type of high gloss paints. The resin never exists as a separate entity, but is 'built-in' by reacting a complex acid with a complex alcohol in the presence of a drying oil.

Synthetic resin paints

This description can be applied to paints which contain substantial proportions of synthetic resins, such as acrylics, polyurethane and epoxides.

Acrylic resin paints   Polymethyl methacrylate which is water-white and holds colour well is the basis of some rapid drying and extremely durable factory finishes and emulsion paints.

Polyurethane paints   Air-drying, single-part paints are used like alkyd gloss paints but have better resistance to water, alkalis and wear. Chemically-curing two-part polyurethane paints are hard, tough, have good resistance to chemicals, and may have better resistance to weather than epoxy paints. However, they do not adhere well to all surfaces and intercoat adhesion may be poor.

Epoxy (epoxide) resin paints

Single-pack epoxy ester paints are tougher and have better resistance to water, alkalis and possibly to abrasion than oil-modified alkyds. In this respect they are similar to the one-pack polyurethane paints.

Two-pack epoxy paints have excellent resistance to abrasion, severe alkaline attack, oils, fatty acids and solvents. Resistance to immersion in water and to continuous condensation is intrinsically poor although it can be improved by heat curing. Two-pack epoxides have great cohesive strength and for that reason must not be applied on plaster. Adhesion to concrete is excellent but steel must be grit blasted and an etching primer may be essential on other metals. They 'chalk' fairly rapidly externally, but further breakdown is slow.

After the catalyst is mixed into the paint the *pot life* is 24 hours or less. At $18°C$ the paint should be hard in six hours and have full chemical resistance in seven days but below $10°C$ the rate of cure is very slow or may cease completely.

Suitable uses include: floors, laboratory furniture and machinery.

Synthetic resin/aggregate finishes.

See 6, page 105.

Cellulose nitrate paints (or 'lacquers')

These paints, based on cellulose nitrate compounds, contain suitable solvents, alkyd resins as plasticizers for flexibility and toughness, and resins for hardness and body. They dry by evaporation of the solvent without any chemical change. Previously applied cellulose nitrate (and also oil-based) paints, would be lifted by brush-applied cellulose nitrate, and for this reason and because it dries very quickly, it is best applied by spraying.

Nitro-cellulose finishes contain less solids than oil or oleo-resinous paints so that more coats are required, but by applying a number of translucent coats graduated colour effects can be obtained.

The paint presents a serious fire risk in storage and during application and the hardened surface has *rapid spread of flame*. It is used for some factory finished components but on the building site its use is mainly confined to 'metallic finishes' on metal balustrades and shop front sections.

Chlorinated rubber paints

These finishes dry by solvent evaporation requiring specially formulated primers and undercoats to resist softening by the solvents in the following coat. The paints offer considerable resistance to a wide range of acids and alkalis, and to sulphur dioxide, white spirit and sea water, and are used in chemical factories, laboratories, gas works, dairies, swimming pools and in marine conditions. They resist mould growth, and resistance to moisture penetration is high, but they are not flexible and resistance to heat is poor. The range of colours is restricted by the requirement for the maximum chemical resistance. Chlorinated rubber paints can be applied by brush, roller or spray.

Bituminous paints

As the term is ordinarily understood, these paints are made from bitumen, asphaltum, pitch or resin, sometimes with heat-treated oil, and solvents. Bituminous paints are described by BS 3416:1961 – amended 1963, *Black bitumen coating solutions for cold application*, and BS 1070:1956 *Black paint (tar base)*. Bituminous products are black, or if pigmented, dark in colour, apart from those which include aluminium to reflect heat and reduce degradation by light. They are largely used for protecting steelwork from corrosion. Suitably formulated as thixotropic or heavy-duty paints, thicknesses up to 0.125 mm can be applied in one coat. They adhere well, are flexible and resist moisture and chemicals, but tend to disintegrate or crack in hot sunlight.

Bituminous paints contain strong solvents and should not, therefore, be applied over paints which contain oil other than red lead primers which are thoroughly hard. Conversely, oil paint is best not applied on bituminous paint – even if a sealer is used to stop the latter bleeding through, movement of bituminous paint is likely to lead to crazing. Special bituminous paints include BS 3416:1961 Type II, which must be free from toxic ingredients, for treating drinking water tanks.

Black Japan, made from a superior grade of bitumen cooked with oil and blended with copal varnish, provides a hard but elastic film which does not bleed, and is heat resisting.

Black varnish consisting of tar thinned with a solvent, often used for dipping cast iron rainwater goods at works, is very cheap but difficult to overpaint satisfactorily.

Water-thinned paints

Water-thinned paints are generally less durable than other paints but easier to apply; a 178 mm brush, a roller or spray can be used. In warm weather they may dry very quickly, in damp weather they may remain wet for many days and in cold weather they may freeze. They are generally permeable to moisture and can be applied to surfaces which are not perfectly dry allowing them to dry out through the paint. The same formulation usually serves as primer, undercoat and finishing coat.

Paints which are thinned with water are:

1 *Limewash* The cheapest finish is slaked lime which has very little binding power and can often be brushed off with the hand. Traditionally, tallow added during slaking gave limewash a degree of durability for external use, although it 'chalked' rapidly with weathering.

2 *Non-washable distemper* (*ceiling* or *soft distemper*) which is whiting (chalk powder) mixed with size (dilute animal glue – BS 3357:1961) in hot water is described in BS 1053:1966 *Waterpaint and distemper for interior use*. It is the cheapest 'domestic' finish but when dry is easily rubbed off and is suitable only on ceilings. However, it gives a flatter matt surface than can be obtained in any

other way and size being soluble, the finish can be easily washed off.

A solution of size with a little whiting (*clearcole*), is applied to surfaces to reduce and equalize their suction before non-washable distemper is applied. (It should never be used below washable distemper or emulsion paints.)

3 *Washable distemper* — also known as *oil-bound water paint*, or just *water paint* — is covered by BS 1053:1966 *Type A*. Consisting of an emulsified drying oil or casein, with pigments and extenders it is provided ready-for-use, or as a paste to be mixed with water or with *petrifying liquid* (a diluted form of medium). The latter helps to seal porous surfaces and to increase the durability of external finishes.

Washable distemper has a matt finish. It is cheaper than most emulsion paints. Hardening takes place slowly as the oil oxidizes and polymerizes and surfaces should not be washed for at least a month, but the best modern products then withstand moderate scrubbing and weather fairly well outdoors.

4 *Emulsion paints* The description *emulsion paint* is applied in particular to paints which are bound with emulsions of vinyl, acrylic and polyurethane polymers. They harden quickly and provide *matt, sheen, lustre* or *gloss* surfaces. A few pigments are not light-fast externally but emulsion paints are tougher, more elastic, and although permeable they are more resistant to wear and weather than washable distemper, while being cheaper both to buy and apply than oi-based paints. Those incorporating vinyl caprone or vinyl versatate and those based wholly on acrylic polymers have the best resistance to alkalis.

Generally, emulsion paints can serve as primer (many adhere even to glossy backgrounds), undercoat(s) and finish coat. They are sometimes used as a primer and undercoats under oil-based paints, but it must be remembered that they are porous and an alkali-resistant primer/sealer may be required. Special primers may be needed on absorptive or powdery surfaces; in particular, on external masonry an oil-based sealer is essential.

5 *Cement paints* — consist of white Portland cement with or without pigments, water repellents, plasticizers and fillers. The need for alkali resistant pigments limits the colour range. A coarse texture and lack of 'flow' makes it difficult to avoid brush marks

so that cement paint is not generally acceptable internally.

It it is used soon after water has been added (paint which has thickened must not be thinned), it adheres well to reasonably porous brickwork, concrete and renderings even if they are damp, but not to timber, metals or gypsum plaster or other types of paint. Absorptive surfaces should be dampened and old surfaces should be treated with a fungicidal wash if required.

Work must not proceed in wet or frosty weather, in a drying wind or direct sunlight. In hot weather each coat should be damped with a fine spray 6 to 12 hours after it has been applied.

6 *Synthetic resin/aggregate finishes* Finishes of this type, although more costly than cement-based paints, are available in bright and light-fast colours, no water need be added, they are easy to apply and are more durable. Lives well in excess of ten years can be expected. Ingredients include water-emulsified synthetic resin binders, and aggregates such as a hard granite derivative and mica which contribute to durability. One product is reinforced with nylon fibres.

Suitable backgrounds are clean, firm and dry brickwork, renderings, concrete and asbestos cement, in all cases constructed to prevent the ingress of water behind the finish. The paint manufacturer's advice should be followed at all stages, including the removal and inhibiting of mould and algae growths, and in sealing chalky or friable backgrounds with a *stabilizing solution*. White or light coloured paints of this type may be applied to mastic asphalt or bituminous felt roofings to reflect solar heat.

The paints are normally water repellent, but not water or vapour proof, allowing a wall to 'breathe'. Where a rain-proof finish is required, as on steelwork or porous 'solid' walls, a bituminous basecoat is needed.

Application should not proceed in wet or frosty weather. Surface finishes range from matt applied by brush, spray or roller, to textured and stippled.

Paints with special properties

Manufacturers should be consulted in selecting paints for special purposes.

Paints with special properties in application

Low-odour paints It is rarely possible to do more than minimize the odour of fresh paints. Masking odours can be a source of contamination.

Quick-drying paints Some paints based on modified alkyd media, epoxy and polyurethane resins dry in 1 to 2 hours and those which dry by solvent evaporation such as chlorinated rubber and cellulose dry faster than oxidizing paints.

Paints for stoving These are usually alkyd/amino or epoxy based, intended for spray application and hardening at temperatures above 66°C in an oven or by infra-red radiation and are considerably harder than air-dried finishes. Urea and melamine form-aldehyde resins blended with alkyd resin produce a colourless stoving enamel which is extremely hard and resistant to alkalis and solvents and is often used on refrigerators.

Paints with special properties in service

Water and chemical resistant paints Paints which have superior resistance to chemical fumes and liquids include chlorinated rubber, bituminous, epoxy and polyurethane which have already been referred to. The two-part synthetic resin paints have greater resistance to chemicals than the one-part paints. Other chemical resistant paints include, *Neoprene* and *Hypalon*. Coal-tar-epoxy and poly-urethane-pitch paints combine the good water, heat and chemical resistance of their constituents. Vinyl paints with special primers to secure adhesion give thin films, but in a sufficient number of coats they are chemically resistant while being flexible and tough.

Fire-retardant paints are available as oil-bound and water-borne finishes. They retard ignition, and particularly, spread of flame over surfaces. Some are *intumescent* and swell when heated forming an insulating porous coating.

Advice as to the efficacy of individual products in a given situation should be obtained from the Fire Research Station, Boreham Wood, Hertford-shire, which issues certificates of classification according to BS 476:Part 7:1971.

Heat resistant paints Typical high grade modern paints can be safely applied to surfaces such as hot water radiators, but manufacturers should be con-sulted as to the suitability of white and pale coloured paints. White silicone paints are very resistant to yellowing at high temperatures and some formula-tions which combine silicone with phenolic, alkyd and epoxy resins, have excellent resistance to high temperatures. One type, pigmented with aluminium powder, withstands temperatures of 535°C in dry conditions and up to 400°C externally. The stoving necessary to polymerize the paint may conveniently be done when objects such as boilers and chimneys are in service.

Fungus-resisting paints Wherever possible the damp conditions which give rise to the growth of moulds should be avoided, but paints which contain fungicides may be required in bakeries, breweries and textile mills. Fungicides which are toxic to humans must not be used where contamination of food or licking by children and animals might occur. Incidentally the life of a fungicide may be shorter than that of the paint in which it is incorporated.

Before painting on infected areas, they must be thoroughly dried and then treated with a fungicidal solution. Some of these cause discoloration, and externally it is safer to use solutions of household bleach or industrial sodium hypochlorite.

Insecticidal paints Paints can be formulated to kill insects on contact in specific environments but they should not be regarded as a primary means of dealing with this problem.

Permeable paints Water thinned paints can be applied on damp plaster, moisture from which they can dry out through the paint film, but claims that specially formulated synthetic resin finishes, includ-ing gloss finishes, are permeable to water vapour should be confirmed by practical tests.

Floor paints One- and two-pack epoxy and poly-urethane paints can improve the appearance of concrete and tiled floors and they are extremely tough and resistant to abrasion. Life, however, is determined by their limited thickness and factors such as bond with the base.

Multi-colour paints contain globules of colour which differ from the main paint and remain separate and float on the surface. When dry, the appearance is of flecks of colour on a background of another colour and there is a very slight texture which disguises minor surface irregularities. Multi-colour paints are suitable for spraying only.

Texture paints — sometimes called 'plastic' paints, but not to be confused with plastics — are very heavily bodied paints with a consistency rather like plaster. The paint can be applied thickly to conceal irregularities in existing surfaces; soon after application it can be worked to form textures and relief patterns and when hard it can be carved.

Imitation stone paint has a fine crushed stone body which gives it an appearance resembling stone and added durability.

Anti-condensation paints have fillers such as cork, which provide some thermal insulation and absorption. If condensation is not too severe it maybe prevented or at least rendered inconspicuous.

'Metallic' paints   These include minute flakes of metals usually in varnish or cellulose media — eg zinc in rust inhibiting paints; aluminium in wood primers and in protective and light reflecting top coats; copper in decorative paints.

Luminous paints   These specialized paints present problems in application which make them unsuitable for site use. There are three types:

Fluorescent paints absorb ultra-violet radiation and re-emit visible light.

Phosphorescent paints absorb energy and emit it as visible light which continues to glow after the source of stimulation has been removed.

Radio-active paints are self-luminous, normally phosphorescent paints in which radio-active compounds activate phosphor.

APPLICATION OF PAINT

Generally, painting should not proceed in wet, damp, or foggy weather, on surfaces below about 4°C, in direct sunlight or in dusty conditions. Each coat should be thoroughly dry before the next coat is applied. Good ventilation is required to dry paint and sometimes to remove noxious fumes. Humid conditions delay drying of ordinary paints and entrapped moisture reduces the adhesion, durability and gloss of finishes, and corrodes ferrous metals. On the other hand, moisture-curing polyurethane and cement paints — although they should not be applied in rain — are best cured in damp conditions.

On the building site, application may be by *brush, hand roller* or *spray*. In the factory, *dipping, flow*

coating, roller coating and other time and labour saving techniques are possible.

Brush

Provided brushes are vigorously manipulated, they displace air and traces of dust and moisture from the surface, and give the best adhesion — which is particularly desirable in priming coats. However, skill is necessary to avoid brush marks and to maintain wet edges when applying paint on large areas.

Rollers

Rollers, which are wider than brushes, hold more paint, require less frequent recharging and save time on large plane surfaces, although a brush is still needed to finish to a line and to paint into internal angles.

Lambswool, mohair and nylon pile and synthetic sponge coverings all slightly stipple surfaces — even of gloss paint.

Spray

Good spraying equipment is costly — particularly the two-pack gun required for paints which harden by catalytic action — and areas which are not to be sprayed must be masked.

The electrostatic method directs and confines spray to the surface being painted, including otherwise inaccessible parts, but it is not easily adapted to site painting.

Lead paint is a health hazard and must not be sprayed, but generally spraying is economical on large areas and on details in relief. It is the only method for applying quick-drying paints such as cellulose, and it leads itself to the production of certain metallic and graded effects. The hot spray process reduces the viscosity of paints without adding solvent. Airless spray restricts overspray and increases productivity but often sufficient continous work cannot be provided in buildings to justify the costly equipment.

Dipping

Dipping is a rapid and economical method of painting those components which allow for adequate drainage, but the requisite close control of the paint and process is not possible on the building site. Other factory processes, which enable excess paint to be recovered, include:

Flow coating in which paint is hosed onto the article and

Roller coating by machine of one or both sides of boards and often continuous lengths of metal sheet.

BACKGROUNDS

Backgrounds must be sound, generally dry, and be properly prepared.

Moisture content

Moisture in backgrounds, or trapped between surfaces and primers or between successive coats of paint, causes loss of adhesion and sometimes leads to blisters in the paint film. Impervious finishes should not, therefore, be applied on damp surfaces unless there is an alternative route for moisture to escape freely. As a rough rule even in good conditions it takes about one week for every 5 mm thickness of wet construction to dry out completely.

The superficial appearance of a surface is not a reliable guide to the moisture content of a construction 'in depth'. Knowledge of the weather conditions during and after construction helps, but it is much better to measure the moisture content directly. Methods include: 1 *Electrical moisture meter.* 2 *Coloured indicator papers*, the significance of colour changes being assessed by reference to a standard colour sheet. Readings should be taken in the centre of a surface at least 300 mm square which has been covered overnight with a glass, metal or polythene sheet. 3 *Hygrometer.* BRE Digest 55 gives recommendations for decoration related to overnight readings of the relative humidity of air in equilibrium with a surface, which are summarized as follows:

Relative humidity per cent	Wall condition	Recommendation
100	Moisture on surface	If decoration *must* proceed wipe surface dry and use a specially formulated, porous, highly pigmented emulsion paint.
	No moisture on surface	If decoration *must* proceed use specially formulated emulsion paint as above, or white cement paint (but not on gypsum plaster).
90 – 75	Drying	As above, and as the surface becomes drier reasonable chance of success extends progressively to: 1 most emulsion paints 2 oil-bound and size-bound distempers 3 wallpaper 4 special types of permeable flat oil paints
Less than 75	Dry	Any treatment

Preparation

Inadequate preparation of backgrounds is a common cause of defective paintwork. Some surfaces require only to be brushed down but others need washing and scraping to remove dirt, dust, loose deposits or defective paint. Oils and stains must be removed by suitable solvents.

Surfaces must have sufficient 'key' for the type of paint which is to be applied. Some proprietary washing solutions slightly etch surfaces while additional key can be provided by a chemical etching solution or by rubbing down with an abrasive. Copper, lead and existing paint containing lead must not be rubbed down dry and it is convenient to combine rubbing down with the washing operation. After rubbing down, etching and washing it is important to remove all residues with clean water. Surfaces must then be dry before ordinary paints are applied.

Previously painted surfaces

For good class work all surface-fixed ironmongery, fittings etc. should be removed before painting. Water soluble paints such as non-washable distemper must always be removed. If other paints have only slightly 'chalked' they provide a good base and key, and one or two coats of new paint usually restore their original condition.

Where a perfect appearance is required, small defects can be 'brought forward' by priming, filling and rubbing down so that the surface is brought into one plane. This, however, is laborious and for large areas where a perfect appearance is desired it is economical to remove all the old paint and treat the surface as being new.

Paint can be removed by:

Burning off — ie softening paint with a blow-lamp and scraping.

Solvent and chemical removers An oil binder is most easily softened, water-thinned paints with a low oil content less readily, and chemically cured resins are very difficult to remove. It is clearly most important to remove all residues before repainting. Water rinseable and solvent rinseable paint removers are described in BS 3761:1970.

Solvent and chemical removers are not effective on structural steel due to its surface texture and the presence of rivets and bolts, and they are not suitable on gypsum plaster.

Steam stripping Softening with steam, followed by scraping, is the only economical way to remove some paint systems and varnishes but the equipment is bulky, the method is suitable only for flat surfaces and it may damage delicate backgrounds.

PAINTING ON VARIOUS BACKGROUNDS

The problems which are peculiar to various backgrounds are dealt with in CP 231:1966 *The painting of buildings*, and some of the more important points are considered here:

Woodwork

Wood changes size with variations in its moisture content; it is liable to attack by fungus, insects and fire. See *MBS: Materials*, chapter 2. Oils and resins contained in certain timbers, and differences between the densities of earlywood and latewood present other problems which are referred to later.

With the high proportion of sapwood (all of which is *non-durable* or worse) contained in much softwood now being imported, it is strongly recommended that softwood for external joinery should be treated with a paintable preservative. Self-draining details and a well maintained impervious paint system, will minimize the movement of timber which cracks paint particularly at joints and allows water to enter.

Because moisture may cause loss of adhesion by paint, and because moisture vaporizing below paint forms blisters, at the time of painting the moisture content of timber should never exceed 18 per cent. To minimize moisture movement, however, its moisture content may require to be as little as 10 per cent for internal joinery. On the other hand it must be remembered that timber can be too dry for its situation.

To obtain a first-class paint finish, the finish on joinery itself must be of very good quality and the thirteen operations described below, which take at least five days to perform, may be needed. However, the 'minimum' treatment on ordinary softwoods is indicated by letter *A–E* — takes four days.

1 *Repair* Large, loose or resinous knots and other gross defects should be cut out and holes plugged with sound wood. Nails should be punched well below surfaces, especially externally.

2 *Rub down* To revive first class painted finishes even the best planed work must be rubbed down with a fine glass paper in the direction of the grain.

3 *Dust off*

4 *Wash with solvent* Oily woods such as teak, afrormosia, gurjun and makoré should be washed with a solvent such as white spirit.

5 *A Knot* Resin which is not sealed always tends to discolour paint even on old wood. If an aluminium primer/sealer is not used two thin coats of *knotting* (shellac in methylated spirit to BS 1336: 1971) must be applied to knots and any other resinous parts of softwoods in an effort to prevent resin staining.

6 *Seal* Wood which has been exposed to the weather becames absorbent and may require: two priming coats, the first well-thinned; the application of a thin coat of a long-oil oleo-resinous varnish; or treatment with boiled oil.

7 *B Prime* The traditional lead-based primer, usually pink in colour due to the inclusion of red lead, possesses the flexibility needed on wood backgrounds. BS 2521 and 2523 are relevant but some manufacturers recommend products with a slightly lower lead content. Emulsion primers, usually based on acrylic polymers, have the advantages of quick drying, freedom from toxic pigments and durability which is said to be equal to that of white lead.

Aluminium primers have an alkyd or oleo-resinous medium which adheres well, even on dense and non-absorbent latewood. They seal against 'bleeding' of resins in softwoods, dispensing with the need for shellac knotting. They are specially recommended on Douglas fir.

A fullcoat of primer should be vigorously brushed in, particular care being taken to fill end grain. Backs of members which will be in contact with external walls should receive at least two coats, preferably of *aluminium wood primer*.

A sound primer applied 'at works' protects joinery from moisture during transport and in storage on the site, but in fact works primers are often inferior and too thin to exclude rain. They should be carefully specified, and on the site damage should be touched up and an extra coat given if the works primer looks thin.

It is important to apply the primer at this stage to prevent loss of oil from stopping (8) and filling (9).

8 *C Stop* All cracks, nail holes and the like should be stopped, preferably with a proprietary *hard stopping*, or with *putty* (BS 544:1969) applied and finished with a knife. Water soluble stopping should not be used outdoors.

9 *Fill* To obtain a first-class smooth surface free even from minor irregularities, a filler is applied with a broad knife. Gypsum plaster or water soluble cellulose-based fillers are satisfactory internally but outdoors a waterproof proprietary paste filler must be used.

10 *Flat down* 'Flatting' with a suitable abrasive is necessary at this stage where a first class finish is required. For ordinary work only hard stopping needs to be rubbed down (this must be done 'wet' if stopping contains lead).

11 *D Apply undercoat(s)* At least two undercoats are needed for good quality work externally, and for first class work internally. Any stopping or filling should be hard.

12 *Flat down undercoats* if a very high gloss finish is required.

13 *E Apply finishing coat(s)* Externally, and for

Background	Exposure	Primer
Non-resinous woods	Externally and internal parts of window frames and sashes, reveals etc.	White lead in linseed oil with not more than 10 per cent red lead, aluminium wood primer or acrylic emulsion primer
	Internally	Leadless primers, eg acrylic emulsions
Resinous woods		Aluminium wood primer
Flat sawn timbers with wide variation between earlywood and latewood eg Douglas Fir	Internally and externally	Aluminium wood primer with leafing aluminium powder and a synthetic varnish medium is 'probably best'
Oily hardwoods washed with solvent eg Teak		Aluminium wood primer or special tenacious 'teak sealer'
Old and thin creosote		Aluminium sealer (two coats)
Thick creosote or bitumen	Externally	Re-apply existing finish

Table 29 Primers on wood

superior quality internal finishes, greater durability is obtained by applying two coats of finishing type paint — one of which may be in substitution for an ordinary undercoat.

Metals

Metals often require to be protected from corrosion — see *MBS: Materials*, chapter 9. Paint can protect from rain and damp, separate dissimilar metals, and protect from contact with, or washings from, woods such as oak, teak and chestnut which contain acids, and form acid vapours.

Metals offer no suction for paint, and grease and fluxes which are often present should be removed with trichloroethylene.

Metalwork which is to be exposed to the weather must be carefully designed. It must be fully accessible for painting and welds should be ground smooth. Pockets and crevices which might retain water must be avoided especially in industrial and marine atmospheres, and where necessary holes should be provided to drain water away.

Ferrous metals

References include:
BRE Digest 70 *Painting metals in buildings — 1 Iron and steel*
BS 5493:1977 *Code of Practice for protection coating of iron and steel structures against corrosion*
Protective painting of structural steel, F. Fancutt, FRIC, AMI and J.C. Hudson, DSc, DIC, ARCS, FIM, Chapman and Hall Ltd.

Ordinary ferrous metals are particularly difficult to protect from corrosion. Essentials are: very thorough preparation of surfaces, a specially formulated paint system including a rust-inhibiting primer, thick and impervious top coats and application by a skilled operative in dry conditions.

Ideal conditions are rarely achieved on the building site and unfortunately, although they are possible in the factory, in fact the ordinary factory primer is often applied over dirt and rust and is of poor quality.

In ordinary, *mild, inland exposures* two priming coats and at least two further coats of air-drying paint with a minimum thickness of 0.125 mm are necessary. (An equal thickness may be obtained with fewer coats of thixotropic or chemically-cured paints.)

In *severe exposures* where heavy industrial pollution occurs, or within two miles of a coast, no paint system is effective unless applied in the factory on galvanized or zinc sprayed metal. Alternatively, vitreous enamelled or plastics coated metal may be used.

Preparation   Fancutt and Hudson have shown that thorough surface preparation increases the life of a paint film four to five times. At present the BRE is not able to recommend primers which are claimed to penetrate or react with rust and advise that the primer should be applied on bright metal. Mill scale and tightly adhering rust on pitted surfaces can only be completely removed by grit or shot blasting[1] or in a factory by acid pickling. Less serious rust, mill scale and old paint can be removed by hand or power tools, or by flame cleaning with oxyacetylene or butane gas (a blow lamp is not effective) followed by brushing. Pickling is effective in the factory, but the use of pickling jellies or pastes is not recommended on the site, where phosphoric acid washes are suitable although less effective than in the factory. (Treating metal with linseed oil while it is still hot after rolling, and weathering to remove rust and scale are no longer recommended.) Degreasing is also best done in the factory. On site, swabs soaked in white spirit should be used and changed frequently to avoid merely spreading grease over surfaces.

Priming   Primers, or the first coats of systems such as zinc-rich and coal-tar epoxy paints which do not require separate primers, should be applied immediately the background has been prepared. Generally the temperature of the air should be above 5°C and its relative humidity not greater than 80 per cent. The temperature of the metal should always be above the dew point of the air. Condensation, including moisture from handling which may not be visible, will lead to corrosion later if it is trapped in the paint film. Flame cleaning has the advantage that it dries surfaces and suitably formulated primers should be applied while the metal is still warm (but not hot).

Brushing is recommended, but roller or spray application of primers may be satisfactory on

[1] BS 4232:1967 *Surface finish of blast-cleaned steel for painting* describes three degrees of finish.

smooth surfaces, provided any tendency to rush the work is resisted. Paint runs away from arrises and a second primer coat is recommended on them. Also, because a second primer coat is of more value than an undercoat, it should be applied where there are specially corrosive conditions and externally, except in inland areas having low rainfall.

For normal paint systems rust-inhibiting primers such as those listed below, are essential.

Red lead in oil, eg BS 2523:1966 — *Tye B* and branded products also containing red iron oxide or graphite.

Metallic lead Like red lead, metallic lead is a 'tolerant primer' ie it is excellent where preparation is not of a high standard and where the primer will not be immediately overpainted.

Calcium plumbate BS 3698:1964 specifies *Type A* — 48 per cent and *Type B* — 33 per cent calcium plumbate oil-based primers. Not all undercoats adhere well to these primers.

Non-toxic primers are now often required and these include:

Zinc chromate Zinc chromate-in-oil primers are particularly useful for priming non-ferrous metals. Suitable formulations give good results on structural steel, although generally red lead-in-oil primers are more effective.

Zinc dust Two-pack zinc-rich epoxy resin-based paints are suitable for use on blast-cleaned metal.

Wash or etch primers These are based on PV butyral resins and phosphoric acid with or without zinc chromate. Available in one- and two-pack forms they can be used as primers on steel which has been acid-pickled or blasted. 'Wash' means that these primers are very thin, and they provide protection for a short time only. Strictly they do not etch although they provide excellent adhesion.

Most other primers, including red (iron) oxide and aluminium, do not possess special rust-inhibiting properties.

Undercoats and finishes Undercoat and finish type paints must be suited to the primer coat as well as to the conditions of exposure.

Paint systems suitable for various conditions of exposure can be taken from table 1 in BRE Digest 70. Examples which provide a high degree of protection include suitably formulated paints of the following types:

Oil modified alkyd
Exterior aluminium pigmented
Micaceous iron oxide
Bituminous and coal-tar with bituminous-aluminium finish
Coal-tar epoxy
Graphite and silica-graphite (for limited applications)

Chlorinated rubber, vinyl, two-pack epoxy and two-pack polyurethane coatings are resistant to severe chemical attack.

Non-ferrous metals

BRE Digest 71 *Painting metals in buildings 2 — Non-ferrous metals and coatings* is a reference.

Generally, non-ferrous metals do not require protection, but externally, zinc coatings on ferrous metals should be painted and aluminium alloys may require to be painted in certain industrial atmospheres, or near the sea.

Table 30 describes preparation and primers for site application. Ordinary undercoats and finishes are usually satisfactory.

The best quality finishes, for example most stoved paints and vinyl, acrylic and viteous enamel coatings, must be applied 'at works'.

Bituminous surfaces

Bituminous surfaces are best painted with bituminous paint. Other types of paint can be applied if a specially formulated sealer is used, but only if the bituminous coating is hard and thin.

Insulating fibre building boards

Factory primed and ivory surfaced boards need no further priming. Ordinary boards can be primed with an oil-based primer to counteract suction and to prevent subsequent water paint raising the surface fibres.

Bitumen impregnated boards should be sealed with preferably two coats of aluminium sealer. Boards impregnated with fire retardant salts and asbestos-faced boards are usually best treated with an alkali-resistant primer.

Sound absorbent tiles and boards

To minimize loss of sound absorption properties paint should be as thin as possible and spray applica-

New metal surface	Site preparation	Suitable primers
Aluminium and Aluminium Alloys[1] – smooth eg sheet, extrusions, aluminized steel	Phosphoric acid washes or Emery (*NOT* wire wool) with white spirit as lubricant or Solvent degreasing with white spirit or white spirit with equal parts of solvent naphtha	Etch-primer[2] plus zinc chromate (*NOT* lead-based primer)
– rough eg castings, aluminium spray	Smooth off nibs with emery paper Clean off dust and dirt	Zinc chromate
		One-pack etch-primer plus zinc chromate
Zinc – sheet, hot-dipped or electro-galvanized[3] coatings	Degrease with white spirit	Calcium plumbate direct, or etch-primer plus zinc chromate
	Weather for several months and wash	Zinc chromate or calcium plumbate
	Phosphoric acid washes and rinse thoroughly	Calcium plumbate
– sprayed or sherardized coatings	Smooth off nibs with emery paper Clean off dust and dirt	One-pack etch-primer preferably plus zinc chromate
Copper and Copper Alloys eg brasses and bronzes	Emery with white spirit (*DO NOT* weather or abrade dry[4]) Phosphoric acid treatments	If painting is essential: *In exposed conditions:* Etch-primer or aluminium pigmented primer *Internally:* Alkyd gloss paint may be applied direct
Lead[5]	Abrade wet (*NOT* dry)[6]	Alkyd gloss direct for small areas – otherwise do not paint
Cadmium coatings	Phosphate treatments (*DO NOT* weather)	Two-pack etch-primer
Chromium and nickel plating	Emery with white spirit	

Table 30   Site preparation and primers for new non-ferrous metals
(Information from BRE Digest 71 *Painting metals in buildings 2 – Non-ferrous metals and coatings,* and other sources)

[1] Aluminium should be protected from alkaline materials such as concrete by an alkali-resistant system (eg chlorinated rubber) or a bitumen-based paint.
[2] A special etch-primer with improved water resistance should be used if exposure to rain or dew is likely before later coats are applied.
[3] The insides of galvanized steel cisterns can be protected against corrosion with a non-toxic bituminous paint to BS 3416, Type 11.
[4] Copper dust settling on surfaces can cause stains when they are subsequently painted.
[5] Graphite-based paints should not be applied directly on metals, particularly on lead.
[6] Lead dust is a health hazard.

tion which avoids paint build-up at the edges of channels or perforations, is preferable.

Hardboards

As with insulating fibreboards, some hardboards are primed or sealed at the factory but a primer-sealer should be used on untreated boards especially under water paints. Externally an aluminium flake primer is suitable. Wood primers are not suitable. Backs and edges should be painted.

Plastics

A tenacious primer is desirable and it may be necessary to rub down shiny surfaces. Paint manufacturers should be consulted in each case.

Paper

Lining paper, wall paper and paper faced boards usually provide uniform suction and if the paper is firmly adherent will accept water-borne paint or an oil-bound primer sealer. Patterned wallpapers should be tested to see if the pattern 'grins through'; if it does it is likely to be more economical to strip the paper and to hang lining paper if this is required.

Fabrics

Hessian, jute and other fabrics can be painted direct with emulsion paints. If the joints spring the problem should be referred to the paint manufacturer.

Plasterwork

Reference should be made to BRE Digests 197 *Painting walls* 1 and 2.

Trouble is likely to follow if an impervious paint is applied before drying of plaster and the structure are complete — a process which normally takes months, especially if the other side cannot dry freely. Distemper and emulsion paint, however, can be applied once the plaster is surface-dry, and an emulsion paint provides a base for a suitable impervious finish when drying is complete.

Dry gypsum plasters are chemically compatible with all except Portland cement paints. Two-pack epoxy paints should be used only after reference to the manufacturer.

If plasters or backgrounds may contain lime or Portland cement it is wise to check for alkalinity with moistened litmus paper and if they prove to be alkaline two coats of alkali-resistant primer should be applied before following with any paint which contains oil.

Sanded, retarded, hemi-hydrate plasters give a good key for paint but absorption is sometimes patchy and in continuously damp conditions they 'sweat out' causing paints to fail. In the lightweight form, they tend to be very smooth and in exceptional cases a special primer-sealer may be needed.

Anhydrous plasters and Keene's cement are harder and less porous than retarded hemi-hydrate plasters and are often finished to almost glass-like smoothness. If they dry too quickly the partially hydrated surface becomes powdery affording a poor key for paint and if 'delayed expansion' of the plaster occurs, breakdown can be complete.

Procedure on new plaster

The processes are:

1 Scrape, 2 Rub down, 3 Dust down, 4 Make good, 5 Prime and 6 Paint. Thus:

1 *Scrape* Plaster and mortar splashes should be carefully scraped off.

2 *Rub down* If it is necessary to rub down to remove irregularities care should be taken to avoid causing variations in the porosity of the surface leading to variations in the sheen of the paint.

3 *Dust down* to remove dust and any efflorescence. The latter must *not* be washed off.

4 *Make good and stop* with plaster of the same type as that used for the surface as a whole.

5 *Prime* Apply a coat of alkali-resistant primer on alkaline surfaces and a well thinned alkali-resisting or *plaster primer* on Keene's plaster. Formerly a *sharp primer following the trowel* (ie a primer with a very small oil content, applied within three hours of plastering being completed) was recommended on Keene's plaster. It was argued that the fresh plaster induced some suction and that this, together with the disturbance caused by the brush, gave good adhesion. In addition, the sharp primer delayed the rate of drying of the plaster, thereby reducing the risk of a *'dry out'* followed by *'delayed expansion'* (see page 64). However, it must never be applied to alkaline surfaces and most proprietary primers are not suitable for 'following the trowel'.

Procedure on old plaster

If surfaces are damp the cause should be removed. Decorations affected by moulds or mildew should be stripped and a mould inhibitor, eg *ICI Mould Inhibitor* or *Santobrite*, should be applied. Unsound plaster should be removed and made good, and cracks and holes should be filled with new plaster of the same type and having the same finish as the old plaster.

Failures often arise because the adhesion of old paint is insufficient to hold fresh paint. Water-soluble paint must always be washed off and the surface allowed to dry. Other old paint which is in poor condition should be removed, or if this is not practicable it may be rubbed and scraped 'dry' and treated with a special penetrating and binding primer.

'*Binding down*', *penetrating* and alkali-resisting primers equalize suction and reduce patchiness in the finish, but on repaired surfaces lining paper (see page 120) may be needed to provide a uniform texture, particularly for gloss paint.

Backgrounds containing Portland cement

Alkalis in lime or Portland cement contained in a structure, rendering, mortar or plaster when carried in solution, cause chemical breakdown of paints containing oil, producing sticky or oily matter (*saponification*), and lime which diffuses from the substrate sometimes becomes 'fixed' in paint producing apparent bleaching. Efflorescent salts may penetrate permeable paints or 'push off' impervious paints during the drying out of concrete and brickwork.

Because new surfaces containing Portland cement are rarely completely dry and may accidentally become wet later, a non-saponifiable alkali-resistant primer is desirable under paints containing oil. Alkaline finishes such as cement and silicate paints are, of course, immune from saponification (but they may present difficulties if it is ever desired to over-paint them with paints containing oil). Ready-mixed synthetic resin/aggregate finishes are suitable and emulsion paints can usually be safely applied on these backgrounds — the first coat being well thinned.

Traces of mould oil must be scrubbed off concrete surfaces using detergent or a solvent which, in turn, must be rinsed away.

Asbestos-cement products which have not been steam cured are highly alkaline when they are new and their porosity is variable. If an impervious finish is applied on one side only, condensation may cause loss of adhesion while carbonation of the untreated reverse side often causes warping and cracking. Before being painted both sides of sheets should be exposed to air for at least ten days to reduce their moisture content and to allow carbonation to take place. Back painting is desirable if the sheet is not fully carbonated and if the finish is impervious. BRE Digest 38 (First series) and D of E Advisory leaflet 28 *Painting asbestos cement*, are useful references.

Brickwork and stonework

Clay bricks contain soluble salts and the mortar is usually alkaline so that generally these surfaces should be treated as for backgrounds containing Portland cement.

On dense and glazed bricks, strongly adhesive primers having penetrating binders are preferable, followed by any paint which is suited to the conditions of exposure. Alternatively, oil-modified alkyd gloss paints may be applied direct after repairing pointing and allowing it to dry out.

Clear finishes

Clear finishes, with or without added colour, enhance the natural appearance of wood and other surfaces, and protect them from knocks and the weather. This protection, however, is inferior to that afforded by opaque finishes.

Materials must be formulated to suit the conditions of use and the substrate. Internally, the main requirements are usually rapid drying, good appearance and resistance to staining and scratching, and a high gloss may be desired. Externally the need for protection limits the choice of materials.

The main clear finishes suitable for common backgrounds are:

115

Internal surfaces

Wood
 oil seals
 wax polish
 French polish
 short-oil varnishes
 spirit varnishes
 synthetic resin finishes
 cellulose lacquers

Paper
 water varnishes

Metals
 cellulose lacquers

External   surfaces

Wood
 preservatives
 oil finishes
 fortified linseed oil
 long-oil varnishes

Brickwork, Stonework, Concrete
 water repellents
 synthetic resin
 finishes

Internal clear finishes on wood and metal are considered first.

Internal surfaces

Internal clear finishes on wood

In general, surfaces must be firm, clean and dry and first-class finishes can only be obtained on smooth surfaces where preparation is thorough. Operations in preparing wood surfaces include:

Bleaching

Lime treatment to give a grey effect and *fuming* to either lighten or darken.

Scraping along the grain.

Sand with garnet paper.

Stop holes and cracks, with hot beeswax, resin and orange lac, plaster of Paris or with whiting and a drying oil — both the latter being coloured to match the wood.

Fill pores (for a first class finish) — usually with a tinted oil-based filler.

Stain — to modify colour — with oil, varnish, wax, or with chemical water stains (which tend to raise the grain). Alternatively, stain may be included in the finish.

Clear finishes suitable for application on internal woodwork are:

1 *Oil seals*
These seals, a form of varnish, often based on tung oil, are used mainly for water and grease resistant, non-slip finishes on wood floors.

2 *Wax polishes*
Wax polish — a paste, liquid or emulsion based on beeswax or other waxes with turpentine or spirits — is fairly easily applied to new wood either directly or — to save time — after 'bodying in' with french polish. (It is also used to maintain all the other clear finishes.) Wax polish is relatively soft and more inclined to collect dirt than other finishes, it is 'whitened' by water and spirits and stained by ink and heat. However, it is not so prone to blooming, crazing or 'orange peeling' and is less likely to show scratches than other finishes. Further, repairs are relatively easy to carry out.

3 *Polymer-based emulsions*
Emulsion polishes based on PVA, acrylic resin and polyethylene are easy to apply and maintain.

4 *French polish*
French polish is costly to apply and is marked by heat, water and spirits. However, it is generally agreed to be the finest internal finish on wood, and it is fairly easy for a skilled polisher to match colours and to repair defects.

After any necessary preparation, the processes are:

Body in   — with lac (a resinous excretion of certain insects) and gums held in a rubber

Body up   — by thin applications of lac held in a rubber using linseed oil as a surface lubricant

Spirit off — polish with a pad of cotton wool soaked in methylated spirit and covered with chamois leather which slightly softens and levels the surface

5 *Cellulose lacquers*
Cellulose lacquers consist of nitro-cellulose with a plasticizer to counteract brittleness and with natural or synthetic resins where gloss is required. The appearance of a cellulose lacquer finish is similar to french polish, although being easier to apply, it is cheaper. Initially, cellulose is more resistant to water, but it is also attacked by spirits. Cellulose deteriorates by cracking so that it must be completely removed before it is renewed. For a first class finish the preparation should be similar to that for french polish but here application must be by spraying in suitable conditions of temperature and humidity. The surface can be *pulled over* rather like the *spiriting off* of french polish, to give a final gloss.

Nitro-cellulose is a serious fire risk and the Petroleum Regulations must be observed in storage and use.

6 Short-oil varnishes

These finishes have a low oil and a high resin content making for high gloss but reducing flexibility, so they tend to fail by cracking and are not suitable externally. Figure 4, page 101 shows the occurrence of oil and resin in various products. Oil varnishes are usually applied with a brush – a simpler proceeding than for french polish or cellulose, but they dry relatively slowly and tend to collect dust. Undercoats are sometimes rubbed down to obtain a first class finish.

Semi-gloss and matt varnishes containing wax *flatting agents* are used as finishes only.

7 Spirit varnishes

Spirit varnishes are made with resins such as shellac and dry quickly by the evaporation of solvents such as alcohol. They remain soluble in the solvent (hence *picture varnish* can be conveniently removed) and as with cellulose, brush application of following coats is difficult. Spirit varnishes are cheap but having a high shellac content they are brittle and inclined to crack. ('Knotting' (see page 109) and french polish are forms of spirit varnishes with lower shellac contents.)

8 Water varnishes

The medium of emulsion paint is a form of water varnish which can be used to glaze emulsion paint or wallpapers.

9 Synthetic resin finishes

One- and two-pack finishes are made from phenol, formaldehyde resins, urea and melamine formaldehydes, polyurethane, polyester, coumarone, indene and epoxy resins together with thinners and catalysts (hardeners).

Although relatively costly, suitable synthetic resin finishes can satisfy one or more exacting requirements such as: extreme hardness; flexibility; resistance to high temperatures – including burning cigarettes; and resistance to water, grease, spirits, acids and alkalis. Synthetic resin finishes are particularly suitable for bar and shop counter tops, laboratory benches and fume cupboards, but not generally for external use.

Surfaces must be free from wax polish and their preparation is similar to that for french polish and cellulose. Synthetic resins dry rapidly, so application must in most cases be by spray – special equipment being required for two-pack finishes.

Patch repairs are very difficult because synthetic resins cannot be removed by normal solvents.

Internal clear finishes on metals

Aluminium alloys, particularly those which are anodized, retain a bright and uniform appearance if they are kept clean. Regular wax polishing is required on copper based metals. Alternatively, cellulose finishes or two coats of *Incralac* or *BNF/CB lacquer* (see page 118) can be applied.

External surfaces

These are mainly applied to wood and sometimes to brickwork, stonework and concrete. Clear finishes lack pigments to filter the damaging ultra-violet radiation and are much less durable than paints.

External clear finishes on wood

Wood which is exposed to the weather often splits and develops a woolly or spongy surface which collects dirt and encourages mould growth; colours are washed out, and bleached by light and eventually all species of timber become grey. In addition, in wet conditions the less durable timbers are attacked by fungus. These effects are minimized by avoiding horizontal surfaces and cavities which could retain water. Table 31 is a useful summary.

Generally, a rather lower standard of surface preparation is acceptable for external than for internal finishes, but any stopping, or filling must be water resistant. Hammering of galvanized nails damages the zinc coating and they should be driven well below the surface to avoid rust stains.

Clear treatments which will help to preserve the natural appearance of timber are:

1 *Preservatives* The sapwood of all timbers and the heartwood of many timbers is readily attacked by fungi and should be preserved if only in order to prevent discoloration by moulds.

2 *Water repellents* applied by brush, especially to end grain, or by dipping in a solution for at least ten seconds can prolong the 'new' appearance of timber for a few years by reducing the surface cracking which results from repeated wetting and drying. Linseed oil alone, is not recommended; it tends to remain sticky and to hold dirt and its effective life is only about six months. BRE Digest 21 states 'on

timber cladding where a high gloss is not required, the appearance can be preserved and the cost of treatment and maintenance reduced by applying, instead of varnish, a single coat of linseed oil fortified with paraffin wax and a fungicide'.

3 *Stains* change the colour of wood and can revive the colour of bleached wood, and water resistant stains are valuable ultra-violet light filters. Some proprietary finishes which include all the above ingredients have preserved the natural colour of Western red cedar for four or more years.

4 *Varnishes* Unlike the above finishes, varnishes attempt to seal timber against the entry of water, but it remains desirable to preserve the less durable wood (as recommended where timber is to be painted, see page 109). Short-oil varnishes, french polish and finishes based on urea formaldehyde, epoxide, vinyl and acrylic resins which contain little, or no oil are generally poor performers externally. Long-oil varnishes including *spar*, *marine* and *exterior varnishes* are most durable clear and glossy finishes, but in spite of their superiority, even on plane and vertical surfaces four coats are unlikely to last more than three years, and fewer coats may deteriorate in a year or so.

Before timber is delivered to the site at least two coats should be applied on all surfaces — especially end grains and backs and at least two further coats should be applied on the site. Extra coats should be given to surfaces which face South, or which are not vertical.

Because unhardened varnishes are extremely sensitive to moisture they should not be applied in damp weather or where condensation might form on the film before it dries.

The appearance of white patches and slight flaking at edges is a signal to recoat surfaces before it becomes necessary to remove all the remaining varnish by the use of a solvent and scraper. Slight discoloration of timber may be removed with glass paper, oxalic acid or white spirit or it may be possible to conceal it by a water stain.

External clear finishes on brickwork, stonework and concrete

BRE Digests 56 and 125 discuss colourless waterproofing treatments for damp walls, some of which remain effective for up to ten years.

Impervious clear finishes are sometimes applied as a protection from soiling and to intensify the colour of marble or concrete, but no attempt should be made to waterproof pervious walling materials where there is no effective damp-proof course.

Water repellents line surface pores without filling them and encourage droplets to form, rather than a continuous film of water. An initial 'duck's back' effect is soon lost, but water repellency of *Silicone-based water repellents for masonry* (BS 3826:1969) — lasts for ten years or more. The latter materials are colourless, although a fugitive dye is sometimes added to assist in obtaining complete coverage in application. Water repellent fluids based on waxes, oils, fats or metallic soaps may retains dirt and cause a slight change in the tone and texture of some surfaces.

Surfaces should be free from cracks, reasonably dry, and free from efflorescence; salts deposited below the film may lead to spalling.

External clear finishes on metals

The only clear finish recommended by the British Non-ferrous Metals Research Association for site application on copper-based metals is *Incralac* which is based on an acrylic resin with a solvent, a corrosion inhibitor, ultra-violet light absorbers and a levelling agent. Metal must be thoroughly cleaned as recommended by the manufacturers of the lacquer. Application must be by spray, and in fine weather. Provided the finish is washed occasionally and not subject to excessive wear, three coats at least 0.025 mm thick have preserved the natural appearance of copper-based metals for five years in London.

BNF/CB lacquer, a two-pack polyurethane based finish is harder than *Incralac* but slow drying limits its use to the factory. Two coats give the requisite 0.025 mm thickness and full hardness can be obtained by stoving.

Vitreous enamel

Vitreous enamel (called *porcelain enamel* in USA) which is glass fused on steel, cast iron, aluminium or copper, is harder than cast-iron and extremely durable. It is attacked by strong alkalis buy many

Finish	Initial treatment	Appearance of wood	Maintenance procedure	Maintenance period of surface finish	Cost of initial treatment	Maintenance cost
Coal tar oils	Vacuum/pressure, hot and cold tank, steeping	Grain visible. Brown to black in colour, fading slightly with age	Brush down to remove surface dirt and brush apply	5–10 years only if original colour is required, otherwise no maintenance	Medium	Nil to low
	Brushing	Grain visible, light to dark brown	Brush down to remove surface dirt	3–5 years or according to colour	Low	Low
Waterborne preservatives	Vacuum/pressure	Grain visible Greenish colour fading with age	Brush down to remove surface dirt	None, unless stained, painted or varnished	Medium	Nil
Organic solvent preservatives	Steeping, dipping, brushing	Grain visible, colour as desired	Brush down and re-apply	3 years or according to colour	Medium to high	Medium
Water repellents	One or two coats, but preferably dip applied	Grain and natural colour visible, becoming darker and rougher textured	Brush down and apply fresh material liberally	4 years or according to colour	Medium to high	Medium
Linseed oil with white spirit	Fibre saturation	Grain and colour unchanged	Brush down, sandpaper and re-apply	6 months	Low	High
Good quality exterior varnish	Four coats minimum	Grain and colour unchanged	Clean and stain bleached areas and apply two more coats	3 years or when a breakdown is imminent	Medium	Medium to high
Polyurethane* (2 pack)	Four coats minimum	Grain and colour unchanged	Completely remove gloss and re-apply	3 years or when a breakdown is imminent	High	High

* These finishes require controlled conditions during application and drying which are not readily obtained on building sites.

Table 31   External clear finishes on woodwork

Based on *Maintaining Exposed Woodwork*, DOE Advisory Leaflet 62, HMSO

enamelled steel advertisements are in good condition after 50 years' exposure externally in industrial climates. Where the finish coats of coloured enamel have been damaged the dark coloured ground coat usually remains intact but where it has also been damaged rust does not creep below it. Exterior finishes should comply with BS 1344:1965:Part 2 (citric acid test) in respect of acid resistance. Designs, which can be in almost any colours, do not fade, stain or discolour.

Finishes can be *gloss, semi-gloss, textured* or *full-matt*. The latter two surfaces collect grime and should not be used externally.

Before enamelling, all fabrication should be completed. The object to be coated is thoroughly cleaned and raised to red heat. A finely pulverized *slip* made from a special form of glass, colour oxides and other ingredients is then sprayed on and flows and bonds with the metal. One-coat finishes are possible on aluminium. On steel at least two coats are required. The ground coat should cover the whole unit — including the back and edges — and for exterior work at least one further coat should do so.

Products should comply with the standards recommended by the Vitreous Enamel Development Council. For example, blemishes should not be visible when a unit is viewed at eye level from a distance of 1500 mm.

BS 3830:1973 describes *Vitreous Enamelled steel building components*

Applications

Wall infill panels — usually metal trays filled with an insulating material and with backs sealed with a vapour barrier;
Signs and advertisements;
Mullions, panels for lifts, escalators etc;
Kitchen furniture;
Chalkboards;
Steel rainwater goods;
Pressed steel and cast iron baths.

Plastics coatings

Plastics coatings on wood, metal and other substrates are warm and smooth to handle, easily cleaned and provide electrical insulation. Generally, they are thicker, tougher and more durable than ordinary paint coatings.

In particular, nylon and PVF coatings are extremely durable but not all plastics coatings are recommended outdoors — polythene, for example, loses its flexibility, and fades in time.

Plastics coatings are applied in the following ways:

1 Melt (or sinter) coatings

Metal articles are coated with powdered or molten plastics which are either self-curing or cured (sintered) by heat. Melt coatings are applied in several ways to give a homogeneous, smooth surfaced coating 0.26 to 1.0 mm thick.

Dipping　Preheated objects are dipped into powder resins such as polythene, flexible PVC, nylon, CAB and epoxies. In a method used mainly for temporary protection of machine parts, cold objects are dipped into molten plastics such as ethyl cellulose. In the *fluidized-bed method*, air is blown through the powder to hold it in suspension.

Flock spraying　Cold powder is sprayed onto preheated objects — where the powder is not self-curing the whole object is sintered after coating.

Electrostatic spraying　Powder sprayed onto cold objects adheres by electrostatic charge and is then sintered.

Flame spraying　A powdered resin such as nylon is melted in a flame gun and projected onto the object — a method liable to degrade the polymer.

Dusting　After dipping in solvents and plasticizer, wood and metal objects are dusted with cellulose acetate powder — giving a hard, high gloss finish.

2 Paste coatings

Heated objects, including complex shapes such as wire mesh, are coated by dipping them in finely divided dispersions of resin in the form of either *organosols* or *plastisols* — which are then coalesced.

Organosols　The resin particles are in a wholly or partly volatile organic liquid. These coatings are thinner and chearper than:

Plastisols　When heated, a plasticizer softens the resin — often PVC or a copolymer — which fuses to a continuous film with little loss of volatile matter. Pastes are spread on fabric, paper and other sheet backings, thickness being controlled by a 'knife'.

3 Solution coatings

Thin coatings – usually of PVC copolymers – can be sprayed on brickwork, concrete and open textured backgrounds such as wood-wool slabs to provide washable dust and vapour-proof barriers. Sprayed skins of this type span small cracks and are sufficiently flexible to accommodate structural movements. One formulation has been certified as having *Class 1 Spread of Flame* (BS 476 test).

Thin plastics coatings applied on aluminium sheet in the factory are more accurately described as a paint deposited from solution, rather than as a plastics coating.

4 Cast resin coatings

Cold, usually liquid, epoxides can be cast round articles which are stoved – usually in a factory. As no solvent is used hardening is rapid and thick coatings are possible.

5 Film and sheet coatings

PVC, ABS, polyurethane and PVF films and sheets can be bonded to asbestos cement, metals and other substrates. Extensive use is made of PVC coated steel for furniture, demountable partitions and external cladding.

Thick PVC films on galvanized steel may be expected to last externally for twenty years although with some colour change. PVF film, although costly, is extremely durable externally. 'Tubes' of cellulose acetate, cellulose nitrate or PVC softened by solvents before being placed over components of uniform section such as handrails, acquire a 'shrink fit' when the solvent evaporates.

Preformed coverings

Preformed coverings such as lining papers, wall papers, Lincrusta-Walton, fabrics and metal foils are considered here. They may save labour and time on the site, and often provide the only economical way of obtaining complex patterns in colours on large areas. Light fastness varies considerably and few of these materials resist strong sunlight. Colours and patterns should be selected from large samples and in the lighting conditions in which they will be used. With the exception of suitable metal foils and special adhesives, these coverings are suitable only in dry conditions.

It is wise to follow the manufacturers' recommendations for hanging various coverings. Methods vary – thus for some materials, the adhesive is best applied to the wall rather than to the back of the hanging and some materials are best jointed by over-lapping adjoining sheets, cutting through both thicknesses and then removing the surplus material.

The following types of thin preformed coverings are described:

Metal foils	Cork
Lining papers	Leather
Expanded polystyrene (lining)	Expanded polystyrene
	Textiles
Wallpapers	Grasscloth etc.
Plastics-faced cloths	Lincrusta-Walton
Wood veneers	Gilding

Metal foils are used for decorative and functional reasons. Underlinings of lead or aluminium foil (or of pitch coated paper) may be required to protect water-sensitive wall coverings while structures dry out from the reverse side. In other cases, metal foil on the inner surfaces of walls and ceilings can serve as a vapour barrier to prevent moisture from the building condensing within the structure.

A two-can epoxy varnish which sets independently of the air and in moist conditions is an effective adhesive for metal foils.

Lining papers are used as coverings on imperfect plaster and similar surfaces, to bridge hair-cracks and give even suction and texture for wall-papers and other thin coverings, and for paint. *Cross lining* is hung horizontally under wall paper to avoid co-incidence of joints in the lining paper and wallpaper.

Colours vary from good white to dark brown.

Qualities are *common pulp* in weights from 165 to 365 kg per ream; *strong brown* – for badly cracked surfaces; *pitch coated* for damp walls, and *cotton backed* for surfaces which are liable to move – eg existing t and g boarding.

Lining papers are 559 and 762 mm x 11 m. There is no selvedge.

Expanded polystyrene is available in widths of 610 mm and thicknesses of 2 mm and 5 mm. In addition to having the merits of paper lining it provides some thermal insulation — often sufficient to prevent surface condensation. Here, suitable solvent-free adhesive is applied to the wall or ceiling.

Wallpapers

Wallpapers vary considerably in character and cost. Patterns have 'repeats' (the distance between identical motifs in any one vertical line) up to 2 m and the size of repeats must be taken into account in estimating quantities. A pattern where motifs are at the same level at the two edges of a paper is called a 'set pattern' and where this does not occur it is called a 'drop' pattern.

Machine-made wallpaper is described by BS 1248: 1954 amended 1967. It covers 533 mm width as hung. Rolls are 10.5 mm ± 1½% long.

Examples include: *pulps*, having a pattern printed directly on paper; *embossed*; *duplex papers* which are two-ply papers; *ingrain* having fibres incorporated in the surface; *varnished* and *plastic emulsion coated 'washable' papers* and *mica surfaced papers* having sheen.

Finishes include *moirés*, a watered silk effect, and *metallic finishes*. Vinyl faced papers including those with gloss and metallic finishes are washable and most domestic stains can be removed. Papers faced with a thin film of PVC are costly, but provide maximum dirt resistance.

Flock papers have patterns in raised pile — produced by blowing wool, nylon, or rayon fibres onto patterns printed in adhesive.

Anaglypta, wet-moulded in high relief from high quality cotton pulp, is provided in natural form or in one colour. It is very tough and the emboss gives the material a high degree of resilience so that it can be used on hair-cracked surfaces which move slightly. High relief patterns and wood textures are provided as panels up to 978 mm square.

Hand-printed paper

This is more costly and the patterns more 'exclusive' than machine printed paper. Colours tend to be denser and do not run downwards — a characteristic of rotary printing by machine. However, patterns are not always so accurate — presenting difficulty in hanging — and some colours are soluble in water.

English hand-printed paper is approximately 533 m by 11 m long.

Hanging wallpapers

A crack-free, smooth and level background is important. Defective plaster should be 'made good' with plaster of the same type, lightly glass-papered and dusted. It should be dry, chemically neutral and have slight suction. Any efflorescent salts should be brushed off 'dry' and a liberal coat of well thinned alkali-resisting primer applied to the surface.

Old wallpaper should preferably be wetted and removed by a stripper. It is shows signs of mould growth, stripping is essential and the surface should be sterilized with a fungicidal wash.

Normally a coat of size is required to equalize and reduce the suction of plaster, but not foamed polystyrene.

Ordinary papers are pasted on the back with flour, starch or cellulose pastes, which provide good 'slip' properties during hanging. Heavy papers are best fixed either with flour or starch pastes with some *Dextrine* (a maize-based paste) added, or with a specially prepared *tub* paste. The addition of about 57 g of washing soda per bucket of paste neutralizes any acid which would darken metallic pigments on papers.

Depressions in the back of anaglypta may be filled with plaster, sawdust and glue size, before fixing, to increase the area for adhesion and the resistance to mechanical damage.

For the best results — especially with heavily grounded papers — edges should be trimmed with a straight edge and knife. In certain cases the edges should be slightly undercut. Before hanging, rolls must be carefully matched for colour.

In hanging, patterns should be matched at eye level to minimize the effects of inaccuracies in printing and of stretch in the paper. Allowing neither too long nor too short a time for the paste to wet the paper, and to reach a stage conductive to good adhesion, is a most important factor in paper-hanging and good pattern matching depends very much on this.

Great care must be taken to avoid paste staining the face of the paper, especially flock papers and those with soluble pigments.

If drying is too rapid, the paper fibres are over-stretched and in drying do not shrink back to their original size, leaving the paper loose and blistered.

Plastics-faced cloths

Strong cotton cloths impregnated with PVC resist normal scratches and scuffing and 'domestic' chemicals and can be cleaned with warm water and mild soap.

They are produced in monochromes and in a large range of patterns, and with plain and textured surfaces, in various widths from 673 mm to 1321 mm.

Surfaces to receive cloths should be prepared as for wallpapers. The adhesive recommended by the manufacturer – which must be mould-inhibiting – may be applied either to the wall or to the back of the cloth.

Allowance of up to 26 mm/m in the length of some cloths must be made for shrinkage which may occur after hanging.

Other preformed coverings

Wood veneers often exotically figured, in varying widths and in lengths up to about 2 m are stocked in the order in which they were sliced from the log so that patterns can be made by matching adjacent veneers. Products mounted on paper, cloth and metal foil backings are easier to bend with than across the grain. An aluminium foil-backed wood veneer has a transparent vinyl coated face.

Textiles The very wide range of materials includes cottons, linen, jute, silk and synthetic fibres. Natural coloured and dyed hessians are available in close, medium and open weaves – either backed or with a paper, foamed plastic or PVA backing. Suitable unbacked materials can be fixed in folds or stretched taut on light frames or horizontal rails. Inexpensive textiles are fixed on surfaces lined with paper tinted to suit the colour of the fabric, paste being applied to the lining paper. Paste is applied to the back of backed materials. Good products can be cleaned with an upholstery fabric cleaner, a vacuum cleaner or by brushing lightly.

Cork is provided on a coloured paper backing 760 mm wide, the colour of which shows through the cork which is extremely thin. It should be hung on a lining paper like wallpaper.

Leather An economical size for cutting cowhide is about 915 mm by 760 mm. It is usually backed with padding such as polyether foam and mounted on blockboard or 6 mm hardboard 'invisibly' fixed to walls.

Expanded polystyrene This hanging, already described as a lining material, must be fixed with a PVA adhesive and painted with emulsion paint. Other adhesives and paints destroy it.

Grasscloth etc Grasses, honeysuckle and bamboos are held together with thread and mounted on backings. After careful trimming, the *cloths* are pasted on the back and applied to previously lined surfaces.

Lincrusta-Walton Lincrusta as it is normally called, is a composition of whiting, wood flour, lithopone, wax and resin with linseed oil as binder, pressed at high temperature on a kraft backing paper giving a more faithful reproduction from the mould than anaglypta. Units of Lincrusta are provided in natural putty colour for painting, and also in colours. Surfaces should be lined before Lincrusta is fixed with a heavy duty adhesive.

Gilding is the application of extremely thin *leaves* of silver, platinum, copper, aluminium, or in particular gold, to surfaces.

Gold leaf is provided in various shades and thicknesses. 23-25 carat English gold of 'double thickness' is used for the best work. Imitation gold tarnishes rapidly if it is not lacquered. A coat of weak parchment size enriches the colour of gold and from time to time the size can be removed together with the dirt adhering to it.

On surfaces other than glass, metal leaves either mounted on paper as a *transfer*, or loose, are applied on *gold size*, the tackiness of which, when the leaf is applied, determines the final lustre of the gilded surface.

Gilding with loose leaf is a very skilled process which requires still air conditions. The leaf is picked up with a special brush (*a tip*) – which has been touched on the hair of the operator and brought into contact with isinglass on glass, and parchment size on other surfaces. On moulded surfaces the leaf is then dabbed and polished with a camel hair *dabber*.

Water gilding – leaf if floated on water on backgrounds covered with a composition of whiting, pipe clay and parchment size, which latter provides adhesion. The method, which gives a brilliant, join-free gold surface is rarely used today except for high class and intricate work such as making picture frames.

123

7 Roofings

THEORY

The solution of the technical and aesthetic problems associated with roofs (the supporting structures), and *roofings* (roof finishes) are essential to the satisfactory performance of the building as a whole. Structural behaviour and roof structure are considered in *MBS: S and F* parts 1 and 2. Some of the more common terms used in connection with roofing are illustrated in figure 5.

With regard to roof finishes the following list gives the more important factors which must be considered.

1 **Appearance** The degree of pitch of the roof surface is a primary design decision. A roof is generally described as either *flat* or *pitched* and it is important to note that a roof is defined as *flat* up to a pitch of 10 degrees to the horizontal (see BS 3589:1963 *Glossary of general building terms*). Where a flat roof is chosen, the appearance of the roof's surface is unlikely to be important, if it is not overlooked from higher levels or used as a terrace or for vehicular traffic. Where a roof is pitched, the colour and texture of the materials used is a very important factor.

2 **Durability** In general terms a roof is more vulnerable to the effects or rain, snow, solar radiation and atmospheric pollution, than any other part of a building. Traditional pitched roof

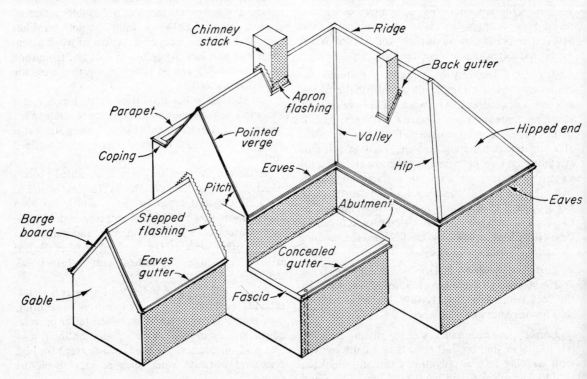

5   *Terms used in connection with roofing*

coverings such as tiles, slates, lead sheet and even thatch remain serviceable for many years but flat roof coverings often have a shorter life. The question of the rate at which water will 'run off' a roof is of fundamental importance. Pitched roofing has a high rate of 'run off' and, provided that the detailing of overlaps or jointing is satisfactory, the materials used to cover pitched roofs will be expected to have a long life. The 'run off' from a truely flat roof is very slow indeed and in practice most materials used for flat roof covering do not remain perfectly level and true after laying. As a result, water is very often retained in shallow result, water is very often retained in shallow pools on the finished roof surface. This is known as *ponding*. It is a prime cause of deterioration because local variations in temperature between the wet and dry area of the roof cause differential thermal movement, which together with accumulations of acid left by evaporating rain cause a breakdown in the roof surface. It is, of course, possible to design roofs to retain a considerable depth of water to protect and insulate the roof surface so that the roof benefits from freedom from diurnal temperature changes. The depth of water must however be sufficient to withstand evaporation and it must not be allowed to stagnate. Because this is difficult in practice, the most satisfactory method is to construct the roof deck so that it slopes or falls towards the roof outlet to a sufficient degree to shed the surface water. The outline of the roof can still retain its flat appearance by the use of a horizontal fascia. A fall of 1 in 80, say 12 mm in 1000 mm, is required for sheet metal covering and mastic asphalt although a greater fall is desirable where possible. Skirtings at all abutments must be at least 150 mm high.

3 **Weather exclusion** Roof coverings are required to prevent the entry of rain, snow and dust and to resist the effects of wind — both wind pressure and the effects of suction.

Rainfall Maps showing an index of driving rain are included in BRS Digest 23. It has been shown that rain penetration depends both on rain amount and wind speed and is governed more by maximum rain intensity rather than total duration or total quantity. This is of particular importance where the roof covering is in the form of separate heavy units made butt jointed as in tiles and slates. This type of covering depends upon the adequacy óf the overlap of the units and the pitch of the roof to shed the water. For details of Rain water pipes and gutters, see MBS *Environment and Services.*

Wind pressure The effect of wind pressure upon a roof depends upon the angle of pitch and the degree of exposure of the roof slope. For a ridge type roof of between 20 degrees and 30 degrees pitch the suction will more or less be equally balanced on both roof slopes. On steeper pitches the negative pressure (the suction) is higher on the leeward side. For shallow pitched roofs up to 20 degrees a suction occurs on the windward side. Modern pitched roofs usually fall into this category and it is in this type of roof that suction may present a serious problem, and in particular where lightweight sheet coverings are used, on a lightweight timber decking. With this construction the roof deck should be securely anchored down and this can be done by making sure that sheeting is firmly fixed to the roof framing and then securing a wallplate by means of galvanized steel straps built in the brickwork. Severe air pressure tends to occur at eaves on a roof particularly in the case of projecting eaves used in conjunction with a low pitch. It is especially important to seal the edges of flat roof coverings to prevent wind entering below. BRE Digest 99, 101 and 105 are concerned with wind loading on buildings and BSCP 3 Chapter V part 2, should be studied.

4 **Fire protection** For England and Wales (excluding the GLC area) the Building Regulations 1976 include structural fire precautions for roofs in Part E. For Scotland the Building Standards (Scotland) (Consolidation) Regulations 1971 include structural fire precautions for roofs. BS 476 Part III:1975 *External fire exposure roof tests* lays down procedures which result in the consideration of the potential fire hazard of roof coverings and supporting systems by their effectiveness in withstanding *external* fire penetration and surface spread of flame. Under earlier editions of this BS, particular forms of roofing systems were designated by two letters — A to D for external fire penetration, and A to D for external surface spread of flame. Certain combinations óf these two letters then decided the permissible

proximity of a building and its roof to a boundary or adjoining buildings in order to avoid the spread of a fire. This designation system is still recognised in the clauses and "deemed-to-satisfy" methods in the present Building Regulation 1976. For example, roofing systems designated AA, AB or AC may immediately adjoin boundaries, whereas roofing systems designated BA, BB or BC must be placed no less than 6,000 mm from boundaries.

However, BS 476:Part 3:1975 has modified the designations, firstly to avoid confusion with the surface spread of flame test characteristics associated with wall and ceiling linings, but also to give actual performance data. The modified designations are P60, P30, P15 and P5: they relate to precise *groups* of the previous two letter designations and reference should be made directly to the BS for clarification.

5 **Thermal Insulation**   *The Building Regulations 1976 Part F* specify that the *maximum* thermal transmittance value, for roofs of houses, flats, and maisonettes should be 0.6 $W/m^2°C$. *Part FF* of these Regulations (*The Building [First Amendment] Regulations 1978* – in force from June 1979) specify the same maximum value for the roofs of other types of buildings, except for factories and storage purposes only. The maximum value for these will be 0.7.$W/m^2°C$.

Thermal insulation may be provided in the roof in one of four ways as follows:

(a)   A layer of insulating material, external to the roof structure but placed immediately below the roof covering. In the case of slates or tiles this could be an insulating quilt laid over the rafters. Flat roof insulation can be an insulating board placed immediately beneath the water-proof covering, and with a vapour barrier below.

(b)   Slabs of weighted insulation material placed externally to the *whole* roof construction including the impervious roof covering. Following German examples, this *'inverted roof'* principle is becoming increasingly used in the UK. Properly executed, it has the advantages of ensuring minimal thermal stressed in both the roof structure and its covering.

(c)   Insulation may be obtained by means of the resistance of the construction of the roof sub-structure. In respect of a flat roof, this would be in the form of a self-insulated roof deck and is an economic form of construction because one material performs both the function of support to the roof surface. and some of the insulation.

(d)   An insulating lining beneath the structure. This type of construction may sometimes be advantageous when rapid changes of interior temperature are expected. A vapour barrier is necessary to prevent condensation within the roof and roofing system.

The most common method of construction is where the insulation is external to the roof structure but immediately beneath the roof covering as described in (a)

(i)   It insulates the structure and thus reduces stress due to temperature change.

(ii)   It can be fully continuous and will thus eliminate cold spots in the construction.

(iii)   It can control condensation by keeping all the construction including its internal surface warm and above the dew point. The necessity for vapour barriers is discussed more fully later.

(iv)   The insulation is simpler and conveniently supported by the structure itself without additional suspension.

6 **Condensation** The atmosphere contains water in the form of water vapour but the amount varies according to the temperature and the humidity. The temperature at which air is saturated is called *dew point* and warm air is able to contain more water vapour than cold air before it becomes saturated. Thus if air containing a given amount of water vapour is cooled there will be a temperature at which condensation of the water vapour into water droplets will occur. Surface condensation occurs when moisture laden air comes into contact with a surface which is at a temperature below the *dew point* of the air. In respect of roof construction surface condensation can be avoided by keeping the internal surface at a temperature above the *dew point* of the

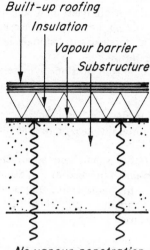

Built-up roofing

Insulation

Vapour barrier

Substructure

No vapour penetration
No surface condensation

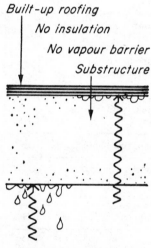

Built-up roofing

No insulation

No vapour barrier

Substructure

Vapour penetration
Surface condensation

6   *Vapour barrier*

internal air. This is done by insulation. Surface condensation can also be avoided by reducing the amount of moist air within the building or within the roof space. This is done by ventilation, and the combination of ventilation and insulation is the best way of preventing surface condensation. The recommended rate of ventilation is 300 mm^2 per 300 mm length of eaves for roof up to 20° pitch.

Where internal environments are warm and humid, the difference in the vapour pressure of the internal atmosphere and the cold external atmosphere may be such that the warm water vapour will move into and through the roof structure towards the coldest side and condense within the roof thickness. This form of condensation is known as *Interstitial condensation*. Where this type of condensation occurs the water will most likely cause the structure to deteriorate, and also part of the moisure may drip back into the building. In such cases a vapour barrier is necessary to prevent this vapour movement and the barrier should be positioned at a point where the temperature remains above the *dew point* of the vapour. The most suitable practical position is to place the vapour barrier on the warmer side of the insulation, since it would also stop the insulation from becoming saturated by condensation and thereby losing its effectiveness. This is illustrated in figure 6. In general terms it is advisable that where moisture sensitive materials are used for roof decking they should be sealed on all surfaces if they are to maintain stability in cases where condensation is likely.

7   **Cost**   In calculating the cost in use of roof covering the cost of maintenance and periodical renewal must be taken into account. Although roof coverings can be replaced and repaired with less disturbance than most other parts of the structure failure will usually involve costly damage to the fabric and its contents. From a study cost analysis on various projects the water proofing element of a flat roofed building represents on an 1.5% of the total cost per unit floor area. This figure applies to water-proofing in respect of built-up felt roofings and similar materials.

SYSTEMS OF CONSTRUCTION

Roof pitches and falls

The roof shape will determine the range of materials from which the choice can be made for the roof finish. The basic form of the roof will either be *flat* or *pitched* or *curved*. Roofs having a fall of less than 10 degrees are technically termed *flat roofs*, and suitable materials for finishes are felt, asphalt and sheet metals such as copper or zinc. These materials will also be suitable for curved roof shapes. For pitched roofs, materials which overlap each other such as slates and tiles or corrugated metal or asbestos cement are also suitable. A material which will be satisfactory on a shallow pitch, or flat roof will also be adequate on a steeper pitch. Modification of flat and sloping roof covering techniques can also be used as cladding for vertical surfaces, eg tiling, slating, and metal sheeting. BS 2717:1965 *Glossary of terms applicable to roof coverings* is a useful reference. Slates or tiles used on pitched roofs need only be supported at intervals by means of battens. Materials such as built-up felt and copper, or jointless materials such as asphalt normally used on flat roofs require continuous overall support in the form of a roof deck.

Roof pitch is the angle of slope to the horizontal. For the normal (symmetrical two slope) pitched roof form shown in figure 7, the pitch can be expressed as rise/span. This method of expressing roof pitch as a fraction for conventional pitched roofs is given, because the relationship of rise to span is more easily used information for setting out on site. Note however that most trade literature in respect of pitched roofing materials indicates roof pitch as the angle of slope.

The minimum pitch at which a material can be laid depends on many factors such as exposure to wind and weather, workmanship, design and type of joints in the roofing, porosity of the roof covering material and its tendency to laminate in frost, and the size of the unit.

As an example for two slope symmetrical roofs, slates laid to an angle of $33\frac{1}{3}°$ would have a pitch of rise/span = 1/3.

Roof fall for 'flat' roofs is expressed as the rise in a stated horizontal distance or run, as illustrated in figure 7.

For flat roofs, asphalt laid at an angle of $\frac{3}{4}°$ would have a 'fall' expressed as 1 in 80 or 12:1000. Table 32 gives the more commonly used coverings related to the minimum pitches and falls at which they should be used.

Roof covering	Angle	Min. pitch	Rise in 1000 mm run
Asphalt: Lead and Copper (with drips)	$\frac{3}{4}°$	—	12 mm
Built up bitumen felt: Zinc (with drips)	1°	—	17 mm
Corrugated asbestos cement sheeting with sealed end laps	10°	1/11	180 mm
Copper and zinc (with welted end seams)	$13\frac{3}{4}°$	1/8	250 mm
Interlocking concrete tiles	$17\frac{1}{2}°$	1/6	333 mm
Corrugated asbestos cement sheeting with 150 mm end laps	$22\frac{1}{2}°$	1/5	400 mm
Slates: min. 300 mm wide	$26\frac{1}{2}°$	1/4	500 mm
Slates: min. 225 mm wide Single lap tiles	$33\frac{1}{3}°$	1/3	670 mm
	35°	1/2·8	715 mm
Plain tiles—concrete —clay	35°	1/2·8	715 mm
	40°	1/2·4	830 mm

Table 32   Pitches and falls

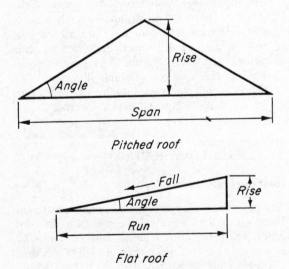

Pitched roof

Flat roof

7   'Pitch' and 'fall'

Roof decking

There are two basic forms which the sub-structure or deck can take, as follows:

(i) *In-situ monolithic* such as reinforced concrete slab   or

(ii) *prefabricated decking and panel units* ranging from thin pre-cast concrete slabs, metal and asbestos cement decking units, to timber and man-made boards such as compressed straw and wood wool.

An in-situ monolithic deck should be designed and constructed so that it does not break-up or crack in a manner which will affect the roof covering. This may be achieved by providing suitable joints. Precise specification and careful site supervision is essential. Screeds which are used to provide falls or insulation should have adequate strength so that they do not cause stresses which will affect the roof covering. It is advisable not to place a vapour barrier underneath water based *insulating* screeds as this will seal any residual moisture content against the impermeable roof covering. The provision of temporary weep holes through the supporting slab will allow this residual moisture to drain away during the remaining construction period, and the provision of strategically placed roof ventilators will avoid the dangers of subsequent interstitial condensation which would otherwise be avoided by the vapour barrier. As an alternative, bitumen coated insulating screed can be used *with* a vapour barrier as these do not use water in their formation.

In-situ or reinforced concrete must be well cured and dry. The surface should be hard and smooth and clean without irregularities and preferably wood floated. Where it would otherwise be of open texture, it must be floated or screeded. Adequate crack control methods including movement joints must be provided in the sub-structure. Lightweight aggregates may be used in in-situ concrete. The types generally in use are either prepared from manufactured materials such as foamed slag, expanded vermiculite, or expanded clay. Lightweight concrete should comply with requirements for ordinary concrete in respect of condition of surface. The water content should be kept to a minimum and sufficient time must be allowed for any water to dry out or disperse. The porous nature and high residual water content of lightweight concrete make it essential to take special precautions to disperse this trapped water so that it does not disrupt the roof finish. The more commonly used prefabricated decking and panel units are listed below.

Pre-cast including pre-stressed concrete beams or slabs

Where this type of structural unit is used for a flat roof deck a 1:4 cement and sand screed of at least 25 mm thick is required. Drainage holes should be provided to prevent water being trapped in the construction after laying.

Lightweight concrete slabs

Where this type of slab is laid carefully a cement/sand screed may not be required. A bitumen emulsion primer should however be applied to the top surface of the slabs as soon as possible after erection to prevent absorption of rainwater.

Asbestos cement

This roof decking is subject to movement due to change of temperature and moisture content. Great care should be taken in fixing to accommodate differential deflection. The hollow decking units are designed to accommodate supplementary insulation, say in the form of a glass fibre quilt or alternatively the asbestos decking can be covered with 12 mm wood fibre insulating boards in panels 1200 mm by 600 mm laid with staggered joints and bonded to the asbestos cement decking with hot bitumen compound.

Metal decking

This form of construction is suitable for both flat and pitched roofs and is usually laid complete with insulation and built-up felt waterproofing as a composite roof construction by specialist sub-contractors. The decking may be of galvanized steel or aluminium formed by a continuous rolled process in a variety of profiles and gauges to suit most span and load requirements. Fibre insulation board, polystyrene, cork or other materials are used in sheet form to give any required insulation value. This insulation is protected by a bituminous felt vapour barrier where necessary. The decking units are fixed by hook bolts or shot firing to the steel supporting structure; the vapour barrier is bonded to the top surface of the metal decking followed by the insulating boards.

129

Timber boarding

The whole of the timber sub-structure should be constructed in accordance with BSCP 112 *Constructional use of timber in buildings*. The construction should minimize the effects of shrinkage, warping and displacement or relative movement of the timber and care should be taken to guard against all conditions which might allow decay through moisture already present in unseasoned timber or resulting from the ingress of water from other parts of the structure or from condensation. To avoid dry rot, ventilation should be provided between roof boarding and the ceiling. BSCP 144: *Roof coverings* stresses the importance of ventilation in roof spaces to avoid fungal growth. Roof boarding should be well seasoned to avoid the tendency to shrink and cup. It should not be less than 25 mm thick and 100 mm wide and should be tongued and grooved. Arrises should be rounded, upstanding edges planed down and nail heads well sunk. The supporting roof construction should be rigid with joists at maximum 450 mm centres and the board fixed by nails at each edge to minimize the risk of curling. Boarding should be laid either in the direction of the fall of the roof or diagonally, and the roof surface should be protected as far as possible from rain during the course of construction.

Plywood

It is essential to supply sufficient support to the plywood and there should be noggin pieces between the joists at sheet edges. Nailing should be at 150 mm centres and at all edges and at intermediate supports. Rafter centres and nail length, according to plywood thickness, are set out below:

Plywood thickness	Rafter centres	Nail length
8 mm	400 mm	38 mm
12 mm	600 mm	38 mm
16 mm	800 mm	50 mm
19 mm	1200 mm	50 mm

Wood-wool slabs

These should be the heavy duty type of slab fixed according to the manufacturers' instructions by clips or screwing to timber joists or steel purlins. The joints between the slabs should be filled with sand and cement and the slab should be topped with a 1:4 sand and cement screed 12 mm thick in bays not exceeding 9 m^2. On roof slopes of more than 20 degrees the screed may be omitted and a sand and cement slurry used instead. Where wood wool units are fixed direct to roof support the span should not exceed 600 mm and the bearing surface at the edge of each unit should not be less than 50 mm and fixed securely at every bearing point. Wood-wool slab units of this nature are usually 50 mm thick and it is important that once fixed, they are temporarily protected by crawling boards to avoid the danger of fracture or collapse under point-loads which could occur during subsequent operations involved in providing the roof covering. To avoid the use of crawling boards, a wood-wool slab unit is available which incorporates a plastic 'safety-net' reinforcement.

Galvanised mild steel channel reinforced wood-wool units must be used for increased loading and/or span requirements. These vary in thickness from 50 mm to 100 mm and span up to 4000 mm: trough section reinforced units capable of spanning 6000 mm are also available.

Note should be taken of the risk of condensation due to the direct conductivity of the steel reinforcing channels, and in order to counteract this, thick slabs are available rebated at the joints to receive inserts to achieve continuity of insulation at each joint. Pre-screeded and pre-felted wood wool slabs are also available. The felt is a protective layer only and does not form part of a built-up felt system. The joints of this type of wood wool slab should be taped immediately the slabs are laid to prevent moisture infiltration.

Compressed straw slabs

These must be of roofing quality which means that they are covered on the external face with an impregnated liner making the unit shower proof for short periods. Each edge of all the units must be fully supported and fixed in accordance with the manufacturer's instructions. Straw board slabs should not be laid unless they can be covered (eg with built-up felt roofing) the same day. A sand and cement screed is not required but instead the joints are taped with strips of roofing felt bonded with hot bitumen compound before the first layer of felt is applied. Thus close co-ordination is essential during the fixing of the deck units and the application of the weather proofing and for this reason it is good practice to allow the deck and built-up roofing to be supplied and fixed by the specialist roofing sub-contractor.

Chipboard

Ordinary chipboard loses strength permanently if it is wet, and moisture resistant quality must be used. BS 5669:1979.

This should be nailed to the joists and to noggins to support all edges. It is recommended that joints be taped with strips of roofing felt bonded with hot bitumen before the first layer of felt is applied. Chipboard does not in itself provide sufficient insulation and should be used in conjunction with an insulating quilt placed over the joists.

Non-structural bases

Insulation boards

Vegetable fibre boards which include those made from wood or cane fibres of natural or regranulated cork, are suitable provided that they are adequately supported. As in the case of timber, care should be taken to guard against decay, particularly through moisture. Where this type of board is laid on concrete or similar materials and where there will be moisture vapour diffusion from within the building a vapour barrier is essential. Mineral fibre and granular boards include those made from glass or mineral fibres, mica or similar granules compressed and bonded with bitumen, synthetic resin or other meterial. When used with metal decking joints in the board must not be made over the trough of the deck or the board will collapse under normal maintenance traffic. Extruded polystyrene is now a commonly used non-structural board and for all practical purposes is vapour proof if the joints are sealed. A vapour barrier can be omitted except in conditions of a very high humidity, eg as found in a laundry.

Wood boards, particle boards, wood-wool slabs and compressed straw slabs, fibre building boards, foamed plastic board are described in *MBS:Materials*. Lightweight concrete for screeds is also described in the *Materials* volume.

Screeds

Mention has been made of the necessity to screed certain decks to provide a smooth surface upon which to lay the roof waterproofing. The selection of a suitable mix and thickness of screed is very

important and whilst the mix mu... that of the sub-structure concret... screed should not be richer than 1 pa... parts sand by volume. They should be ... cement ratio and laid in areas not exce... even if they are reinforced. The minimu... should be 25 mm except where they a... topping on wood-wool slabs when the ... thickness can be reduced to 13 mm. Ad... insulation can be provided by using a ligh... concrete screed but in such cases entrapped... is always a problem and if allowed to remain... seriously reduce the thermal insulation value of... screed and may cause blistering of the roof fin... where built-up felt, asphalt or single layer roofi... is used. It is customary to provide a topping o... 12 mm of sand cement immediately after light-weight concrete has been laid — this provides a surface which will shed water to pre-arranged temporary drainage holes in the roof structure. These drainage holes should pass through the screed and the roof deck at the lowest part of the roof and be positioned in any depression where water collects. The problems that may arise where water is trapped in a screed are more fully discussed on page 139.

ROOFING MATERIALS

Mastic asphalt

Mastic asphalt is a mixture of several materials and is prescribed for various purposes such as roofing, flooring and tanking by a series of British Standard Specifications. The specifications relevant to asphalt for roofing are as follows. BS 1162 *Mastic asphalt for roofing (natural rock asphalt aggregate)*; BS 988 *Mastic asphalt for roofing (limestone agregate)*. Where the roof is liable to be used by vehicular traffic say for car parking, the British Standards are BS 1446 *Mastic asphalt (natural rock aggregate) for roads and footways* and BS 1447 *Mastic asphalt (limestone aggregate) for roads and footways*. As will be seen from the British Standards, asphalt consists of an asphaltic cement and an aggregate. The asphaltic cement will consist of bitumen from petroleum distillation or a blend of this bitumen with Trinidad Lake Asphalt. The choice is then between rock asphalt from Switzerland, France or Sicily which is a limestone naturally impregnated with about 6% bitumen or a natural ordinary crushed limestone. Mastic asphalt produced from the natural rock asphalt is lighter in colour but is about one-third more expensive than the crushed limestone material. The British Standards permit alternative percentages of Trinidad Lake asphalt which may be incorporated in the asphaltic cement. These are specified in BS 988 as Table III, columns 1, 2 and 3 and in BS 1162 as Table II, columns 1 and 2. The specifier should thus indicate which composition of asphaltic cement is required in accordance with the British Standards. The Code of Practice CP 144: *Roof coverings* Part 4 *Mastic asphalt* requires the use of black sheathing felt to BS 747 type 4A (i) as an isolating membrane under the asphalt. *Black sheathing felt* is available with either a bitumen or a pitch saturant. On wet construction decks the bitumen impregnated type must be employed whilst on decks of dry construction either the bitumen or the pitch impregnated type may be used.

Roofing asphalt can be used either to form a continuous waterproof covering over either, flat, pitched or curved surfaces and can be easily worked round pipes, roof lights and other roof projections. It can be laid on most types of rigid sub-structure such as concrete either precast or in situ, timber boarding or a variety of proprietary structural deck units.

Durability

Mastic asphalt when laid by a good specialist roofing sub-contractor on a sound base will not require major repairs for at least 60 years. When repairs are required they should always be carried out by a specialist. Eventually, exposed mastic asphalt is broken down by acids in the atmosphere and by ultra-violet radiation. So a special surfacing such as stone chippings, greatly increase the durability of the covering. Special surfacing is also necessary where there will be pedestrian or vehicular traffic.

Mastic asphalt is a dense material and being a very dark colour the uncovered material absorbs the heat very readily and especially where insulation is laid below the asphalt. To counteract this, a wide range of chippings is available for applying to the surface of asphalt roofing to give a high degree of reflection. Various coloured granites, white limestone, calcined flint and white spar usually in sizes up to 13 mm are the most widely used. Reflec-

tive chippings are suitable for use on roofs up to 10 degree pitch. They are embedded in a layer of bitumen dressing compound to form a textured surface.

Thermal insulation

For general comments on thermal insulation standards for roofs see page 126. Table 33 indicates forms of construction [A-F] and the nearest *readily available* thicknesses of various insulation boards (1-3) which each give a 'U' value within the Building Regulations 1976 and the Building (First Amendment) Regulations 1978 mandatory maximum of $0.6W/m^2°C$. The Table allows for top surface chippings on 20 mm mastic asphalt and black sheathing felt — the effects of a vapour barrier beneath the insulation quoted has also been allowed for but *not* the effects of an applied ceiling.

It should be remembered that insulation within the roof construction leads to a reduction in temperature variations in the roof structure, thereby minimizing thermal movement.

Vapour barrier

It is necessary to provide a vapour barrier on the warmest side of the insulation. The vapour barrier may consist of a layer of roofing felt with sealed laps but the best type incorporates an impermeable metal foil. A good example of a proprietary vapour barrier supplied by specialist asphalt contractors consists of a sheet of aluminium foil protected by a coating of bitumen on both sides and reinforced with a sheet of glass fibre tissue. The vapour barrier should be folded back at least 225 mm over the outer edges of the insulating layer and the asphalt roofing bonded to the overlap as shown in figure 8.

Fire resistance

Asphalt for roofing achieves the designation AA under the test requirements of BS 476 Part 3 *External fire exposure roof tests*. See also page 125 for general comments.

Application of asphalt

In-situ concrete, precast concrete beams and slabs, wood-wool slabs, timber construction, asbestos cavity decking, compressed strawboard and metal decking are all suitable methods of construction for the sub-structure upon which asphalt may be laid.

	Sub-structure	Insulation		
A	150 mm solid concrete slab or 125 mm hollow precast concrete beams with 25 mm sand/cement structural screed.	1 2 3	30 polyurethane board 75 mm cork board 69 mm fibre insulation board (2 x 25 mm and 1 x 9 mm boards laminated)[1]	
B	50 mm wood-wool slabs with 13 mm sand/cement screed.	1 2 3	20 mm polyurethane board 38 mm cork board 50 mm fibre insulation board (2 x 25 mm boards laminated)[1]	
C	50 mm compressed straw boards	1 2 3	20 mm polyurethane board 38 mm cork board 44 mm fibre insulation board (1 x 25 mm and 1 x 19 mm boards laminated)[1]	
D	25 mm flax board	1 2 3	25 mm polyurethane board 50 mm cork board 57 mm fibre insulation board (1 x 25 mm and 1 x 19 mm and 1 x 13 mm boards laminated)[1]	
E	25 mm deal boards	1 2 3	25 mm polyurethane board 75 mm cork board 63 mm fibre insulation board (2 x 25 mm and 1 x 13 mm boards laminated)[1]	
F	Metal decking	1 2 3	30 mm polyurethane board 75 mm cork board 69 mm fibre insulation board (2 x 25 mm and 1 x 19 mm boards laminated).[1]	

Table 33   Mastic asphalt covered flat roofs having U values not exceeding $0.6 W/m^2 °C$

[1] flame resistant type

In all cases the sub-structure must be strong enough to prevent excessive deflection. And in particular where metal decking is used the deflection limit must be reduced 1/325 of the span instead of the more normal 1/240. For timber, flax board, plywood, strawboard or metal decking a timber kerb on which expanded metal is fixed as a key for asphalt, is required at walls. An air space between the wall and kerb allows for movement as shown in figure 8.

Timber rolls, similar to those shown in figure 22 are required to prevent water being blown over verges. With a sub-structure formed of wood wool, strawboard, timber or plywood, provision must be made for ventilation between the roof deck and the ceiling. The sub-structure on which the asphalt is to be laid should ensure the rapid dispersal of rainwater, and so provide falls not less that 1 in 80. Any change in

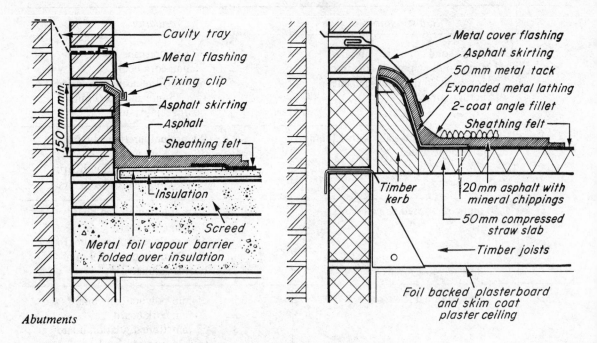

Abutments

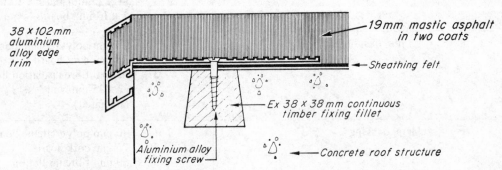

Aluminium verge trim for small roofs

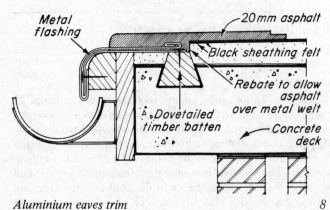

Aluminium eaves trim

8 *Asphalt details: abutments, eaves and verge*

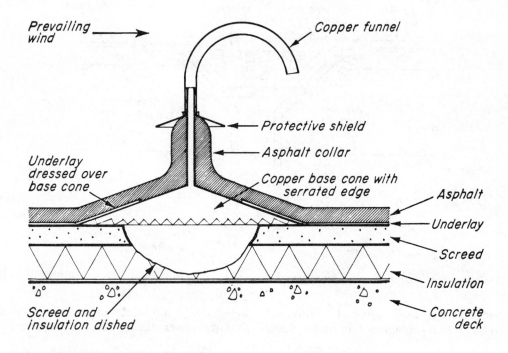

Prevailing wind

Copper funnel

Protective shield

Asphalt collar

Copper base cone with serrated edge

Underlay dressed over base cone

Asphalt

Underlay

Screed

Insulation

Concrete deck

Screed and insulation dished

9   'Parovent' copper ventilator

the direction of the roof surface in buildings shaped as letter T or L indicates the need for movement joints should be continuous through the entire structure, including roof, walls and upstands, as shown in figure 13, which is similar in one of those illustrated for built-up felt roofing in figure 26.

To assist in drying out screeds used in connection with concrete decks and to release trapped moisture, it is good practice to install drying vents. A proprietary example is shown in figure 9.

On flat roofs and roofs up to 30 degrees pitch the roofing asphalt is laid with a wooden float in two coats breaking joint to a minimum thickness of 20 mm on an underlay of black *sheathing felt* laid loose with 50 mm lapped joints. The asphalt surface should be dressed with reflective mineral chippings to reduce the temperature induced by solar heat and to protect it from UV radiation and fire. On flat roofs and foot traffic the asphalt should be laid in two coats to a minimum total thickness of 25 mm. On slopes of over 30 degrees the asphalt is applied without sheathing felt in three coats, the first coat being applied very thinly with a steel trowel. The second and third coats are then applied breaking

joint to give a total thickness of not less than 20 mm. Where the asphalt is laid on vertical or sloping surfaces of more than 30 degrees a positive key is required. In the case of sloping surfaces over 10 degrees formed in timber boarding a layer of black sheathing felt is nailed to the timber boards and bitumen coated expanded metal lathing is then fixed at 150 mm centres with galvanized clout nails or staples to form the key for the asphalt which is then applied in three coats. In all cases where the asphalt is laid on flat or slightly sloping roofs, clean sharp sand is rubbed evenly over the surface of the asphalt whilst it is still hot. This breaks up the skin of the bitumen brought to the surface by the wooden float at the time of application. The object of this is to minimize the gradual crazing of the surface due to the action of the sun.

Details at abutments and edges are shown in the drawings as follows: figure 8 Abutments, eaves and verge; figure 10 Cast iron outlet with grille; figure 11 an alternative type of outlet made from gun metal or spun steel which has a domed grating and a clamping device which allows the grating to be tightened against the waterproofing; figure 12

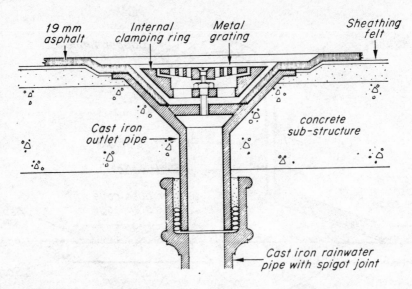

10   Asphalt details: cast iron rainwater outlet for balcony

Projections through roof; figure 13 Movement joint. Where there is continuous foot traffic, mastic asphalt can be protected with concrete, asbestos or glass fibre-cement tiles or with a jointed screed.

(a) *Concrete or asbestos cement tiles*   Concrete tiles are approximately 300 mm x 300 mm x 25 mm thick, asbestos cement tiles are also 300 mm x 300 mm but usually available in two thicknesses 25 mm and 8 mm. They are lighter than the concrete tiles and thus can be used where weight is an important consideration. The tiles are laid in bays of maximum 9 m^2 with 25 mm joints between the bays which are filled with bitumen compound. The tiles are set 25 mm back from the base of angle fillets and the margin is completed with bitumen compound. A bitumen primer is applied to the surface of the mastic asphalt roof covering and to the backs of the tiles and allowed to dry. The tiles are then bedded in hot bitumen bonding compound, taking care not to squeeze the compound upwards between the individual tiles.

(b) *Jointed screed.*   A cement and sand screed 25 mm thick is laid on a separating membrane of building paper and grooved into a 600 mm square tiled pattern. The screed should be laid in bays of not more than 9 m^2 with a 25 mm joint between the bays. The grooves and joints can be filled with hot bitumen compound on completion.

11   Asphalt details: spun steel rainwater outlet

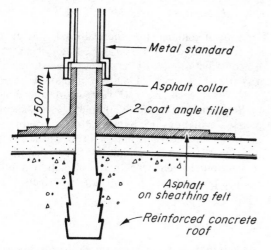

Asphalt finish to metal standard

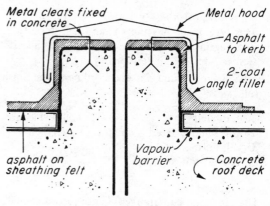

Twin kerb expansion joint

13   Asphalt: movement joint

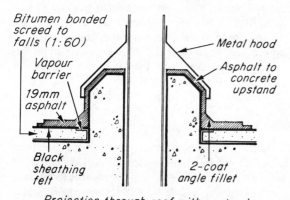

Projection through roof with upstand

12   Asphalt: projections through roof

Bitumen felt roofing

('Built-up' roofing)

Terms

The following terms are commonly used in connection with multi-layer sheet roofing.

(i)   *Built-up roofing*   two or more layers of bitumen roofing fused together on site with bitumen compound. For flat roofs, three layer specifications are recommended, and for pitched roofs, two layers are usual.

(ii)   *Roof sub-structure*   the element of a building on which built-up roofing is directly laid.

(iii) *Vapour barrier*   a special material interposed between roof surface and the insulation to prevent transmission of moisture or moisture vapour into the insulation. See page 127.

(iv) *Layer*   a single thickness of bitumen roofing. The word *ply* is not synonymous with layer but is a term sometimes used to denote the thickness of the bitumen sheet.

(v)   *Under-layer*   an unexposed layer in built-up roofing.

(vi) *Cap-sheet*, an exposed or final layer in built-up roofing.

(vii)*Movement joint*   break or joint in the roof substructure where relative movement of the elements of the structure would otherwise affect the roof covering. The movement may be caused by moisture changes, thermal changes, loadings or subsidence.

Materials

BS 747 is the *Specification for Roofing Felts*. There are three main types used in built-up felt roofing as detailed below.

BS Class 1 *Bitumen felt (fibre base)*

This material has great flexibility and is used extensively in specifications which are generally lowest in cost.

BS Class 2 *Bitumen felt (asbestos base)*

The asbestos base is relatively inert and provides improved fire resistance.

137

BS Class 3 *Bitumen felt (glass fibre base)*

This type of felt has high dimensional stability, is proof against decay and is used where the Specifition calls for the highest quality.

The BS subdivides the classes according to the finish as follows:

A saturated
B fine sand surfaced
C self finish
D coarse sand surfaced

E Mineral surfaced
G venting base
   layer

The use of the saturated felts is not recommended for the lower layers of the roof on reinforced felt, (Class F, is used as an underlayer beneath slates or tiles, over rafters).

Each type of felt is further subdivided according to its weight per 11 m $\times$ 0.9 m roll. The heavier felts are normally used as a top layer and thus taking into account the different types, finishes and weights available, the specifier has a wide choice. The Felt Roofing Contractors Advisory Board, list 18 sample Specifications for typical conditions in their Booklet *Built-up Roofing* which is a very good reference.

It is usual to use a protective finish on the top layer of built-up felt roofing to give a reflective finish and protect the bitumen from sunlight or to provide a wearing surface. Stone chippings 10 mm to 13 mm size are often used bedded in bitumen and there is a wide range of types, Derbyshire, White Spar and Leicester Red granite being examples. If the roof is to withstand foot traffic the spar finish will not be suitable because of the danger of the sharp granules cutting the felt. Thus for promenade roofs concrete grc or asbestos tiles should be used.

In general, for roofs not taking foot traffic (except for maintenance) the main area will be stone chippings; edges and upstands will be in mineral surfaced felt and gutters in self finished felt.

Durability

Successful built-up felt roofing is dependent on the correct specification for each situation. Good materials, careful detailing and correct application are all necessary and so since supervision is difficult the contract should be carried out by a specialist contractor experienced in this type of work.

Thermal insulation

For general comments on thermal insulation standards for roofs see page 126. Table 34 indicates forms of construction [A-F] and the nearest *readily available* thicknesses of various insulation boards [1-3] which each give a 'U' valve within the Building Regulation 1976 and the Building [First Amendment] Regulations 1978 mandatory maximum of 0.6 W/m^2 °C. The Table allows for top surface chippings on three layers of built up felt — the effects of a vapour barrier beneath the insulation quoted has also been allowed for but *not* the effects of an applied ceiling.

Vapour barrier

Condensation is liable to occur on the internal surfaces of a roof construction within a building if the temperature and humidity of the air inside is appreciably higher than the outside temperature and humidity. Thus a vapour barrier will be required on the underside of the insulating layer below the built-up roofing. The barrier should incorporate an impermeable metal foil, and the type and application detailed in the notes on asphalt, page 132, is suitable for use with built-up felt roofing.

Fire resistance

External fire designations for various weatherproofing specifications are set out in the 'deemed to satisfy' section of The Building Standards (Scotland) (Consolidation) Regulations 1971, and The Building Regulations 1976 for England and Wales. See also page 125.

Where stone chippings are used as topping all felt flat roofs have the highest AA BS 476 Part 3 fire rating. On pitched roofs the rating varies according to the type of felt in each layer and the combustibility of the roof deck. Asbestos felt has the best fire resistance and most Local Authorities require its use.

Application of built-up felt roofing

Hollow precast concrete beams or slabs, in-situ concrete, aerated concrete, wood wool slabs, compressed straw slabs, timber construction or asbestos cement or metal decking are all suitable roof decking for built-up felt roofing. The use of these materials is more fully discussed on page 128. All built-up felt roofing should be carried out in accordance with the

	Sub-structure		Insulation
A	150 mm solid concrete slab *or* 125 mm hollow precast concrete beams with 25 mm sand/cement structural screed	1 2 3	30 mm polurethane board 75 mm cork board 69 mm fibre insulation board (2 x 25 mm and 1 x 19 mm boards laminated).[1]
B	50 mm wood-wool slabs with 13 mm sand/cement screed.	1 2 3	20 mm polyurethane board 50 mm cork board 50 mm fibre insulation board (2 x 25 mm boards laminated.)[1]
C	50 mm compressed straw boards	1 2 3	20 mm polyurethane board 38 mm cork board 44 mm fibre insulation board (1 x 25 mm and 1 x 19 mm laminated.)[1]
D	25 mm flax board	1 2 3	25 mm polyurethane board 50 mm cork board 57 mm fibre insulation board (1 x 25 mm and 1 x 19 mm and 1 x 13 mm boards laminated.)[1]
E	25 mm deal boards	1 2 3	25 mm polyurethane boards 75 mm cork board 63 mm fibre insulation board (2 x 25 mm and 1 x 13 mm boards laminated.)[1]
F	Metal deck	1 2 3	30 mm polyurethane board 75 mm cork board 75 mm fibre insulation board (3 x 25 mm boards laminated).[1]

Table 34   Built-up felt covered flat roofs having maximum U values not exceeding $0.6W/m^2{}^\circ C$

[1] flame resistant type

requirements of CP 144 Part 3 1970 *Built-up bitumen felt*. It is necessary to provide falls to clear the water from a flat roof and a minimum of 17 mm in 1000 mm is recommended (1 degree slope). The first layer of roofing felt is fixed by nailing, or by full bonding or by partial bonding according to the nature of the sub-structure. Partial bonding to the deck prevents the formation of blisters in the waterproof due to vapour pressure, and gives a measure of freedom of movement between the roof deck and covering.

BRE Digest 51 *Developments in roofing* discusses at length the problem of water vapour in the roof deck, particularly in connection with lightweight screeds. The sources of screed moisture are as follows

(i)   mixing water
(ii) rain water during the drying out period and
(iii) condensation formed within the building.

The effect of a saturated screed is as follows

(i)   diminished thermal insulation

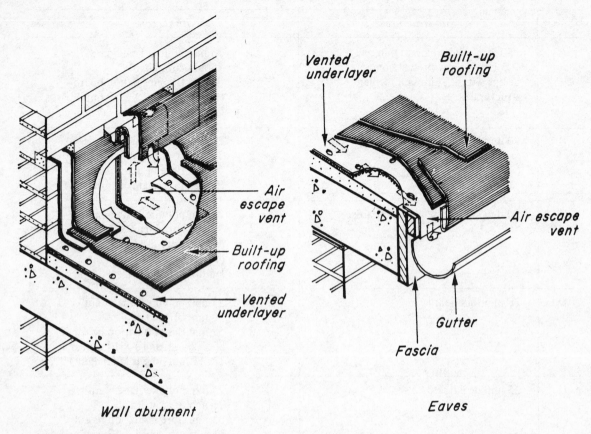

Wall abutment

Eaves

14   Water vapour release: vented underlay

(ii) blistering and damage to water-proofing by vapour pressure

(iii) staining of internal decoration.

Experiments at the Building Research Station with an exposed aerated screed found that after four wet days and with subsequent shielding from further rain complete drying out needed 36 good summer days or 180 winter days. Research and long observation has revealed that nearly all roof blisters are caused by the entrapping of constructional moisture in the roof deck. Solar heat vapourises this moisture and causes considerable pressure which weakens the bond between the roofing layers and the roof substructure. Ventilation of the roof deck, below built-up felt roofing, can be obtained in several ways:

(i) *deliberately isolating the first layer of felt* by means of uniform granules on the underside. This first layer is of perforated glass fibre felt laid dry on the sub-structure and the bonding bitumen of the upper layer penetrates the perforations automatically to give 10% bonding. Precautions must be taken to release pressure through special vents at eaves and abutments as shown in figure 14. The specially prepared base sheet is known as a *vented underlayer* or *venting base layer*.

(ii) *partial bonding* or *frame bonding* where provision must be made for the release of pressure by the installation of special perimeter details. Figure 15 shows typical patterns of partial bonding. Partial bonding, or vented underlay must always be used on a screeded finish; a vented underlay is in fact recommended for most roof decks (except timber boarding) due to the possibility of moisture being trapped during construction.

(iii) *installing proprietary plastics or metal breather vents* spaced in accordance with the manufacturers' instructions with various types specially designed to

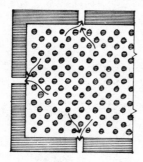

Spot sticking

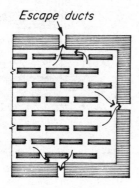

Strip sticking

15   *Watervapour release: frame bonding*

dry out wet screeds and/or to act as pressure release vents. Note that this type of ventilation is also suitable for asphalt roofing.

BSCP 144 Part I:1968 *Built-up bitumen felt* states that where roofs of timber joists with timber boards, compressed straw slabs, flax board, particle board or plywood decks are constructed so that there is a space between ceiling and deck, this space must be ventilated to the open air to avoid fungal growth. Minimum ventilation is given by 300 mm² opening per 300 mm run on two opposite sides of the building. Provision must be made for a free air path from one side to the other. Where the width of the roof between openings is greater than 12 m the size of the openings should be doubled. Vents should be preferably located in the walls rather than roof. The ceiling below a ventilated roof space should be free from gaps and holes and have no vapour permeability.

The following are three typical examples of built-up felt roofing specifications.

1   *Timber deck* – built-up roofing with chipping finish. The first layer is laid, starting at and parallel to the lower edge or eaves, at right angles to the direction of fall, and secured by large headed galvanized clout nails spaced at 50 mm centres along the laps and stagger nailing at 150 mm centres over the sheet. First layer to be self-finished asbestos base felt weighing not less than 13.6 kg per 10 m² roll. Second and third layers to be self-finished fibre base felt weighing not less than 13.6 kg per 10 m² roll continuously bonded to the first layer and to each other with bitumen compound applied hot. All layers fixed breaking joint, 50 mm side laps, 75 mm end laps. Top surfaced with 10 mm diameter stone chippings, embedded in bitumen dressing compound and laid shoulder to shoulder.

2   *Fully bonded specification* – built-up roofing with mineral surface finish. Two layers asbestos based self finish felt weighing 27.2 kg per 20 m² and one layer asbestos based mineral surfaced felt weighing 36.2 kg per 10 m². The first layer fully bonded to the deck and subsequent layers continuously bonded with hot bitumen compound. The three layers laid breaking joint. 50 mm side laps, 75 mm end laps.

3   *Vented underlay specification* – built-up roofing with mineral surface finish. First layer glass fibre based mineral surfaced vented underlay weighing 31.8 kg per 10 m² (proprietary material) fixed to the roof deck simultaneously with the second layer and to the third layer with hot bitumen compound. The two top layers to be glass fibre based felt weighing 18.1 kg per 10 m². Surfaces to be covered with approved mineral chippings. All laps 50 mm, and to run with the slope of the roof.

In view of the very many alternative specifications possible in built-up felt roofing and the various weights and types of felt available, it is advisable to take advice from the specialist contractor regarding the intended specification with regard to suitability and cost. Typical details of three-layer built-up felt roofing are shown in the following figures. Figure 16 flashing to brick parapet; figure 18 detail at

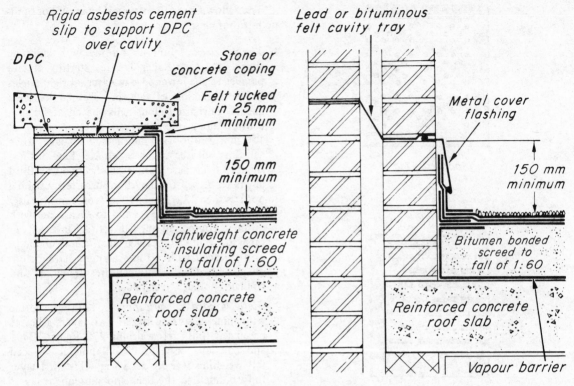

16 *Built-up felt roofing: flashing to brick parapet* 18 *Built-up felt roofing: abutment*

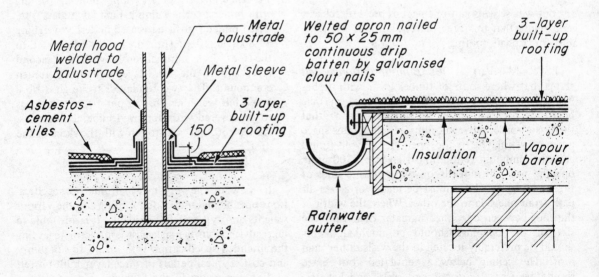

17 *Built-up felt roofing: balustrade fixing* 19 *Built-up felt roofing: welted apron to eaves*

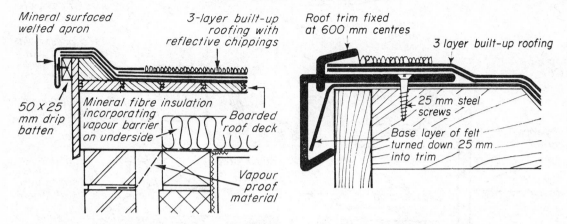

20　*Built-up felt roofing: welted apron to verge*

22　*Built-up felt roofing: grp verge trim*

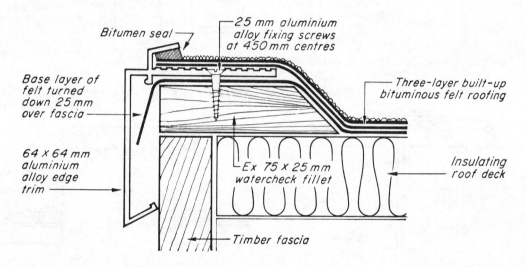

21　*Built-up felt roofing: aluminium verge trim*

abutment: figure 17 detail showing a balustrade fixing; figure 19 welted apron to eaves; figure 20 welted apron to verge.

As an alternative to the welted drip shown at the verge, aluminium trim is available in various depths and profiles to receive the built-up felt and asphalt. A typical profile is shown in figure 21. The welted drip (figure 20) is formed by nailing the felt to a timber strip and returning the felt over the roof surface lapping with the roof covering according to the direction of the fall. The depth of the apron can be varied but will not be satisfactory if it is less than 50 mm. The aluminium trim is 'built-in' to the three-layer felt system as shown, and because of the possibility of electrolytic action between steel and aluminium, it is fixed with stainless steel or aluminium alloy screws at 450 mm centres. The trim is produced in standard lengths of 3.050 m, the longer pieces are jointed by a spigot and a 3 mm gap should be left between each length to allow for expansion. A glass fibre reinforced polyester resin verge trim is shown as an alternative detail figure 22. Since there is no possibility of electrolytic action galvanized steel screws can be used for fixing. Because of the lower thermal expansion of this material, it is not necessary to leave a gap between the lengths of trim. Built-up

143

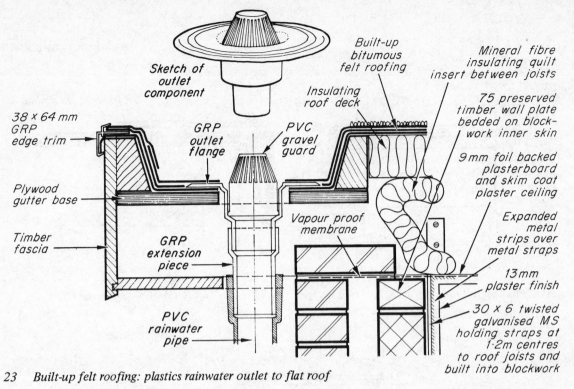

Sketch of outlet component

38 × 64 mm GRP edge trim

Built-up bitumous felt roofing

Insulating roof deck

Mineral fibre insulating quilt insert between joists

75 preserved timber wall plate bedded on blockwork inner skin

GRP outlet flange

PVC gravel guard

9 mm foil backed plasterboard and skim coat plaster ceiling

Plywood gutter base

Timber fascia

GRP extension piece

Vapour proof membrane

Expanded metal strips over metal straps

13 mm plaster finish

PVC rainwater pipe

30 × 6 twisted galvanised MS holding straps at 1·2m centres to roof joists and built into blockwork

23   *Built-up felt roofing: plastics rainwater outlet to flat roof*

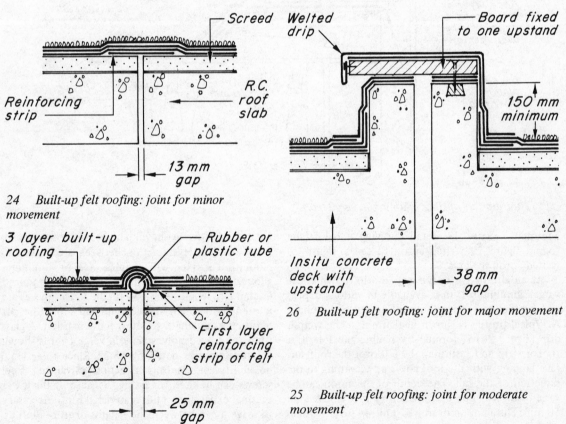

Screed

Welted drip

Board fixed to one upstand

Reinforcing strip

R.C. roof slab

150 mm minimum

13 mm gap

24   *Built-up felt roofing: joint for minor movement*

3 layer built-up roofing

Rubber or plastic tube

First layer reinforcing strip of felt

Insitu concrete deck with upstand

38 mm gap

25 mm gap

26   *Built-up felt roofing: joint for major movement*

25   *Built-up felt roofing: joint for moderate movement*

felt roofing will often be detailed to incorporate an internal or *secret gutter*. A typical detail incorporating a plastics outlet component is shown in figure 23.

In order to prevent the failure of the roofing due to movement in the structure it is necessary to incorporate joints in the roof finish which will accommodate relative movement, figures 24, 25 and 26 illustrate suitable joints for minor, moderate and major movement respectively.

Single layer sheeting

Bitumen/asbestos

A proprietary sheet roofing composed of asbestos and bitumen is available, manufactured by the Nuralite Co Ltd. The material is applied in a one-layer technique and is laid either as roll-cap roofing, a 'twin-rib' system, or factory bonded to flaxboard, wood chipboard or plywood decking.

The roll-cap technique is a method of laying standard 2438 mm x 914 mm sheets to near flat or pitched roofs having a minimum fall of 17 mm per 1 m. The technique can be used on steeper pitches up to vertical. The finished appearance resembles the roll technique as used for zinc, copper, lead or aluminium. The laying is carried out in accordance with CP 143 Part 8 1970. The roof has drips at 2300 mm across the slope and 32 mm x 44 mm wood rolls at 840 mm apart down the slope.

The 'twin-rib' system is an application of the standard sheets to near flat or pitched roofs having a minimum fall of 12 mm in 1 m, up to vertical. The edges of the sheets are jointed impermeable by heat and pressure, using prefabricated cover strips. The sheets are secured to the decking by nailing or screwing at the top and through the base ribs and the centres of sheets secured by adhesive.

Prefabricated cover flashings and other roofing components are manufactured for use in conjunction with the sheets. These components are also available for use with corrugated roofing sheets, and patent glazing. The joints in the pre-fabricated 'decking' systems are made by heat welding of a jointing strip. Manufacture and site installation of the flax board 'deck' system is covered by Agrément Certificate No 69/29. Traditional *Nuralite* systems are normally fixed by the Contracting and Plumbing trades. The cost of the material compares favourably with that of other roofings of similar durability. Its appearance is initially black slowly weathering to mottled grey, and it has a thermal expansion slightly greater than copper but less than zinc or lead. The same manufacturers market the *Nuraphalte* system using 1219 mm square sheets. The sheets are 'joggled' on two adjacent sides in order to form overlap joints. The sheets are laid starting at the lowest point of the roof and arranged so that the joints are diagonal. *Nuralite* and *Nuraphalte* are guaranteed by the manufacturers for 25 years provided the materials are laid in accordance with their recommendations. CP 143 Part 8 1970 covers the recommendations for laying fully supported semi-rigid asbestos bitumen sheet roofs using the roll cap and rib systems.

Vinyl/Asbestos

This roofing material by the Marley Company is suitable for low pitched roofing (minimum fall 12 mm in 1 m). The sheeting is laid in one layer and the joints are solvent welded. It is necessary to vent roof decks where lightweight screeds are used to prevent the moisture and rain absorbed during the curing period causing the sheets to blister (as with built-up felt). Where insulation is provided immediately below the waterproof sheeting, the insulation accelerates the heat build-up from sunshine on top of the roof and so increases the vapour pressure and the need to ventilate. The roof sheeting is cold bonded to the roof and breather vents and ducts are located at 6 m centres. The technique is illustrated in figure 27.

The breather vent, abutment duct detail and verge duct detail are illustrated in figures 28, 29 and 30 respectively. *Marleydek* is covered by Agrément Certificate No. 16.

Synthetic rubber/asbestos

This is a single layer system based on Du-Pont *Hypalon* synthetic rubber, laminated with asbestos. It is marked under the trade name *Uniroof* and is covered by Agrément Certificate No 68/19. There are several other proprietary plastics membrane sheets available and manufacturers' advice should be sought regarding performance. In general the costs of plastics or elastomer sheet roofings are higher than for typical built-up bitumen felt systems.

145

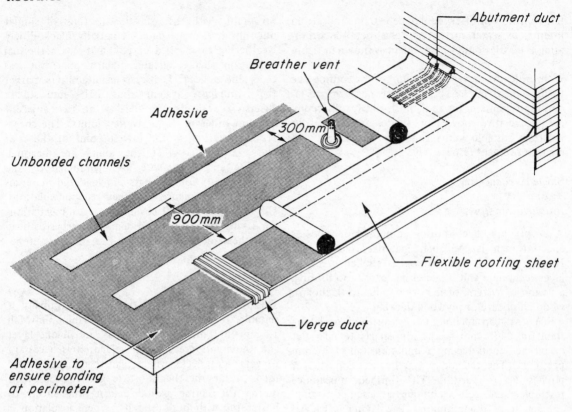

27   *Vinyl asbestos: sheet roofing*

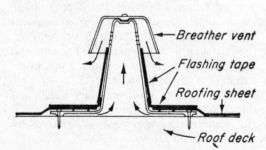

28   *Vinyl asbestos: detail of vent*

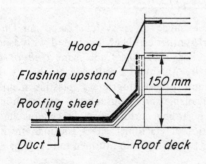

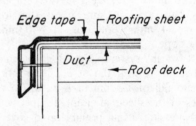

29   *Vinyl asbestos: verge duct*

Brushed or sprayed finishes

Elastomeric materials such as neoprene for brushing or spray application are known to be extremely durable but there is limited experience of their use as in situ roof coverings in this country. Advice should be obtained from the manufacturers and the materials should be laid by contractors appointed by them.

30   *Vinyl asbestos: abutment duct*

Fully supported metal sheets

Fully supported sheet metal roofing has standing seams, rolls, drips and welted joints to connect the sheets. These roof coverings are suitable provided access is restricted to maintenance personnel. For purposes such as escape in case of fire and for maintenance inspections duck boards should be provided to distribute weight evenly without restricting the flow of rainwater.

With the exception of lead, sheet metal roof coverings are much lighter than tiles and slates and differences in weight between copper, zinc and aluminium are not significant. Correctly laid lead and copper roof covering have given trouble-free protection for buildings for centuries but premature decay can result from bimetallic electrolytic action or in the presence of corrosive agents. For instance, timber such as Western Red Cedar and those treated with corrosive preservatives should not be used for the duck boards. Lead can be perforated by constant concentrated dripping of water from roofs upon which algae are growing. See *Corrosion of Metals: MBS: Materials*, chapter 9. Durability increases with the pitch of roofs and all the metal sheets can be fixed at any pitch or vertical.

Sheet metal gauges are compared in table 72, *MBS: Materials*, page 181.

Methods of fixing

The principles of fixing are the same for all sheet metals. Stresses which could arise from constant thermal movements will cause fatigue and should be minimized by reducing friction between the metal and the decking by providing joints at suitable centres, designed to absorb movement.. Sheet metals are laid in bays with their lengths in alignment with the fall of the roof. The sheets are turned up to form upstands against abutments and these are protected by cover flashing being taken into a raked joint in the case of brickwork or a raglet groove in the case of masonry or concrete. The cover flashing is retained by wedges and afterwards pointed. Joints in the direction of the fall are formed into rolls. Rolls with solid cores are preferable where there may be foot traffic and also on flat roofs since their greater height is an advantage. An alternative to the roll is a standing seam. Differences between the properties of the metal

determine the techniques for laying, thus lead is malleable but roofing grades of copper and aluminium are less so and zinc is relatively stiff. In consequence lead can be formed into complex shapes by bossing, copper and aluminium can be formed into standing seams and welts while details in zinc roof covering are generally restricted to simple folds, the sheets being preformed before being placed in position. Joints across the fall are formed as follows

(a) in pitches up to 5 degrees, as steps called *drips* — these are at least 50 mm high.

(b) pitches over 5 degrees, as welts

(c) for very steep pitches in lead, laps are satisfactory. Where the longitudinal joints are standing seams welts across the fall must be staggered to avoid the problem which arises if the corners of four sheets coincide.

Underlays

Underlays are required

(a) to allow free movement of the metal

(b) to prevent corrosion by screeds or timbers

(c) for sound deadening. Rain and hail can be very nosiy on copper, aluminium and zinc sheets.

Lead, copper and zinc sheets should be laid on an inodorous felt (BS 747 Type 4A (ii) Brown no. 1 inodorous felt) butt jointed and fixed with clout nails. The same felt is suitable for aluminium which is laid over timber boarding but on other bases BS 747 Type 1 C self-finished bituminous felt 13.6 kg per roll, should be used below aluminium. The underlay in this case should be laid with 75 mm laps sealed with cold bonding mastic and covered overall with waterproof building paper (BS 1521) to prevent possible adhesion between the metal and the underlay. Underlays should be dry when the roof coverings are laid, and this is particularly important in the case of inodorous felt.

Lead

This is described in CP 143 11:1970 *Sheet roof and wall coverings — lead.* The metal is discussed in *MBS: Materials,* Chapter 9. The use of this extremely durable roof covering is limited by its

147

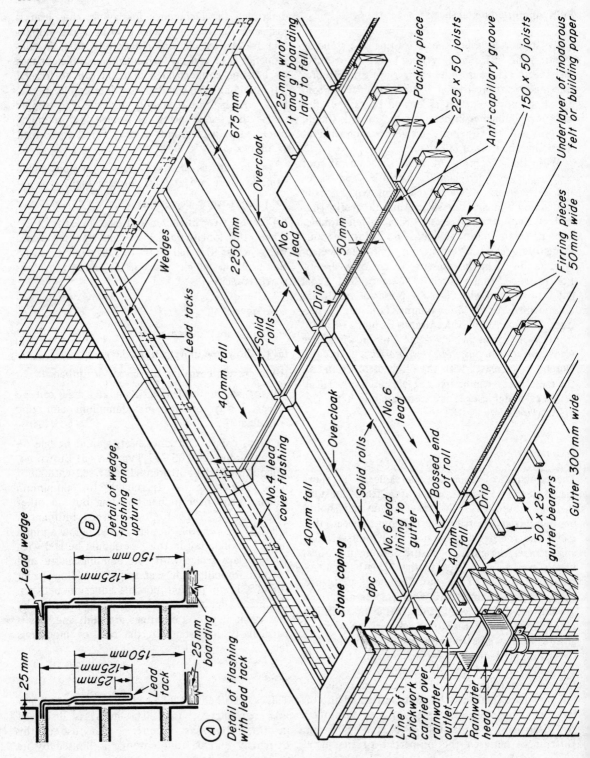

Wedges

Lead tacks

675 mm

Overcloak

25mm wrot 't and g' boarding laid to fall

Packing piece

225 x 50 joists

Anti-capillary groove

150 x 50 joists

Underlayer of inodorous felt or building paper

2250 mm

No. 6 lead

50 mm

Drip

Solid rolls

40mm fall

No.4 lead cover flashing

No. 6 lead

Overcloak

Firring pieces 50mm wide

Solid rolls

40mm fall

Stone coping

No. 6 lead lining to gutter

Bossed end of roll

Drip

50 x 25 gutter bearers

Gutter 300 mm wide

dpc

40mm fall

Line of brickwork carried over rainwater outlet

Rainwater head

Detail of wedge, flashing and upturn

Lead wedge

150 mm

125 mm

ⓑ

25 mm

150 mm

125 mm

25 mm

Lead tack

25 mm boarding

Detail of flashing with lead tack

ⓐ

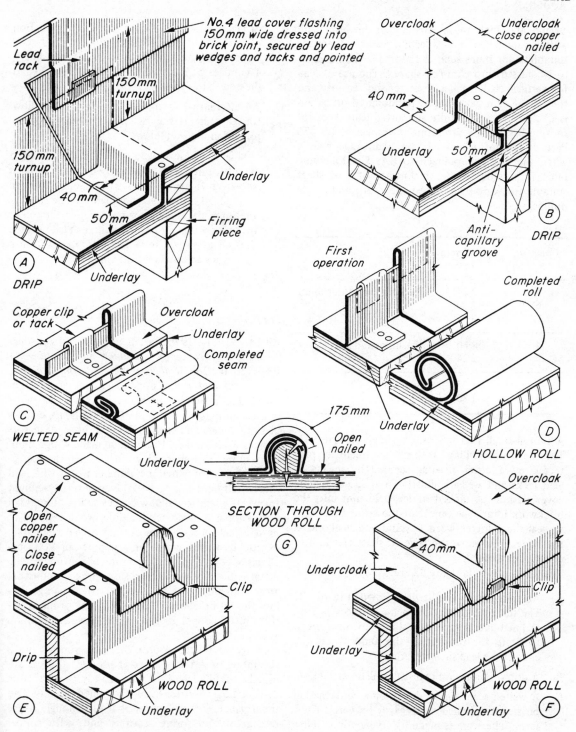

A DRIP

Lead tack

No.4 lead cover flashing 150 mm wide dressed into brick joint, secured by lead wedges and tacks and pointed

150 mm turnup

150 mm turnup

40 mm

50 mm

Underlay

Firring piece

Underlay

B DRIP

Overcloak

Undercloak close copper nailed

40 mm

Underlay

50 mm

Anti-capillary groove

C WELTED SEAM

Copper clip or tack

Overcloak

Underlay

Completed seam

D HOLLOW ROLL

First operation

Completed roll

Underlay

Anti-capillary groove

175 mm

Open nailed

Underlay

G SECTION THROUGH WOOD ROLL

E WOOD ROLL

Open copper nailed

Close nailed

Clip

Drip

Underlay

F WOOD ROLL

Overcloak

40mm

Undercloak

Clip

Underlay

Underlay

32   Joints used in lead roofing

weight and high initial cost. It is however still widely valued for its malleability and consequent suitability for items such as flashings which require to be bossed into complex shapes. The use of lead for vertical cladding has been revived recently and the use of thin gauge metal premounted on panels is likely to increase. Fully supported lead sheet for roofing has an AA fire rating in respect of BS 476 Part 3[1] except where laid on plain edge boards when the rating is reduced to BA. The following table is a guide to the thicknesses of lead sheet suitable for various uses, and the appropriate code number.

Code No	Thickness mm	Use
5	2·24	Roofing and gutter lining
6	2·50	
7	3·15	
4	1·80	Flashings and lead 'slates'
5	2·24	
3	1·25	Soakers
4	1·80	

A typical small lead flat roof is shown in figure 31. The upstand flashing at each abutment is protected by a cover flashing secured by means of lead tacks and wedges, illustrated at A and B. The cover flashing is tucked at least 25 mm into the brickwork joint. The object of the cover flashing is to seal the joint between upstand and wall and at the same time, allow the covered sheet freedom to contract or expand.

The joints shown in figure 32 are:

A   An enlargement of the drip shown in figure 31. The flat roof consists of plane surfaces slightly inclined and separated by low steps or *drips* to facilitate the run off at the joints where the ends of the lead sheets overlap.

B   A drip with a groove to resist capillary attraction.

C   A welted seam for a joint running with the fall on steeply pitched surfaces or on vertical surfaces. The seam is made by fixing copper clips

or tacks at about 600 mm centres at the junction of the sheets. The clips should be 'dead soft' temper and cut from 24swg (0.559 mm sheet). The edges of the sheets are then turned up and dressed flat as shown.

D   An alternative to the welted seam is a hollow roll of lead. It was extensively used on steep pitches in old buildings.

E, F and G   These show a solid roll, made over a wood former. This joint is used on flat roofs as shown in figure 31 or as a ridge joint. Wooden rolls of 38 mm to 50 mm diameter are fixed at the joint either by screwing through the roll or by using a double headed nail. The lead is then dressed as shown in G being formed well into the angles to obtain a firm joint.

Copper

CP 143:Part 12 1970 (metric units) describes *Sheet roof and wall coverings – copper:* and the relevant BS is 2870:1968 *Rolled copper and copper alloys, sheet strip and foil.* Copper is strong in tension, tough, ductile and in suitable tempers it is malleable, but has negligible creep. See *MBS: Materials,* chapter 9. Roof sheets and flashings should be in dead soft temper. Welts and folds should be made with a minimum number of sharp blows rather than the succession of taps with which the plumber works with lead sheet. Half-hard temper metal is sometimes required for weatherings to window frames and copings. Like lead, copper is extremely durable. When exposed to most atmospheres a thin coating of basic sulphate of copper forms which in a number of years becomes green. This coating protects the underlying metal from continuing corrosion—even in industrial areas. Copper is not attacked by other metals. Fixings should be copper. The coefficient of linear expansion of copper is less than for lead, aluminium and zinc.

Fully supported copper sheet for roofing has a fire rating of AA in respect of BS 476[1]. Sheets are usually supplied in 1.22 x 61 m, 1.83 x 0.91 m or 2.44 x 1.22 m sizes. Strip is supplied in coils. The usual gauge is 0.559 mm (24 swg) although a very satisfactory pre-formed roofing unit, with copper sheet, factory bonded to 50 mm compressed straw-board or 25 mm chipboard uses embossed copper

[1] See page 125.

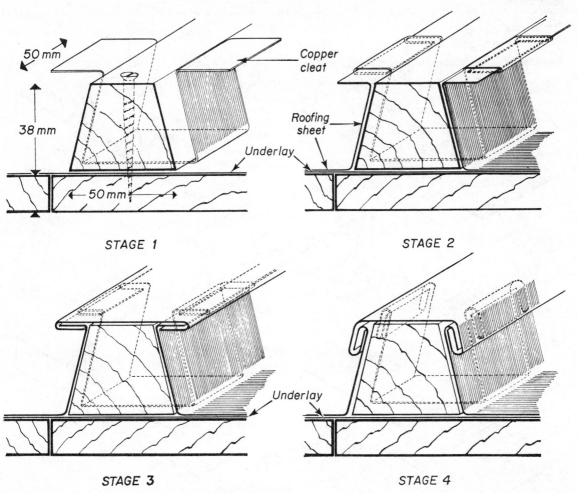

50 mm

38 mm

50 mm

Copper
cleat

Roofing
sheet

Underlay

STAGE 1

STAGE 2

Underlay

STAGE 3

STAGE 4

33   *Copper roofing: batten roll*

sheet of 0.315 mm (30 swg).

Timber decking upon which copper roofing is to be laid should be free from 'spring', tongued and grooved 25 mm minimum thickness. Heads of nails should be punched in, and the boarding laid either diagonally or in the direction of fall. Other dry decking materials are suitable provided that they are dimensionally stable. Concrete decks should be screeded, and preferably sealed with a coat of bitumen

It is necessary to use an underlay of impregnated flax (inodorous) felt, whatever the decking material. The underlay is secured to timber decks by cooper nails and laid butt jointed. The underlay lessens the possibility of 'wearing' the copper as it expands and contracts, and deadens the drumming sound of rain. The minimum fall for copper roofing is 12 mm in 1 m (1 in 80), and drips 63 mm deep, spaced not more than 3 m apart should be used in roofs of 5 degree pitch or lower.

There are two traditional methods of forming the longitudinal joints in copper roofing: 1 the *standing seam*, and 2 the *batten* or *wood roll*.

1   *Standing seam*   The three processes in the formation of a standing seam in copper are shown in figure 34.

2   *Wood roll*   This method uses timber battens to form a shaped wooden core against which the

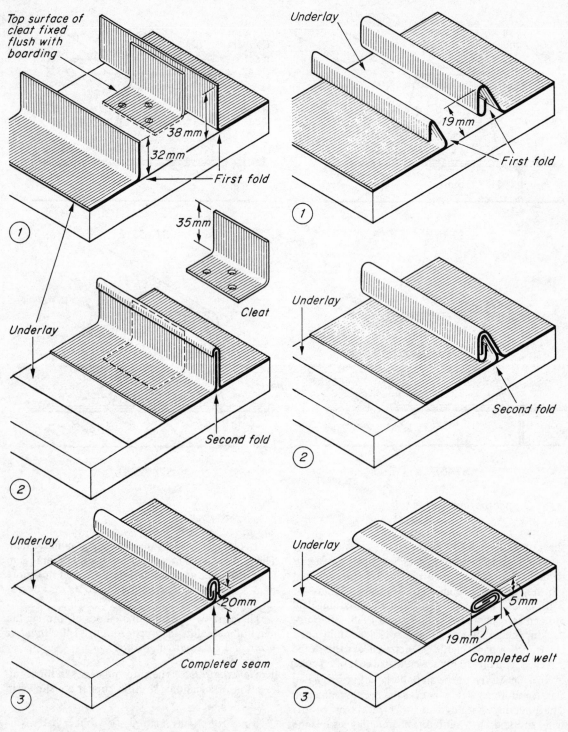

Top surface of
cleat fixed
flush with
boarding

38 mm

32 mm

First fold

①

35 mm

Cleat

Underlay

Second fold

②

Underlay

20 mm

Completed seam

③

Underlay

19 mm

First fold

①

Underlay

Second fold

②

Underlay

5 mm

19 mm

Completed welt

③

34   *Copper roofing: standing seam*

35   *Copper roofing: welted joint*

edges of the sheet are turned up. A prepared capping strip is then welted to the flanges. The timber battens are screwed to the decking and the roof sheeting is secured to the battens by means of 50 mm wide copper strips. The four stages in the formation of a batten roll are shown in figure 33.

Transverse joints in each case are formed by double lock cross welts (or for very flat roofs — drips). The formation of a double-lock cross welt is shown in figure 35 and the application of the standing seam method is shown in figure 36. *Long strip 'economy' roofing* can be used where the total distance between eaves and ridge does not exceed 8.5 m. Expansion cleats in the standing seam joint allow movement over this length.

A proprietary roofing material utilizes an indented copper sheet (42 gauge) backed with bitumen and laid as a top layer of built-up felt roofing on an underlayer of asbestos or glass fibre based bitumen felt. This copper/bitumen roofing gives the appearance of traditional copper at less cost.

Zinc

CP 143:Part 5 describes *Zinc sheet Roof and Wall Coverings.* The metal is considered in *MBS: Materials*, chapter 9. The minimum thickness of zinc sheet for roofing should not be less than 0.78 mm. In average urban conditions the maintenance-free life of zinc roofing conforming to the CP should not be less than 40 years for a roof laid to the minimum fall of 1 in 80 (approx. 1°). In rural areas or by the sea, and with steeper pitches, the life will be longer. Zinc is attacked by acids and water must not be allowed to drain from Western Red Cedar shingles on to a zinc roof, nor should drainage from copper pipes discharge on to zinc. The coefficient of thermal expansion of zinc is greater than that of copper, but slightly less than lead. Standard sizes of zinc sheet are 2400 mm and 210 mm x 920 mm and as continuous strip in widths of up to 1 m. Zinc provides one of the lightest roof coverings which although less durable than lead or copper has the lowest first cost. Zinc sheet for roofing has a fire rating AA in respect of BS 476[1]. Typical details of a flat roof covered in zinc sheet are shown in figure 37. The formation of the batten roll is shown at A

[1] See page 125.

and the treatment of the sheeting at the junction of a drip and roll is shown at B. Detail C shows the formation of a 'dog ear' at an internal corner and a detail of a holding down clip is hsown at D. Saddle pieces are formed on the ends of cappings at walls and drips as shown at E and where a roof abuts the wall at a drip, a corner piece is welted to the upper sheet as shown at F.

Aluminium

Since aluminium forms a protective oxide when exposed to the atmosphere the alloy used for roofing is normally extremely durable even in industrial and marine atmospheres. Precautions must however be taken to avoid a galvanic attack with other materials and aluminium should be protected from wet concrete and mortar. timbers containing acid and preservatives are also dangerous to the sheeting. Fully supported aluminium sheet for roofing has a fire rating AA in respect of BS 476. The techniques of laying aluminium fully supported roof coverings are similar to those of copper, see CP 143 Part 15: 1973 *Sheet roof and wall coverings: aluminium*, which sould be consulted for detailed information. Aluminium sheet for roofing should comply with BS 1470:1972 *Wrought aluminium and aluminium alloys for general engineering purposes — sheet and strip*. Aluminium is the lightest of roofing metals — it has ample strength and ductivity and creep is not significant. Hand forming is easiest in soft temper and high purity metal. It has a high reflectivity to solar heat. The durability of high purity aluminium is good in normal atmospheres provided it is washed by rain. However, it must not be used in contact with copper or copper alloys.

Fixings should be preferably of aluminium but where steel is used it should be galvanized. Water must not be allowed to drain on to aluminium from copper roofing and particularly not from copper expansion pipes.

Corrugated sheet roofing

Asbestos cement sheet

Asbestos cement is described in *MBS: Materials*, chapter 10. A comprehensive range of asbestos coment components in the form of corrugated sheets and accessories are available for use in the covering of pitched roofs. Although complex roof

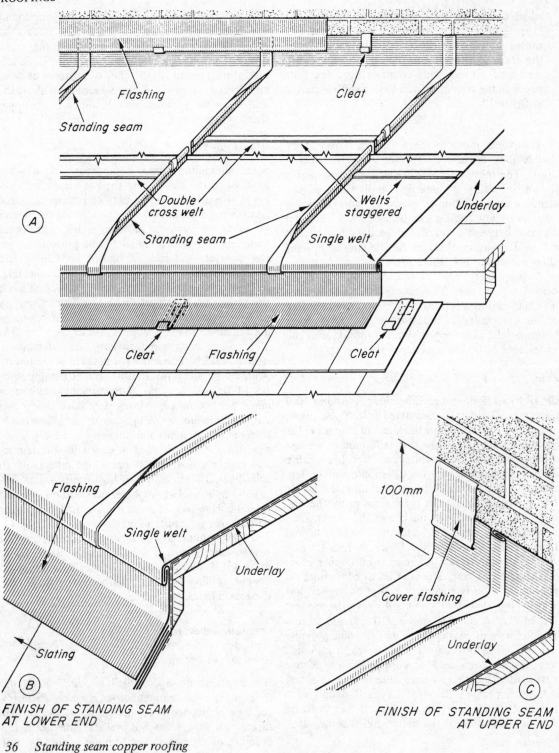

Flashing

Standing seam

Ⓐ

Double cross welt

Standing seam

Welts staggered

Single welt

Underlay

Cleat

Flashing

Cleat

Flashing

Single welt

Underlay

Slating

Ⓑ

FINISH OF STANDING SEAM
AT LOWER END

100 mm

Cover flashing

Underlay

Ⓒ

FINISH OF STANDING SEAM
AT UPPER END

36   Standing seam copper roofing

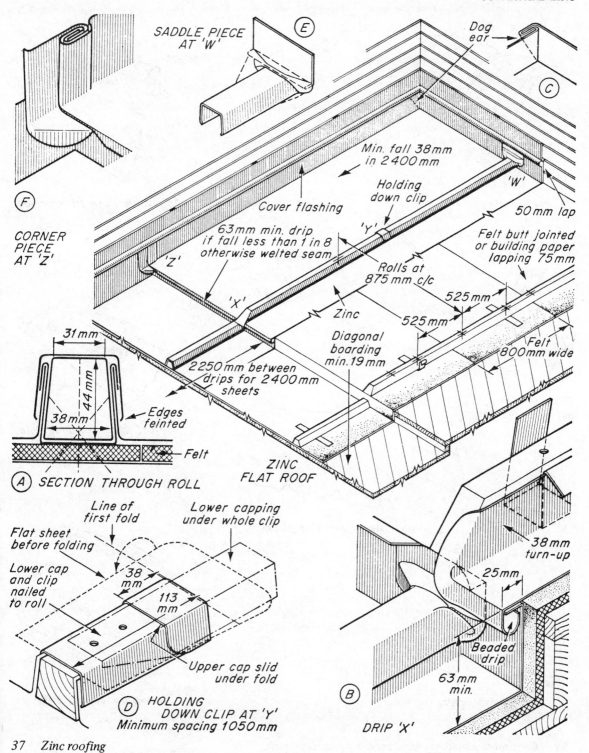

SADDLE PIECE AT 'W'

E

Dog ear

C

F

CORNER PIECE AT 'Z'

Min. fall 38mm in 2400mm

Cover flashing

Holding down clip

'W'

50 mm lap

63mm min. drip if fall less than 1 in 8 otherwise welted seam

'Y'

Felt butt jointed or building paper lapping 75mm

'Z'

'X'

Rolls at 875 mm c/c

525mm

Zinc

525mm

Felt 800mm wide

31mm

44mm

Diagonal boarding min.19mm

2250mm between drips for 2400mm sheets

38mm

Edges feinted

Felt

A SECTION THROUGH ROLL

ZINC FLAT ROOF

Line of first fold

Lower capping under whole clip

Flat sheet before folding

Lower cap and clip nailed to roll

38 mm

113 mm

Upper cap slid under fold

D HOLDING DOWN CLIP AT 'Y'
Minimum spacing 1050mm

38mm turn-up

25mm

Beaded drip

63 mm min.

B DRIP 'X'

37   Zinc roofing

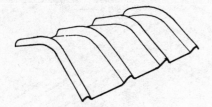

Cranked crown sheet

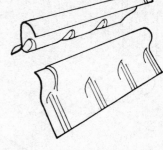

Adjustable close-fitting ridge

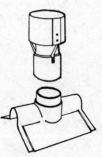

Ridge soaker with
extractor ventilator

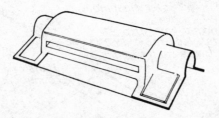

Ridge ventilator

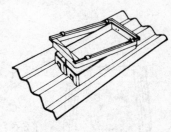

Roof light – opening type

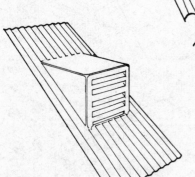

Dormer ventilator

Apron flashing piece

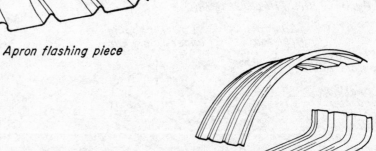

Curved and curved-end tiles

38   Corrugated asbestos cement sheet roofing: accessories

BS profile class		Min/max lengths	Roof pitch	Maximum purlin centres:mm
1	5·5 mm 25 mm 102 mm lap ⊢648 mm net cover⊣ ⊢750 mm nominal width⊣	1225 to 3050	10° min	925
2	6·0 mm 54 mm 70 mm lap 146 mm nominal 1016 mm net cover 1086 mm nominal width	1525 to 3050	10° min	1375
3	6·0 mm 51 mm 76 mm lap 339 mm 339 mm 1016 mm net cover 1092 mm nominal width	1525 to 3050	10° min	1375
4	6·0 mm 80 mm 90 mm lap 250 mm 250 mm 1000 mm net cover 1090 mm nominal width	1675 to 3650	4° min	1800
5	9·0 mm 83 mm 90 mm lap 250 mm 250 mm 1000 mm net cover 1090 mm nominal width	1825 to 3650	4° min	1975

39   *Corrugated asbestos cement sheet roofing: profiles*

shapes can be covered by asbestos cement sheets, maximum economy is achieved where the roof is simple in plan shape. The roof should also be planned so that the purlin spacing allows the use of standard sheets without cutting to waste. Figure 38 gives an idea of the range of accessories available for use with standard profile sheets. Note that certain of the roof ventilators have integral soaker flanges and so dispense with the need of separate flashings. BS 690: Part 3:1973, the relevant British Standard, separates the sheeting for roofing and vertical cladding into five profile classes according to depth and minimum loadbearing capacity. Fittings are detailed in BS 690: Part 6: 1976. Figure 39 gives a range of the more commonly used profiles for roof sheeting. Metal fixing accessories are covered by BS 1494:1967 Part I *Fixings for sheet roof and wall coverings.* Asbestos cement sheets may be coloured by factory applied processing in a range of subdued colours giving a high resistance to fading. Profiled translucent sheeting

made from glass fibre reinforced polyester-resin, and transparent sheets from rigid pvc are manufactured for use with the various asbestos cement resin, and transparent sheets from rigid pvc are factured for use with the various asbestos cement sheet sections to give a natural diffused daylighting, and are available clear, or in a range of colours. The thermal transmittance (U) through a single layer of unlined asbestos cement roof sheeting is approximately 6.1 W/m² deg C, so it is not acceptable under the current Building Regulations for dwellings. See page 126. A method of insulating asbestos cement roofs which satisfies the Regulations, and which does not require the use of additional supporting members, is to incorporate a top corrugated sheet with an associated lining panel of asbestos cement. BS 690 Part 5:1975 is relevant to lining sheets and panels. The cavity between the two layers of asbestos cement accommodates an additional insulant in the form of a glass fibre or mineral wool mat 60 mm thick which improves the insulation value of the structure and at the same time restricts the flow of free air circulating within the cavity. This system of construction thus improves insulation and helps to provide a reasonable dust tight covering. Several types of sandwich construction are available and two typical profiles are illustrated in figure 40. However, insulated double cladding can also be arranged with asbestos cement or timber spacer pieces fixed between the lining panels and corrugated sheets as indicated in figure 41. This method avoids compression of the insulation infill by the superimposed weight of the top sheeting

BS profile class		Thermal insulation 'U' approx.	
		Sandwich (25mm glass fibre insulant)	Single skin
2		1·00 W/m² deg C	6·1 W/m² deg C
3		1·00 W/m² deg C	6·1 W/m² deg C

40   Corrugated asbestos cement sheet roofing: insulated double cladding profiles

Thermal insulation ('U' valve) for quilt thickness

60mm	80mm	100mm
0·55	0·46	0·41

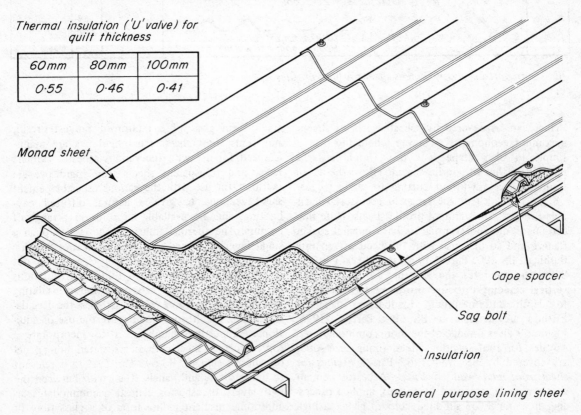

Monad sheet

Cape spacer

Sag bolt

Insulation

General purpose lining sheet

41   Corrugated asbestos cement sheet roofing: insulated double cladding profile 2 (improved)

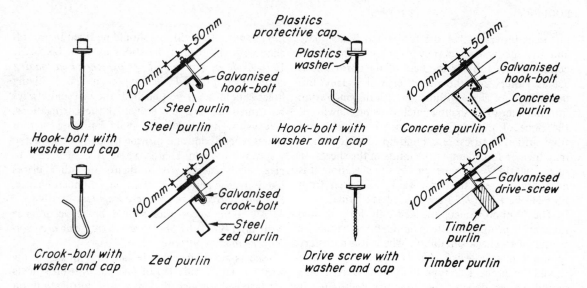

42   Corrugated asbestos cement sheet roofing: purlin fixings

and thereby provides a further improved U value. The mandatory U values of 0.6 or 0.7 W/m²°C for roofs of non-domestic buildings (see page 126), makes it will be essential to use spacers in sandwich construction. Figure 41 indicates that the U value has been improved from 1.0 to 0.55 W/m²°C and by increasing the insulation mat thickness to 80 mm or 100 mm, the U values become 0.46 and 0.41 W/m²°C respectively.

Where is is considered necessary to provide insulated natural lighting panels in conjunction with the insulated roofing, hermetically sealed insulated rooflights or translucent lining panels are available. As an alternative to sandwich construction satisfactory thermal insulation can be obtained by 'under drawing' or lining the roof above or below the purlin by suitable rigid sheet of insulation material such as fibre building board or plasterboard which incorporates insulation.

Fixing for asbestos cement sheeting should not be rigid since allowance must be made for slight movement. Usual fixings are various types of hook bolts which pass through the asbestos sheet and clip round steel or concrete purlins, or drive screws into timber purlins or timber plugs in concrete purlins as shown in figure 42. In order to accommodate movement and render the detail weathertight a plastic washer with a separate dome shaped cap-seal is used, as shown in figure 43. Alternatively galvanized steel or bitumen washers are available. The minimum pitch of the roof will vary according to the profile of the sheet and the degree of exposure of the site. Sheets are designed to provide resistance to the penetration of rain at end and side laps with-

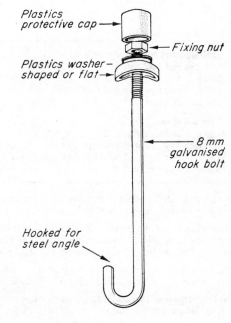

43   Detail of hook bolt

159

out seals provided that the roof pitch is adequate and the site is not severely exposed. Where such conditions are fulfilled the base of the corrugations act as gutters and the rainwater will usually run down the roof slope without the risk of penetration into the interior. A shallow pitch or wind blowing at the slope of the roof may reduce the velocity of flow sufficient to cause a build-up of water which may then be forced under the joints in the sheets. In such conditions, or to prevent dust penetration, it is necessary to seal the laps. Table 35 taken from BS 5247:Part 14 1973 may be used as a guide.

The 4° pitch is recommended only for a limited number of profiles and the manufacturers should be consulted to check suitability. Where it is necessary to use a mastic seal 8 mm extruded mastic strip should be used. The type and method of laying should be as directed by the manufacturers. It should be borne in mind however that the efficiency of the seal can be affected by the temperature at which it is laid and it is recommended that a routine check be made on the compression of mastic laid during winter months.

Laying procedure Sheets should be fixed in accordance with the recommendations made in BS 5473: 1976 *Code of Practice of performance and loading criteria for profiled sheeting in building*. Fixing holes should never be punched, they should always be drilled through the crown of the corrugations. Always use roof ladders to avoid damaging the roof sheets when fixing and provide properly constructed walkways or roof boards where it is necessary to give regular access to rooflights or other places likely to need periodical attention, and maintenance. See *Safety Health and Welfare Regulations* 1948.

All fixing accessories should be in accordance with BS 1494:1967 *Specification of fixing accessories for building purposes Part I*.

Sheets are designed to be laid smooth side to the weather with a side lap of one corrugation. Sheets are fastened through the crowns of corrugations on each side of the side laps except at each intermediate purlin where one fixing only on the overlapping side is adequate. The laying procedure is shown in figure 44. Working upwards from the eaves sheets may be laid either from left to right, or right to left, but it

Lap treatment*	Minimum sheet pitch†	
	Profile class 3 and 4 BS 690 : Part 3	Profile class 1 and 2 BS 690 : Part 3
(a) **Sheltered and normal sites**‡		
150 mm end laps unsealed	22½°	22½°
300 mm end laps unsealed	15°	15°
150 mm end laps with end laps sealed	15°	10°
150 mm end laps with side end laps sealed	10°	4°
(b) **Exposed sites**		
150 mm end laps unsealed	25°	25°
150 mm end laps with end laps sealed	17½°	15°
150 mm end laps with side and end laps sealed	15°	10°
300 mm end laps with side and end laps sealed	10°	4°

* The table should be used as a guide for roof slopes up to 32 m in length. For recommendations for roof slopes over 32 m in length, the manufacturer's advice should be sought.

† Pitches detailed above are the minimum for the sheeting as laid, therefore it is important that the pitch of the rafter is designed to take into account the lapping of the sheeting including mastic (which reduces the pitch by ½° for unsealed laps and by 1° for sealed laps) and the deflection of the supporting structure due to live and dead loads.

‡ The degree of exposure to be taken for design purposes is a matter of experience coupled with local knowledge, and the above table should be regarded as a guide. In case of doubt the advice of the manufacturer should be sought.

For the purpose of this table, an exposed site is one where the wind suction on any part of the roof cladding exceeds 1200 N/m^2 when calculated in accordance with CP 3 : Chapter V : Part 2.

Table 35B. Minimum sheet pitches and corresponding lap treatments

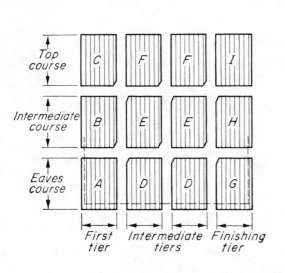

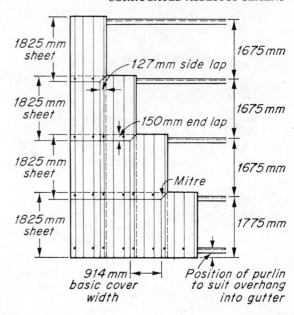

44   Corrugated asbestos cement sheet roofing: laying procedure

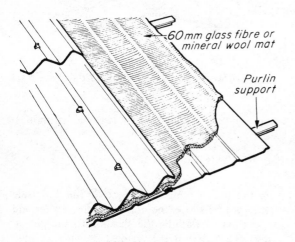

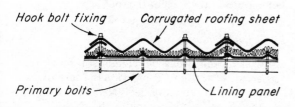

45   Corrugated asbestos cement sheet roofing: laying procedure

is advisable to commence at the end away from the prevailing wind. The starter sheet and the last sheet to be fixed are laid unmitred; all other sheets require mitring where the overlap occurs as shown.

With insulated double cladding the fixing procedure is similar. The lining panels are first laid mitred as for the roofing sheets except that they are laid smooth side to the underside. The sheets are secured with a short bolt through the intermediate corrugation. Lining panels are then overlaid with a glass fibre or mineral wool insulating mat which should have a minimum 100 mm lap to all joints. The laying of the final covering sheet then proceeds as before. A typical double cladding unit is shown in figure 45. Figure 46 shows a typical roof sheeting arrangement using single skin construction suitable for a storage building where space heating is not required. Detail A shows the finish at the eaves. The sheets should not have an unsupported overhang of more than 300 mm beyond the eaves purlin and the details is completed by an eaves filler component. Details B and C show the method of construction where a translucent rooflight is used. The translucent sheet is unmitred, and 13 mm diameter sealing strips are used at the end laps. Detail D shows a close fitting ridge. Because it is in two parts, it is adjustable to suit various degrees of slope. An alternative apex

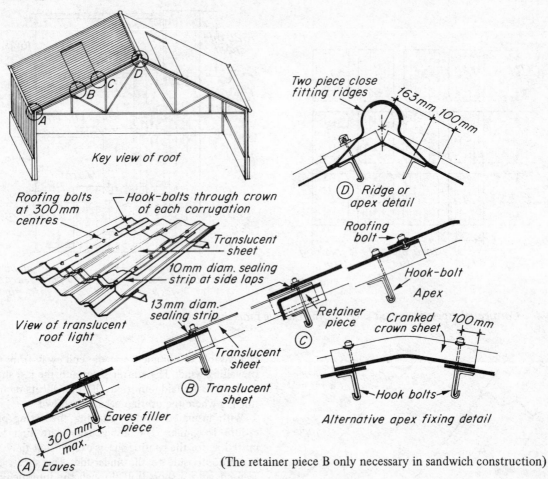

Key view of roof

Two piece close fitting ridges

163 mm   100 mm

D Ridge or apex detail

Roofing bolts at 300 mm centres

Hook-bolts through crown of each corrugation

Translucent sheet

10 mm diam. sealing strip at side laps

View of translucent roof light

Roofing bolt

Hook-bolt

Apex

13 mm diam. sealing strip

Retainer piece

Cranked crown sheet

100 mm

Translucent sheet

C

Hook bolts

Alternative apex fixing detail

B Translucent sheet

300 mm max.

Eaves filler piece

A Eaves

(The retainer piece B only necessary in sandwich construction)

46   *Corrugated asbestos cement sheet roofing: single skin construction*

detail is shown using a cranked crown sheet. The correct positioning of the top purlin is important and should be arranged so that the hook bolt fixing is not less than 100 mm from the end of the crown sheet.

Figure 47 illustrates the use of insulated double cladding. The eaves detail at A indicates the use of eaves filler pieces and a method of fixing an asbestos gutter by means of front and back plates. B shows a typical end lap detail at an intermediate purlin. Detail D is a section through the roof verge and illustrates the barge board component which provides a neat finish between the vertical cladding and roof sheeting. Details E, F and G show the method of detailing the translucent roof sheeting.

Note the use of the closure piece on the underside of the roof. H shows the use of a valley gutter and the method of flashing the sheets into the gutter. J gives the fixing of the cranked crown sheet and lining panel at the apex of the roof.

Profiled aluminium

Corrugated and troughed aluminium sheet roofings are dealt with in CP 143 Part 1. The alloy used for this type of roof covering is NS 3 H to BS 1470, and the sheets should comply with BS 4868:1972. The behaviour of aluminium when exposed to the atmosphere is discussed on page 155. Profiled sheets are available with a plain finish or with a

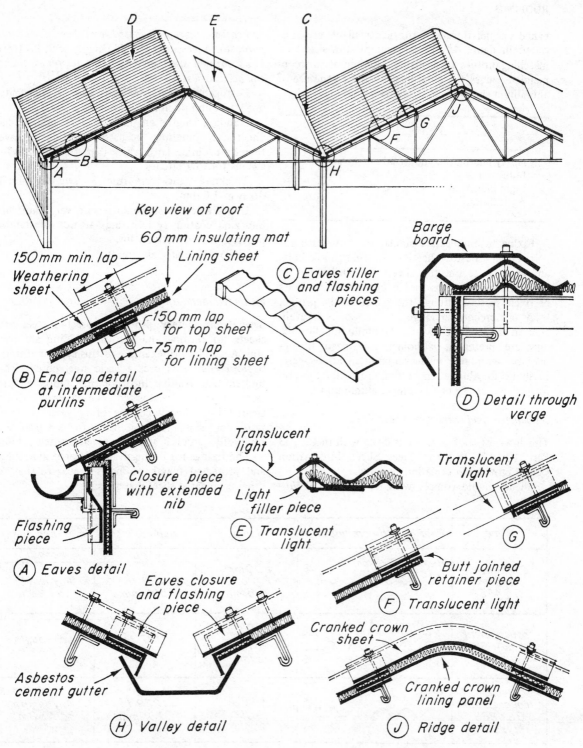

Key view of roof

150 mm min. lap
Weathering sheet
60 mm insulating mat
Lining sheet
150 mm lap for top sheet
75 mm lap for lining sheet

B End lap detail at intermediate purlins

C Eaves filler and flashing pieces

Barge board

D Detail through verge

Closure piece with extended nib
Flashing piece

A Eaves detail

Translucent light
Light filler piece

E Translucent light

Translucent light

G

Butt jointed retainer piece

F Translucent light

Eaves closure and flashing piece
Asbestos cement gutter

H Valley detail

Cranked crown sheet
Cranked crown lining panel

J Ridge detail

47   Corrugated asbestos cement sheet roofing: insulated double cladding fixing details

baked enamel finish. BS profiles available are illustrated in figure 48. Translucent plastics sheets of matching profiles are available. The minimum recommended gauges for durability related to the use of aluminium sheeting is as follows:

Use	Swg
Heavy and marine industrial	18
Industrial	20
Light industrial	22
Agricultural	24

Fixing techniques are similar to those used for corrugated asbestos sheeting, in that hook bolts are used to secure the sheets to purlins but in addition, the side laps should be secured by bolts or rivets passing through the crown of the profile.

A comprehensive range of accessories is available in 20 and 22 swg, and aluminium alloy fixings are preferable although galvanized fittings may be acceptable in a non-polluted atmosphere. Flashings for aluminium roofing are preferably preformed and of ½H or ¾H temper aluminium.

Galvanized steel corrugated sheet

This low-cost roof covering is dealt with in CP 143 Part 10:1973 and the Steel Sheet Information Centre provides information and advice.

Sheets should comply with BS 3083:1959 *Hot-dipped galvanized corrugated steel sheets for general purposes.* Accessories should comply with BS 1091: 1963 *Pressed steel gutters, rainwater pipes, fittings and accessories.*

Corrugated sheets are normally 76 mm pitch but a 127 mm pitch is also available.

Standard lengths are 1220 to 3660 mm. Longer sheets can sometimes be used from ridge to eaves, thereby avoiding laps, which is particularly advantageous for low pitches.

Thickness gauges are from 30 swg–0.3 mm to 16 swg–1.6 mm.

Unprotected steel would have a very short life, but zinc coating (galvanizing) affords substaintial protection at a relatively low cost.

See *MBS: Materials,* chapter 9.

Protected metal roofing

Several proprietary profiled protected steel core sheets for roofing and vertical cladding are available. A well known example of this type of material (*Colour Gabestos*) uses a basic steel core, with a molten zinc coating incorporating a bonded protective layer of asbestos felt. The material is finally treated by a heavy coating of polyester resin to resist corrosion. The material is formed into 'box rib' profiles and is available in several muted colours,

The fixings for both galvanized corrugated sheet, and protected metal roofing is similar to that for other corrugated sheet materials.

Type	Profile with nominal pitch		Gauge	Available sizes (max. and min.)	
				Width	Length
Corrugated sheet BS 4868 type S	76·2mm 76·2mm	19 mm	1·00 mm to 0·5 mm	1118 to 508 mm	Any length to 1·22 m
Trough sheet BS 4868 type A	127 mm	38·1 mm	0·9 mm to 0·7 mm	1187 to 579 mm	Any length to 7·62 m
Heavy trough sheet BS 4868 type B	130·2 mm	44·5 mm	1·2 mm to 1·00 mm	1229 to 705 mm	Any length to 7·62 m

48   Corrugated aluminium roofing sheet profiles

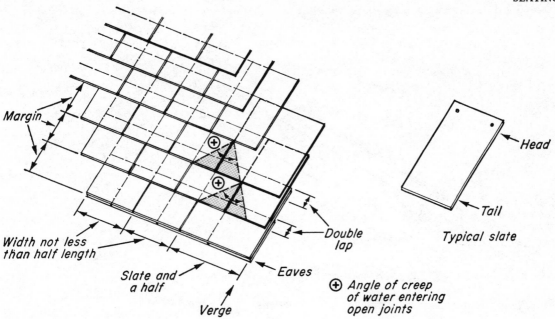

49 *Angle of creep in slating*

Slating

Code of Practice for Slating and Tiling BS 5534: 1978 Part 1—Design

Natural slates

Roofing slates are obtained from Wales, North Lancashire, Westmorland and Cornwall. Slates should comply with BS 680:1971 Part 2 *Roofing slates.* See *MBS: Materials,* chapter 4. There are more than 20 'standard' sizes of slate varying from the largest at 610 mm long by 355 mm wide and the smallest at 255 mm long to 150 mm wide.

When rainwater falls on to a pitched roof it will fan out and run over the surface at a given angle. This angle will depend upon the pitch of the roof and is commonly referred to as the *angle of creep*, see figure 49. The steeper the pitch the narrower the angle will be and this can be used as a guide to minimum width of the slate that can be used. It follows that the shallower the pitch the wider the slates will have to be and as a general principle the more exposed the position of the roof the smaller the slate and the steeper the pitch must be. Thus the larger unit is laid on the shallower pitch.

The following list gives a range of the metric equivalent sizes of slate most commonly used together with the recommended minimum rafter pitch.

Sizes of slates: length x width (mm)	Minimum pitch
305 x 205	45°
330 x 180	40°
405 x 205	35°
510 x 255	30°
610 x 305	25°
610 x 355	22½°

The thickness of slates varies according to the source, those from Westmorland and North Lancashire being relatively thick and coarser in surface texture. The thickest slates from any quarry are called *Bests* or *Firsts*, and the thinner slates, seconds and thirds. Thus, this description does not refer to quality, but is an indication of thickness. Where slates supplied vary in thickness the thinner slates should be used at the ridge and the thicker slates at lower courses.

Each row of slates is laid starting from the eaves, and is butt jointed at the side and overlapped at the head (see figure 49). Slates are laid *double lap* with special slates at the eaves and verge. This means that there are two thicknesses of slate *over* each nail

165

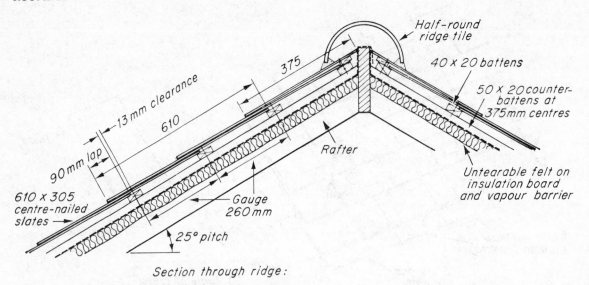

Section through ridge:

50   *Slating: centre nailed slates showing counter battens*

hole as protection, making in all, three thicknesses of material at the overlaps[1]. The side joint should be left very slightly open so that water will drain quickly. Each slate is nailed twice. The slate should be holed so that the 'spoiling' will form a counter sinking for the nail heads. The slates are best holed by machine on the site so that the holes can be correctly positioned by the fixers. The nails should be of yellow metal, aluminium alloy, copper or zinc. They are 32 mm long for the lighter and smaller slates up to 63 mm long for the heavier slates. Galvanized nails are not recommended. The slates may be either centre nailed or head nailed. For centre nailing, the nail holes are positioned by reference to the gauge and lap so that the nails just clear the head of the slates in the course below. Centre nailed slates on battens and counter battens on felt are illustrated in figure 50. For head nailed slates the holes will be positioned about 25 mm from the upper edge of the slate. Head nailed slates on battens and counter battens on felt are illustrated in figure 51. The holes should not be nearer than 25 mm to the side of the slate. Centre nailing gives more protection against lifting in the wind or chattering. The technique of head nailing should therefore only be used on smaller sizes of slate. Because of the angle of creep the width of slate is chosen having in mind the pitch of the roof, the shallower the pitch the larger the unit re-

[1] See figures 57 and 58 (fixing detail)

quired. The head-lap is chosen according to the degree of exposure, and in relation to the pitch, since the steeper the pitch the quicker the run off. The following minimum laps can be taken as a guide for moderate exposure.

rafter pitches — 22¼°   head laps — 100 mm
— 25°   — 90 mm
— 30°   — 75 mm
— 40°   — 65 mm

For severe exposure, that is to say on sites which are elevated, near the coast or where heavy snowfall is common the lap should be further increased as follows:

rafter pitches — 25°   head laps — 100 mm
— 30°   — 75 mm

(See BS 5534:Part1:1978 and BRE Digest 23.)

Vertical slating should have a minimum lap of 30 mm

Centre nailed and head nailed

Before setting out the slating the distance from the centre to centre of the battens must be worked out. This distance is known as *gauge* and is equal to the *margin* which is the amount of exposed slate measured up the slope of the roof. The gauge may be worked out as follows:

First decide on the head lap required with regard to the degree of exposure, say for example 90 mm

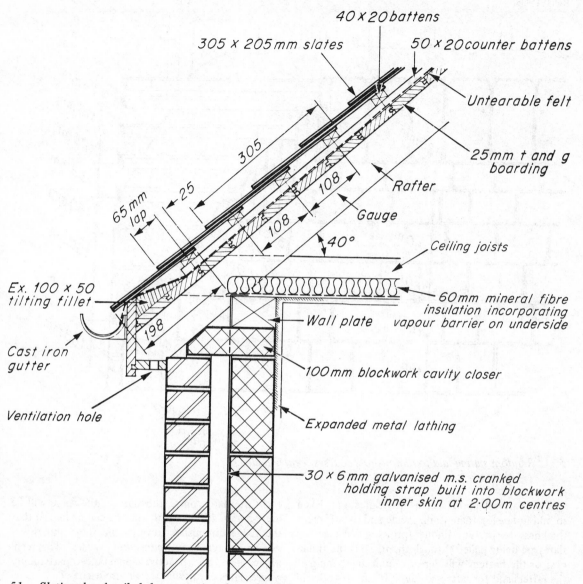

40 × 20 battens

305 × 205 mm slates

50 × 20 counter battens

Untearable felt

25 mm t and g boarding

305

25

Rafter

65 mm lap

108

108

Gauge

108

40°

Ceiling joists

Ex. 100 × 50 tilting fillet

198

60 mm mineral fibre insulation incorporating vapour barrier on underside

Wall plate

Cast iron gutter

100 mm blockwork cavity closer

Ventilation hole

Expanded metal lathing

30 × 6 mm galvanised m.s. cranked holding strap built into blockwork inner skin at 2·00 m centres

51   *Slating: head nailed slates: section through eaves*

at 25° pitch, using 610 mm × 305 mm slates. Then for centre nailed slates:

$$\text{gauge} = \frac{\text{length of slate} - \text{lap}}{2}$$

$$= \frac{610 - 90}{2}$$

$$= 260 \text{ mm (see figure 50).}$$

If the slates are head nailed allowance must be made

for the fact that the nail holes are positioned 25 mm from the top of the slates. For example, 65 mm lap for 305 mm × 205 mm slates at 40° pitch:

$$\text{Gauge} = \frac{\text{length of slate} - (\text{lap} + 25 \text{ mm})}{2}$$

$$= \frac{305 - (65 + 25)}{2}$$

$$= 108 \text{ mm (see figure 51).}$$

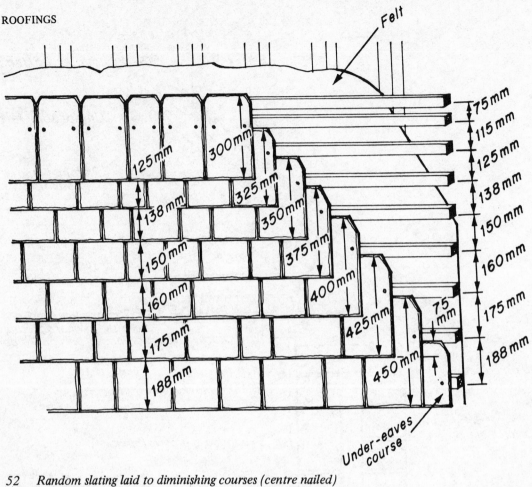

52 Random slating laid to diminishing courses (centre nailed)

The battens upon which the slates are fixed should not be less than 40 mm wide and of sufficient thickness to prevent undue springing back as the slates are being nailed through them. Thus the thickness of the battens will depend upon the spacing of the rafters and for rafters at say 400 mm to 460 mm centres the battens should be 20 mm thick.

Eaves courses of slates must always be head nailed and the length of the eaves slate is thus worked out as follows:

Length of slate at eaves = gauge x lap x 25 mm
Therefore previous example

= 108 + 65 + 25 = 198 mm

In order that the maximum width of lateral cover is maintained the slates are laid half-bond so that the joints occur as near as possible over the centre of slates in the course below. This means that in each alternate course the slate at the verge will be *'slate and a half'* in width. Slating can be laid so that the gauge diminishes towards the ridge and this is known as laying in *'diminishing courses'*. This technique gives an attractive appearance, particularly where slates of *random widths* are used.

It requires skilled craftsmanship to ensure correct bonding, and minimum lap should be specified which can be increased by the slaters as required to maintain the diminishing margins. The technique is shown in figure 52 in which random width slates are illustrated.

Slating should overhang slightly at the verge in order to protect the structure below. The average overhang of the slate is 50 mm and the edge of the slate is supported by using an undercloak of slate or plain asbestos cement sheeting bedded on the walling. The verge should have an inward tilt and, the bedding mortar is usually 1:5 cement/sand by volume. The detail is shown in figure 53. Alternatively, the roof structure, supported on sprockets built into the brickwork may overhang the wall and be finished off with a timber *barge board*. The verge slating will then project slightly beyond the bargeboard.

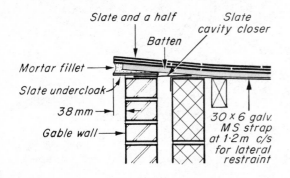

53 Slating: verge detail

Hips can be finished with lead rolls or with tiles but for the steeper pitches the neatest solution is to cut the slates and mitre them along the head using metal soakers lapped and bonded with each course and nailed at the top edges. Specially wide slates should be used so that the side bond is maintained when the slate is cut. Valleys are usually formed by having a dressed metal valley gutter and raking cut slates. As with hips specially wide slates are required so that they are sufficiently wide at their tails when cut. The slates are not bedded and do not have an undercloak. The traditional techniques for the *swept valley* formed by cutting slates to special shapes, and the *laced valley* require skilled craftsmen. Details are shown in figure 54. The flashing details where a chimney projects through a tiled roof are illustrated in figure 59.

Asbestos cement slates

These should comply with BS 690:1071 *Asbestos cement slates and sheets*. Properties are discussed in *MBS: Materials*, chapter 10.

The loss of cement from the exposed surfaces slowly exposes the asbestos fibres. Fixing details, and typical details at eaves, verge, ridge and valley are shown in figure 55.

Tiling

Plain tiles

Plain tiles are available in clay or concrete. Like slates they are laid in bond with double laps and have no interlocking joints. Nearly all plain tiles are cambered from head to tail so that they do not lie flat on each other, which prevents capillary movement of water between the tiles when they are laid on the roof. Some also have a camber in the width, but usually only on the upper surface. It should be noted that the camber in the length of the tile reduces the effective pitch, normally by about 9 degrees at 65 mm lap. Special tiles are available for use as ridges and to form hips and valleys; also *'tile and a half'* for verges. Each plain tile has two holes for nailing and most are provided with nibs so that they may be hung on to the battens, see figure 57.

Clay plain tiles and fittings should comply with BS 402: Part 2 1970 *Plain clay roofing tiles and fittings*. Sizes in mm: plain tile 265 long x 165 wide: Eaves and topcourse tiles 190 long x 165 wide: 'Tile and a half' 265 long x 248 wide; thickness is 10 to 15 mm. There is a limited production in certain districts of hand-made tiles which are now only used for special work. These are slightly thicker than the machine-made tiles, varying between 13 mm and 16 mm. Special length tiles are required at eaves and at top courses.

Well burnt clay tiles are not affected by atmosphere and are resistant to frost. The minimum rafter pitch recommended in BS 5534: Part 1:1978 is 40 degrees.

Concrete plain tiles should comply with BS 473/ 550 (Combined) Part 2 1971 *Concrete roofing tiles and fittings*. The fittings include half-round, segmental, hogsback and angular ridge and hip tiles, bonnet hip tiles and valley and angle tiles. The metric equivalent standard size for concrete plain tiles is 265 mm x 165 mm x approximately 10 mm thick. Concrete plain tiles usually cost less than clay tiles. They are usually faced with coloured granules which give a textured finish and are manufactured in a wide range of colours.

Concrete tiles as a result of their density and absence of any laminar structure when manufactured in accordance with the British Standard are not affected by frost. The minimum rafter pitch for these tiles recommended in BS 5534 in order to

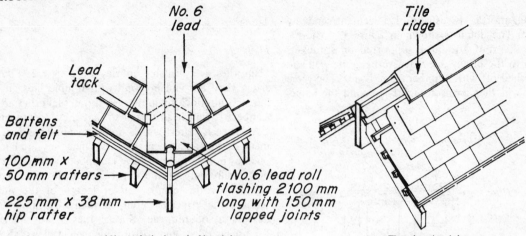

No. 6 lead

Lead tack

Battens and felt

100 mm x 50 mm rafters

225 mm x 38 mm hip rafter

No.6 lead roll flashing 2100 mm long with 150 mm lapped joints

Tile ridge

Hip with lead flashing

Typical ridge

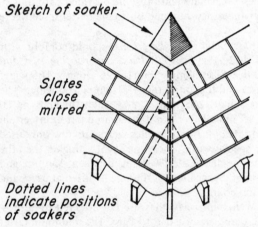

Sketch of soaker

Slates close mitred

Dotted lines indicate positions of soakers

Hip with lead soakers

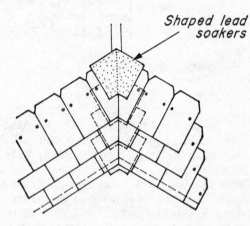

Shaped lead soakers

Mitred valley

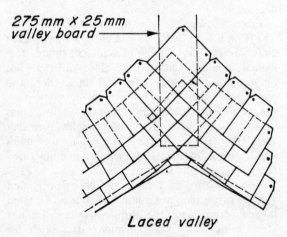

275 mm x 25 mm valley board

Laced valley

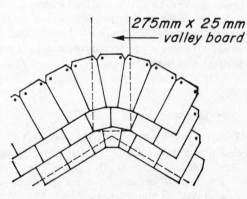

275 mm x 25 mm valley board

Circular swept valley

54   Slating: hips, ridge, and valleys

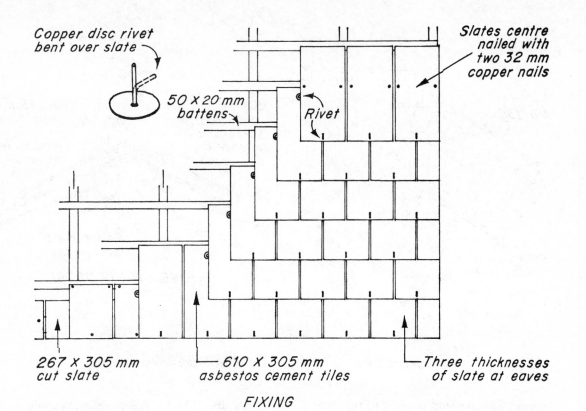

Copper disc rivet bent over slate

50 x 20 mm battens

Rivet

Slates centre nailed with two 32 mm copper nails

267 X 305 mm cut slate

610 X 305 mm asbestos cement tiles

Three thicknesses of slate at eaves

FIXING

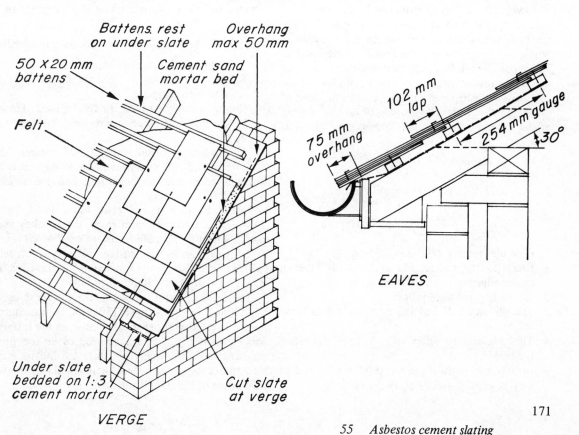

Battens rest on under slate

Overhang max 50 mm

50 x 20 mm battens

Cement sand mortar bed

Felt

Under slate bedded on 1:3 cement mortar

Cut slate at verge

VERGE

75 mm overhang

102 mm lap

254 mm gauge

30°

EAVES

55   *Asbestos cement slating*

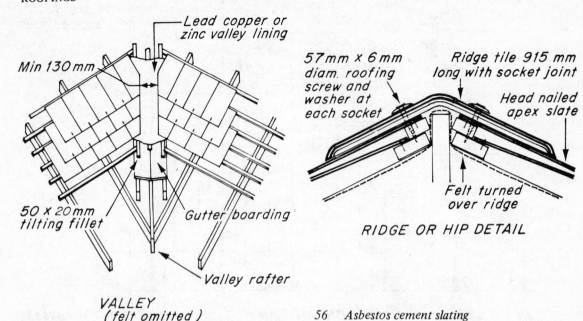

VALLEY
(felt omitted)

RIDGE OR HIP DETAIL

56   Asbestos cement slating

prevent rain and snow penetrating the joints is 35°, 5° lower than the less frost resistant clay tiles.

The lap for both clay and concrete plain tiling must not be less than 65 mm for moderate exposure. Where exposure is severe this should be increased to 75 mm or 90 mm. It should be noted that increasing the lap decreases the pitch of individual tiles and for this reason the lap must never exceed one third of the length of the tile. The gauge — or normal spacing of the battens — on the roof slope is worked out as follows:

$$\text{Gauge} = \frac{\text{length of tile} - \text{lap}}{2}$$

For standard 265 mm × 165 mm tiles the

$$\text{gauge} = \frac{265 \text{ mm} - 65 \text{ mm}}{2} = 100 \text{ mm}$$

Plain tiles require nailing as follows:

1 Every fourth course and at the ends of each course adjacent to abutments and verges.
2 All cut tiles in swept valleys.
3 The tile and half and the adjacent tile in laced valleys.
4 Tiles adjacent to valley tiles, but not the valley tile itself.
5 In exposed positions every third course and in very exposed positions every course.

6 See BS 5534 for special recommendations for extra nailing at steep pitches of 50 degrees and over.

Nails should be made from the following materials:

(a) Aluminium alloy complying with BS 1202 Part 3. These are extensively used and have excellent resistance to corrosion.
(b) Copper complying with BS 1002 Part 2. These have a high resistance to corrosion, but tend to be soft.
(c) Silicon-bronze of an alloy of 96% copper, 3% silicon and 1% manganese. These have also a high resistance to corrosion, and are much harder than copper.

Figure 58 is a typical plain tiling detail sheet showing the construction at ridge, verge, valley and eaves. Note that an underlay of *untearable felt* must be provided under the battens. The type of felt (which must also be used in slating) is classified in BS 747:1970. Class F Reinforced felt.

The felting is laid parallel to the ridge and each tier should be overlapped 150 mm at horizontal joints. The felt will sag slightly between the rafters, which, providing it is not allowed to be too pronounced, will allow any moisture to find its way into the eaves gutter, where there should be ample turn down of the felt into the gutter.

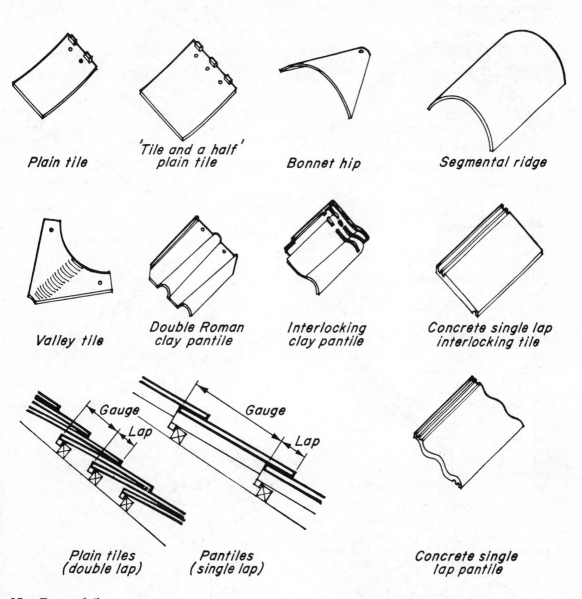

Plain tile

'Tile and a half' plain tile

Bonnet hip

Segmental ridge

Valley tile

Double Roman clay pantile

Interlocking clay pantile

Concrete single lap interlocking tile

Gauge

Lap

Gauge

Lap

Plain tiles (double lap)

Pantiles (single lap)

Concrete single lap pantile

57   Types of tiles

The *Building Regulations 1976* require that the thermal insulation (U) of the roof and ceiling combined shall be not more than 0.6 W/m²°C in houses, flats and maisonettes. The U value of tiles over felt including the ceiling is 2.22 W/m²°C, and so insulation will be required. This must always be provided with a vapour barrier and can be installed either immediately over the rafters ('warm' roof construc-tion — see figure 50) or between the ceiling joists ('cold' roof construction — see figure 51). If the latter technique is used, care must be taken to see that water tanks, etc positioned within the roof space are also insulated. Descriptions of numerous 'deemed-to-satisfy' methods of achieving the man-datory U value for domestic roofs are given in Schedule 11, Part III: Tables 5 and 6 of the Building

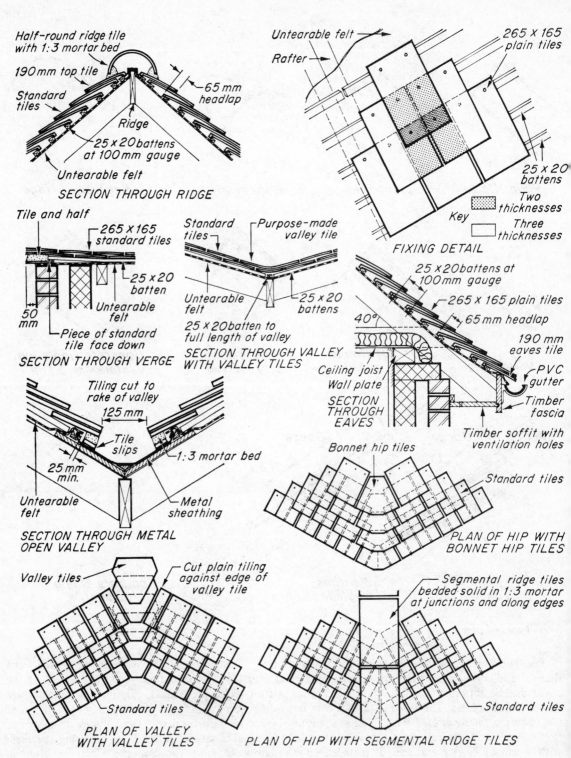

Half-round ridge tile with 1:3 mortar bed
190 mm top tile
Standard tiles
65 mm headlap
Ridge
25 x 20 battens at 100 mm gauge
Untearable felt

SECTION THROUGH RIDGE

Tile and half
265 x 165 standard tiles
25 x 20 batten
Untearable felt
50 mm
Piece of standard tile face down

SECTION THROUGH VERGE

Standard tiles
Purpose-made valley tile
Untearable felt
25 x 20 battens
25 x 20 batten to full length of valley

SECTION THROUGH VALLEY WITH VALLEY TILES

Tiling cut to rake of valley
125 mm
Tile slips
1:3 mortar bed
25 mm min.
Untearable felt
Metal sheathing

SECTION THROUGH METAL OPEN VALLEY

Valley tiles
Cut plain tiling against edge of valley tile
Standard tiles

PLAN OF VALLEY WITH VALLEY TILES

Untearable felt
Rafter
265 x 165 plain tiles
25 x 20 battens
Key
Two thicknesses
Three thicknesses

FIXING DETAIL

25 x 20 battens at 100 mm gauge
265 x 165 plain tiles
65 mm headlap
190 mm eaves tile
40°
Ceiling joist
Wall plate
PVC gutter
Timber fascia
SECTION THROUGH EAVES
Timber soffit with ventilation holes

Bonnet hip tiles
Standard tiles

PLAN OF HIP WITH BONNET HIP TILES

Segmental ridge tiles bedded solid in 1:3 mortar at junctions and along edges
Standard tiles

PLAN OF HIP WITH SEGMENTAL RIDGE TILES

58   Plain tiling (double lap)

Regulations 1976 and include the following examples:

(a) Tiles on battens over felt underlay enclosing ventilated roof space with either 60 mm minimum thickness mineral fibre laid over rafters, or 50 mm expanded insulation board laid over rafters.

(b) Tiles on battens over felt underlay enclosing ventilated roof space with either 46 mm minimum thickness mineral fibre above, but in direct contact with the ceiling, or 34 mm minimum thickness of foamed polystyrene insulating board, fixed above ceiling but incorporating and enclosed air space.

Tiled roofs for other than domestic buildings should also follow these examples. Counterbattens are required whenever boarding or rigid sheeting is used over rafters. They should be laid on the line of each rafter over the sheeting and the felt underlay. By this means the tiling battens are raised clear of the underlay by the thickness of the counterbattens (see figures 50 and 59) so allowing any wind-blown water penetration to drain away on the felt into the eaves gutter. The tiling battens, fixed to the correct gauge for the tiles concerned, should be a minimum of 25 mm x 20 mm when the supporting rafters are spaced at maximum 380 mm centres.

Where plain tiling abuts a chimney or other projection through a roof, the junction between the tiling and the brickwork must be made watertight by the use of metal flashings. Figure 59 shows the method of forming a back gutter and the use of stepped and apron flashings in lead. The same techniques are also applicable to slated roofs. The tiling (or slating) is weathered against the abutting wall by a series of lead soakers, one to each course, laid between the tiles or slates with an upstand against the wall. A lead flashing cut from a strip of lead sheet, the lower edge following the rake of the roof and the upper edge stepped to follow the coursing of the brickwork, is fixed over the upstands of the soakers. The horizontal edges of the steps are turned about 25 mm into the joints of the brickwork, secured by lead wedges and pointed in The flashing is dressed round the front of the stack after the front apron has been fixed. The front of the chimney stack is flashed by a lead apron carried well down on to the tiles or slates. The top edge of the apron is turned into a horizontal brickwork joint, wedged and pointed in. The flashing to the back of the chimney is formed as a short valley gutter with a separate lead cover flashing, the top edge of which is turned, fixed into the brickwork joint with lead wedges and pointed. The lead should be carried over a tilting fillet well back under the eaves course of tiling above the chimney and should be dressed carefully over the tiles or slates at each end of the gutter to ensure a close fit.

Single lap tiles

The shaped side lap in single lap tiling takes the place of the bond in plain tiling and in slating, and because of this the protection at the head lap can be reduced to two thicknesses of material. In this category of tiling there is a single overlap (double thickness) of one tile upon the other. This technique includes pantiling and is of ancient origin. In this country pantiling was first used in Eastern England, the influence probably coming from the Dutch craftsmen. Many types of single lap tiles are available, examples of which are shown in figure 60 and 62. Nearly all single lap tiles are of the interlocking pattern. Some types of interlocking tile have anti-capillary grooves at the head-lap of the tiles. This makes it possible to lay these tiles on roofs of comparatively flat pitch. The amount of side lap is determined by the shape of the tile. Head lap should never be less than 75 mm.

Certain patterns of single lap tiles can be laid at variable gauge. This should be used to avoid cutting tiles at top courses.

Figure 62 shows typical details of concrete tiles with interlocking side lap. Each alternate course of tiles is shown nailed but, in certain severe exposure conditions, each tile in each course must be nailed. (See CP 3 Chapter V: *Loading* Part 2 1972 *Wind loads*.) The eaves course of tiles projects about 50 mm over the edge of the fascia board and the felt underlay is drawn taut and fixed in this case by a proprietary eave clip nailed to the top edge of the fascia board. Purpose made valley tiles on felt underlay form the valley detail. Alternatively, the valley could be lined with metal sheeting over valley boards. Verges hsould overhang about 50 mm and the undercloak can be formed from natural slate, asbestos-cement strip as shown, or plain tiles. The ridge is covered in the example by a segmental ridge tile bedded and pointed in 1:3 cement/sand mortar.

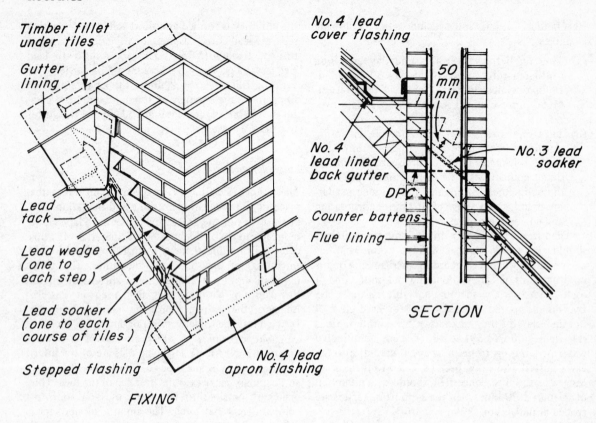

Timber fillet
under tiles

Gutter
lining

Lead
tack

Lead wedge
(one to
each step)

Lead soaker
(one to each
course of tiles)

Stepped flashing

No. 4 lead
apron flashing

FIXING

No. 4 lead
cover flashing

50 mm min

No. 4
lead lined
back gutter

DPC

Counter battens

Flue lining

No. 3 lead
soaker

SECTION

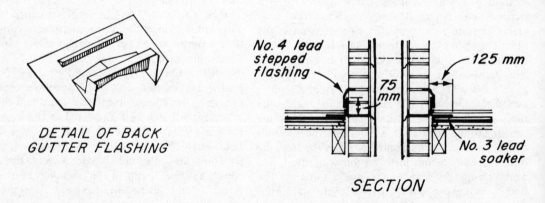

DETAIL OF BACK
GUTTER FLASHING

No. 4 lead
stepped
flashing

75 mm

125 mm

No. 3 lead
soaker

SECTION

59   *Lead flashings to chimney: plain tile or slate roof coverings*

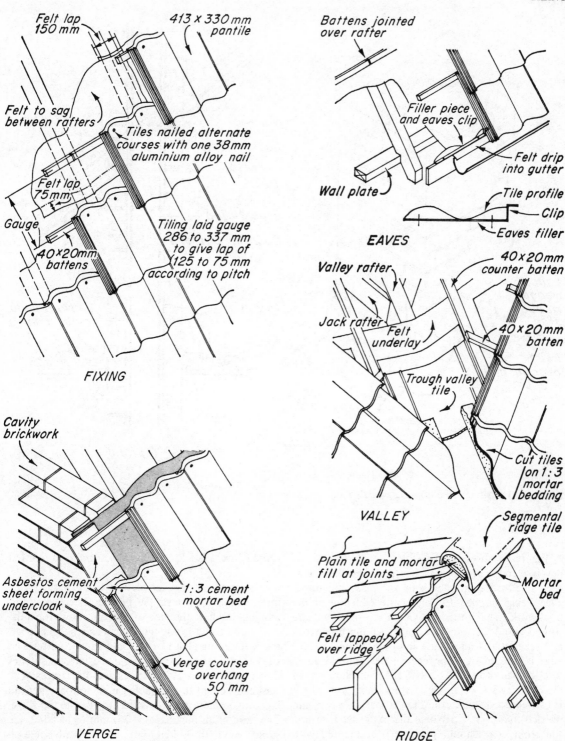

Felt lap
150 mm

413 × 330 mm
pantile

Felt to sag
between rafters

Tiles nailed alternate
courses with one 38mm
aluminium alloy nail

Felt lap
75 mm

Gauge

40×20mm
battens

Tiling laid gauge
286 to 337 mm
to give lap of
125 to 75 mm
according to pitch

FIXING

Cavity
brickwork

Asbestos cement
sheet forming
undercloak

1:3 cement
mortar bed

Verge course
overhang
50 mm

VERGE

Battens jointed
over rafter

Filler piece
and eaves clip

Felt drip
into gutter

Wall plate

Tile profile

Clip

Eaves filler

EAVES

Valley rafter

40×20mm
counter batten

Jack rafter

Felt
underlay

40×20mm
batten

Trough valley
tile

Cut tiles
on 1:3
mortar
bedding

VALLEY

Segmental
ridge tile

Plain tile and mortar
fill at joints

Mortar
bed

Felt lapped
over ridge

RIDGE

60   *Pantile roofing (single lap)*

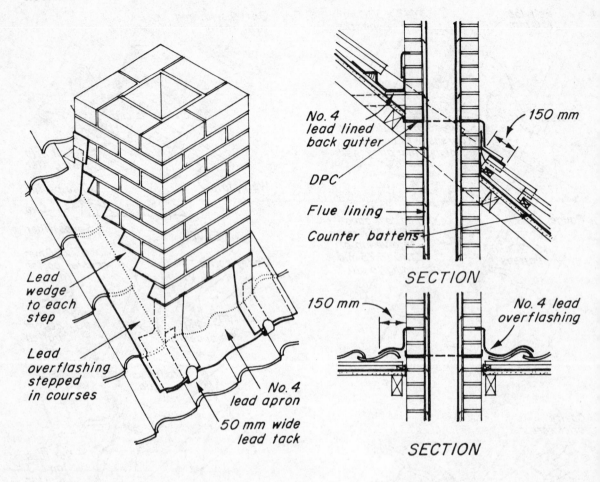

No. 4
lead lined
back gutter

DPC

Flue lining

Counter battens

150 mm

SECTION

150 mm

No. 4 lead
overflashing

SECTION

Lead
wedge
to each
step

Lead
overflashing
stepped
in courses

No. 4
lead apron

50 mm wide
lead tack

61   *Lead flashings to chimney: pantile roof covering*

Figure 61 shows lead flashing details to a chimney in a roof covered with pantiles. The flashing at each side of the chimney is in one piece, the upper edge being stepped to follow the coursing of the brickwork. The horizontal edges of the steps are turned about 25 mm into joints of the brickwork and secured by lead wedges and pointed in. The free edge is dressed over the nearest tile roll and down into the pan of the tile beyond the roll. The front of the chimney stack is flashed with a lead apron which is carried down on to the tiles at least 125 mm and dressed to a close fit. Where the exposure is severe, the front edge should preferably be secured with lead tacks as shown. The top edge of the apron is turned into a brickwork joint, wedged and pointed in.

Figure 62 shows the details using a single lap interlocking tile of simple profile. The neat interlocking detail at the side of the tile allows the adjacent units to lie in the same plane, giving an appearance of slating. Tiles of this and similar pattern on sites of moderate exposure can be laid on pitches down to between 22½ degrees and 15 degrees. The tiles can be laid to a variable gauge, so that the head lap can be increased to avoid cut tiles at the ridge. The minimum headlap is 75 mm. The tiles are shown laid with broken joint and this is advisable on roofs of less than 30 degrees pitch. Where tiles are

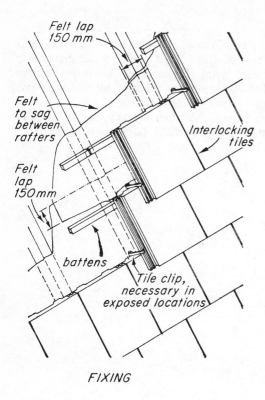

Felt lap 150 mm

Felt to sag between rafters

Interlocking tiles

Felt lap 150 mm

battens

Tile clip, necessary in exposed locations

FIXING

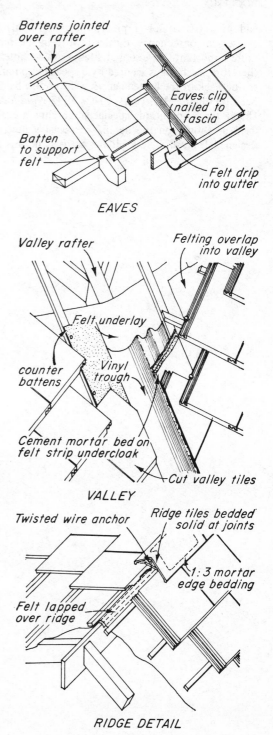

Battens jointed over rafter

Eaves clip nailed to fascia

Batten to support felt

Felt drip into gutter

EAVES

Valley rafter

Felting overlap into valley

Felt underlay

counter battens

Vinyl trough

Cement mortar bed on felt strip undercloak

Cut valley tiles

VALLEY

Twisted wire anchor

Ridge tiles bedded solid at joints

1:3 mortar edge bedding

Felt lapped over ridge

RIDGE DETAIL

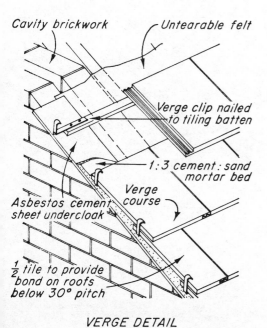

Cavity brickwork

Untearable felt

Verge clip nailed to tiling batten

1:3 cement: sand mortar bed

Verge course

Asbestos cement sheet undercloak

$\frac{1}{2}$ tile to provide bond on roofs below 30° pitch

VERGE DETAIL

62   Interlocking concrete: tiling details

laid on roofs of lower pitch, the wind uplift increases. In consequence, the need for fixing becomes more important. On exposed sites, at lower pitches therefore, each tile is secured by a special clip nailed to the back of the batten carrying the course below. See CP 3 Chapter V *Loading* Part 2 1972 *Wind loads*. Under these conditions special verge clips are also used as shown on the detail. A special valley tile designed for use at low pitches is used in this ex-ample to form the valley gutter as an alternative to a metal open valley. The ridge tile is fixed by means of a special wire twisted around a nail driven into the ridge board. In addition, the ridge tiles are bedded solid at joints in 1:3 sand and cement mortar and edge bedded along both sides.

For details of dormer windows and skylights in pitched roofs see *MBS: Components* Chapter 6, page 197.

CI/SfB

The following information from the *Construction Indexing Manual 1976* is reproduced by courtesy of RIBA Publications Ltd.

Used sensibly and in appropriate detail, as explained in the manual, the CI/SfB system of classification facilitates filing and retrieval of information. It is useful in technical libraries, in specifications and on working drawings. *The National Building Specification* is based on the system, and BRE Digest 172 describes its use for working drawings.

The CI/SfB system comprises tables 0 to 4, tables 1 and 2/3 being the codes in most common use. For libraries, classifications are built up from:

Table 0	Table 1	Tables 2/3	Table 4
-a number code	-a number code in brackets	-upper and lower case letter codes	-upper case letter code in brackets
eg 6	eg (6)	eg Fg	eg (F)

An example for clay brickwork in walls is: (21) Fg2, which for trade literature, would be shown in a reference box as:

The lower space is intended for UDC (Universal decimal classification) codes – see BS 1000A 1961. Advice in classification can be obtained from the SfB Agency UK Ltd at 66 Portland Place, London W1N 4AD.

In the following summaries of the five tables, references are made to the six related volumes and chapters of *Mitchell's Building Series* in which aspects of the classifications are dealt with. The following abbreviations are used:

Environment and Services	*ES*
Materials	*M*
Structure and Fabric, Part 1	*SF (1)*
Structure and Fabric, Part 2	*SF (2)*
Components	*C*[1]
Finishes	*F*[1] [2]

Table 0 Physical Environment
(main headings only)

Scope: End results of the construction process

0	Planning areas
1	Utilities, civil engineering facilities
2	Industrial facilities
3	Administrative, commerical, protective service facilities
4	Health, welfare facilities
5	Recreational facilities
6	Religious facilities
7	Educational, scientific, information facilities
8	Residential facilities
9	Common facilities, other facilities

---

[1] Previously part of – *Components and Finishes*
[2] The *Finishes* chapters in the *CF* volume were numbered

CF (1971)	*F* (1979)
12	1
13	2
14	3
15	4
16	5
17	6
18	7

TABLE 1

Table 1 **Elements**

Scope: Parts with particular functions which com bine to make the facilities in table 0

(0-) Sites, projects
Building plus external works
Building systems *C 11*

(1-) Ground, substructure

(11) Ground

(12) Vacant

(13) Floor beds *SF (1)* 4, 8; *SF (2)* 3

(14), (15) Vacant

(16) Retaining walls, foundations *SF (1)* 4; *SF (2)* 3. 4

(17) Pile foundations *SF (1)* 4; *SF(2)* 3, 11

(18) Other substructure elements

(19) Parts, accessories, cost summary, etc

(2-) Structure, primary elements, carcass

(21) Walls, external walls *SF (1)* 1, 5; *SF (2)* 4, 5, 10

(22) Internal walls, partitions *SF (1)* 5; *SF (2)* 4, 10; *C 9*

(23) Floors, galleries *SF (1)* 8; *SF (2)* 6, 10

(24) Stairs, ramps *SF (1)* 10; *SF (2)* 8, 10

(25), (26) Vacant

(27) Roofs *SF (1)* 1, 7; *SF (2)* 9, 10

(28) Building frames, other primary elements *SF (1)* 1, 6; *SF (2)* 5, 10
Chimneys *SF (1)* 9

(29) Parts, accessories, cost summary, etc

(3-) Secondary elements, completion of structure

(31) Secondary elements to external walls, including windows, doors *SF (1)* 5; *SF (2)* 10; *C* 3, 4, 5, 7

(32) Secondary elements to internal walls, partitions including borrowed lights and doors *SF (2)* 10; *C* 3, 7

(33) Secondary elements to floors *SF (2)* 10

(34) Secondary elements to stairs including balustrades *C* 8

(35) Suspended ceilings *C* 10

(36) Vacant

(37) Secondary elements to roofs, including roof lights, dormers *SF (2)* 10; *C* 6

(38) Other secondary elements

(39) Parts, accessories, cost summary, etc

(4-) Finishes to structure

(41) Wall finishes, external *SF (2)* 4, 10; *F* 3, 4, 5

(42) Wall finishes, internal *F* 2, 4, 5

(43) Floor finishes *F 1*

(44) Stair finishes *F 1*

(45) Ceiling finishes *F* 2

(46) Vacant

(47) Roof finishes *SF (2); F* 7

(48) Other finishes

(49) Parts, accessories, cost summary, etc

(5-) Services (mainly piped and ducted)

(51) Vacant

(52) Waste disposal, drainage *ES* 13 /*ES* 11, 12

(53) Liquids supply *ES* 9, 10; *SF (1)* 9; *SF (2)* 6, 10

(54) Gases supply

(55) Space cooling

(56) Space heating *ES* 7; *SF (1)* 9; *SF (2)* 6, 10

(57) Air conditioning, ventilation *ES* 7; *SF (2)* 10

(58) Other piped, ducted services,

(59) Parts, accessories, cost summary, etc
Chimney, shafts, flues, ducts independent *SF (2)* 7.

(6-) Services (mainly electrical)

(61) Electrical supply

(62) Power *ES* 14

(63) Lighting *ES* 8

(64) Communications *ES* 14

(65) Vacant

(66) Transport *ES* 15

(67) Vacant

(68) Security, control, other services

(69) Parts, accessories, cost summary, etc

(7-) Fittings with subdivisions (71) to (79)

(74) Sanitary, hygiene fittings *ES* 10

TABLE 2

(8-) **Loose furniture, equipment** with subdivisions (81) to (89)

Used where the distinction between loose and fixed fittings, furniture and equipment is important

(9-) **External elements, other elements**
(90) External works, with subdivisions (90.1) to (90.8)
(98) Other elements
(99) Parts, accessories etc. common to two or more main element divisions (1 -) to (7 -)
Cost summary

Note: The SfB Agency UK do not use table 1 in classifying manufacturers' literature

---

Table 2 **Constructions, Forms**

Scope: Parts of particular forms which combine to make the elements in table 1. Each is characterized by the main product of which it is made.

A   Constructions, forms – used in specification applications for Preliminaries and General conditions
B   Vacant –   used in specification applications For Demolition, underpinning and shoring work
C   Excavation and loose fill work
D   Vacant
E   Cast in situ work *M* 8; *SF (1)* 4, 7, 8; *SF (2)* 3, 4, 5, 6, 9

Blocks
F   Blockwork, brickwork
Blocks, bricks *M* 6, 12; *SF (1)* 5, 9 *SF (2)* 4, 6, 7
G   Large block, panel work
Large blocks, panels *SF (2)* 4

Sections
H   Section work
Sections *M* 9; *SF (1)* 5, 6, 7, 8; *SF (2)* 6
I   Pipework
Pipes *SF (1)* 9; *SF (2)* 7

J   Wire work, mesh work
Wires, meshes
K   Quilt work
Quilts
L   Flexible sheet work (proofing)
Flexible sheets (proofing) *M* 9, 11
M   Malleable sheet work
Malleable sheets *M* 9
N   Rigid sheet overlap work
Rigid sheets for overlappings *SF (2)* 4; *F* 7
P   Thick coating work *M* 10, 11; *SF (2)* 4;
F 1, 2, 3, 7
Q   Vacant
R   Rigid sheet work
Rigid sheets *M* 3, 12, 13; *SF (2)* 4; *C* 5
S   Rigid tile work
Rigid tiles *M* 4, 12, 13; *F* 1, 4
T   Flexible sheet and tile work
Flexible sheets eg carpets, veneers, papers, tiles cut from them *M* 3, 9; *F* 1, 6
U   Vacant
V   Film coating and impregnation work *F* 6;
M 2
W   Planting work
Plants
X   Work with components
Components *SF (1)* 5, 6, 7, 8, 10; *SF (2)* 4;
C 2, 3, 4, 5, 6, 7, 8
Y   Formless work
Products
Z   Joints, where described separately

Table 3 **Materials**

Scope: Materials which combine to form the products in table 2

---

a   **Materials**
b, c, d,   Vacant

Formed materials e to o
e   **Natural stone** *M* 4; *SF (1)* 5, 10; *SF (2)* 4
e1   Granite, basalt, other igneous
e2   Marble
e3   Limestone (other than marble)

TABLE 3

e4	Sandstone, gritstone
e5	Siate
e9	Other natural stone

f   **Precast with binder** *M* 8: *SF (1)* 5, 7, 8, 9, 10 *SF(2)* 4 to 9; *F* 1

f1   Sandlime concrete (precast)
Glass fibre reinforced calcium silicate (gres)

f2   All-in aggregate concrete (precast) *M* 8
Heavy concrete (precast) *M* 8
Glass fibre reinforced cement (gre) *M* 10

f3   Terrazzo (precast) *F* 1
Granolithic (precast)
Cast/artificial/reconstructed stone

f4   Lightweight cellular concrete (precast) *M* 8

f5   Lightweight aggregate concrete (precast) *M* 8

f6   Asbestos based materials (preformed) *M* 10

f7   Gypsum (preformed) *C* 2
Glass fibre reinforced gypsum *M* 10

f8   Magnesia materials (preformed)

f9   Other materials precast with binder

g   **Clay (Dried, Fired)** *M* 5; *SF (1)* 5, 9, 10; *SF (2)* 4, 6, 7

g1   Dried clay eg pisé de terre

g2   Fired clay, vitrified clay, ceramics
Unglazed fired clay eg terra cotta

g3   Glazed fired clay eg vitreous china

g6   Refractory materials eg fireclay

g9   Other dried or fired clays

h   **Metal** *M* 9; *SF (1)* 6, 7, *SF (2)* 4, 5, 7

h1   Cast iron
Wrought iron, malleable iron

h2   Steel, mild steel

h3   Steel alloys eg stainless steel

h4   Aluminium, aluminium alloys

h5   Copper

h6   Copper alloys

h7   Zinc

h8   Lead, white metal

h9   Chromium, nickel, gold, other metals, metal alloys

i   **Wood** including wood laminates **M** 2, 3; *SG (1)* 5 to 8, 10 *SF (2)* 4, 9; *C* 2

i1   timber (unwrot)

i2   Softwood (in general, and wrot)

i3   Hardwood (in general, and wrot)

i4   Wood laminates eg plywood

i5   Wood veneers

i9   Other wood materials, except wood fibre boards, chipboards and wood-wool cement

j   **Vegetable and aminal materials** – including fibres and particles and materials made from these

j1   Wood fibres eg building board *M* 3

j2   Paper *M* 9, 13

j3   Vegetable fibres other than wood eg flaxboard *M* 3

j5   Bark, cork

j6   Animal fibres eg hair

j7   Wood particles eg chipboard *M* 3

j8   Wood-wool cement *M* 3

j9   Other vegetable and animal materials

k, 1   Vacant

m   **Inorganic fibres**

m1   Mineral wool fibres *M* 10; *SF (2)* 4, 7
Glass wool fibres *M* 10, 12
Ceramic wool fibres

m2   Asbestos wool fibres *M* 10

m9   Other inorganic fibrous materials eg carbon fibres *M* 10

n   **Rubber, plastics, etc**

n1   Asphalt (preformed) *M* 11; *F* 1

n2   Impregnated fibre and felt eg bituminous felt *M* 11, *F* 7

n4   Linoleum *F* 1

Synthetic resins n5, n6

n5   Rubbers (elastomers) *M* 13

n6   Plastics, including sythetic fibres *M* 13
Thermoplastics
Thermosets

n7   Cellular plastics

n8   Reinforced plastics eg grp, plastics laminates

TABLE 3

n9   Other rubber, plastics materials eg mixed natural/synthetic fibres

o   **Glass** *M* 12 *SF (1)* 5; *C* 5
o1   Clear, transparent, plain glass
o2   Translucent glass
o3   Opaque, opal glass
04   Wired glass
o5   Multiple glazing
o6   Heat absorbing/rejecting glass
     X-ray absorbing/rejecting glass
     Solar control glass
o7   Mirrored glass, 'one-way' glass
     Anti-glare glass
o8   Safety glass, toughened glass
     Laminated glass, security glass, alarm glass
o9   Other glass, including, cellular glass

Formless materials p to s
p   **Aggregates, loose fills** *M* 8
p1   Natural fills, aggregates
p2   Artificial aggregates in general
p3   Artificial granular aggregates (light) eg foamed blast furnace slag
p4   Ash eg pulverized fuel ash
p5   Shavings
p6   Powder
p7   Fibres
p9   Other aggregates, loose fills

q   **Lime and cement binders, mortars, concretes**
q1   Lime (calcined limestones), hydrated lime, lime putty, *M* 7
     Lime-sand mix (coarse stuff)
q2   Cement, hydraulic cement eg Portland cement *M* 7
q3   Lime-cement binders *M* 15
q4   Lime-cement-aggregate mixes
     Mortars (ie with fine aggregates) *M* 15; *SF (2)* 4
     Concretes (ie with fine and /or coarse aggregates) *M* 8
q5   Terrazzo mixes and in general *F* 1
     Granolithic mixes and in general *F* 1
q6   Lightweight, cellular, concrete mixes and in general *M* 8

q7   Lightweight aggregate concrete mixes and in general *M* 8
q9   Other lime-cement-aggregate mixes eg asbestos cement mixes *M* 10

r   **Clay, gypsum, magnesia and plastics binders, mortars**
r1   Clay mortar mixes, refractory mortar
r2   Gypsum, gypsum plaster mixes *SF* 2
r3   Magnesia, magnesia mixes *F* 1
r4   Plastics binders
     Plastics mortar mixes
r9   Other binders and mortar mixes

s   **Bituminous materials** *M* 11; *SF (2)* 4
s1   Bitumen including natural and petroleum bitumens, tar, pitch, asphalt, lake asphalt
s4   Mastic asphalt (fine or no aggregate), pitch mastic
s5   Clay-bitumen mixes, stone bitumen mixes (coarse aggregate)
     Rolled asphalt, macadams
s9   Other bituminous materials

Functional materials t to w
t   **Fixing and jointing materials**
t1   Welding materials *M* 9; *SF(1)* 5
t2   Soldering materials *M* 9
t3   Adhesives, bonding materials *M* 14
t4   Joint fillers eg mastics, gaskets *M* 16
t6   Fasteners, 'builders ironmongery'
     Anchoring devices eg plugs
     Attachment devices eg connectors *SF (1)* 6, 7
     Fixing devices eg bolts, *SF (1)* 5
t7   'Architectural ironmongery' *C* 7
t9   Other fixing and jointing agents

u   **Protective and Process/property modifying materials**
u1   Anti-corrosive materials, treatments *F*6
     Metallic coatings applied by eg electroplating *M* 9
     Non-metallic coatings applied by eg chemical conversion

TABLE 4

u2	Modifying agents, admixtures eg curing agents *M* 8	**z**	**Substances**
	Workability aids *M* 8	**z1**	By state eg fluids
u3	Materials resisting specials forms of attack such as fungus, insects, condensation *M* 2	**z2**	By chemical composition eg organic
		z3	By origin eg naturally occurring or manufactured materials
u4	Flame retardants if described separately *M* 1	**z9**	Other substances

u5 Polishes, seals, surface hardners *F* 1: *M* 8

u6 Water repellants, if described separately

u9 Other protective and process/property modifying agents, eg ultra-violet absorbers

v **Paints** *F* 6

v1 Stopping, fillers, knotting, paint preparation materials including primers

v2 Pigments, dyes, stains

v3 Binders, media eg drying oils

v4 Varnishes, lacquers eg resins
Enamels, glazes

v5 Oil paints, oil-resin paints
Synthetic resin paints
Complete systems including primers

v6 Emulsion paints, where described separately
Synthetic resin-based emulsions
Complete systems including primers

v8 Water paints eg cement paints

v9 Other paints eg metallic paints, paints with aggregates

W **Ancillary materials**

w1 Rust removing agents

w3 Fuels

w4 Water

w5 Acids, alkalis

w6 Fertilisers

w7 Cleaning materials *F* 1
Abrasives

w8 Explosives

w9 Other ancillary materials eg fungicides

x **Vacant**

y **Composite materials**
Composite materials generally *M* 11
See p. 63 *Construction Indexing Manual*

Table 4   **Activities, Requirements**
(main headings only)

Scope: Table 4 identifies objects which assist or affect construction but are not incorporated in it, and factors such as activities, requirements, properties, and processes.

Activities, aids

(A) Administration and management activities, aids *C* 11; *M* Introduction

(B) Construction plant, tools *SF (1)* 2; *SF (2)* 2, 11

(C) Vacant

(D) Construction operations *SF (1)* 11; *SF (2)* 2, 11

Requirements, properties, building science, construction technology
Factors describing buildings, elements, materials, etc

(E) Composition, etc

(F) Shape, size, etc

(G) Appearance, etc *M* 1; *F* 6

Factors relating to surroundings, occupancy

(H) Context, environment

Performance factors

(J) Mechanics *M* 9; *SF (1)* 3; *SF (2)* 4

(K) Fire, explosion *M* 1; *SF (2)* 10

(L) Matter

(M) Heat, cold *ES* 1

(N) Light, dark *ES* 1

(O) Sound, quiet *ES* 1

(Q) Electricity, magnetism, radiation *ES* 14

(R) Energy, other physical factors *ES* 7

(T) Application

TABLE 4

Other factors

(U) Users, resources

(V) Working factors

(W) Operation, maintenance factors

(X) Change, movement, stability factors

(Y) Economic, commerical factors *M* Introduction; *SF (1)* 2; *(SF (2)* 3, 4, 5, 6, 9

(Z) Peripheral subjects, form of presentation, time, place — may be used for subjects taken from the UDC (*Universal decimal classification*), see BS 1000A 1961

Subdivision: All table 4 codes are subdivided mainly by numbers

Contents of other volumes

The reader is referred to the five other related volumes in *Mitchell's Building Series* for the following:

Environment and Services　Peter Burberry

1 General significance
2 Moisture
3 Air movement
4 Daylighting
5 Heat
6 Sound
7 Thermal installations
8 Electric lighting
9 Water supply
10 Sanitary appliances
11 Pipes
12 Drainage installations
13 Sewage disposal
14 Refuse disposal
15 Electricity and Telecommunications
16 Gas
17 Mechanical conveyors
18 Firefighting equipment
19 Ducted distribution of services

Materials　Alan Everett

1 Properties generally
2 Timber
3 Boards and slabs
4 Stones
5 Ceramics
6 Bricks and blocks
7 Limes and cements
8 Concretes
9 Metals
10 Asbestos products
11 Bituminous products
12 Glass
13 Plastics and rubbers
14 Adhesives
15 Mortars for jointing
16 Mastics and gaskets

Structure and Fabric　Jack Stroud Foster

Part 1
1 The nature of buildings and building
2 The production of buildings
3 Structural behaviour
4 Foundations
5 Walls
6 Framed structures
7 Roof structures
8 Floor structures
9 Fireplaces, flues and chimneys
10 Stairs
11 Building operations and site preparation

Structure and Fabric　Jack Stroud Foster
　　　　　　　　　　　　Ray Harington

Part 2
1 Contract planning and site organization
2 Contractors' mechanical plant
3 Foundations
4 Walls and piers
5 Multi-storey structures
6 Floor structures
7 Flues and chimeny shafts
8 Stairs, ramps and ladders
9 Roof structures
10 Fire protection
11 Site preparation and temporary work

Components　Harold King
　　　　　　　revised by Derek Osbourn

1 Component design
2 Joinery
3 Doors
4 Windows
5 Glazing
6 Roof lights
7 Ironmongery
8 Balustrades
9 Demountable partitions
10 Suspended ceilings
11 Industrialized system building

Index